PETER OAKES is Tutor in Biblical Studies at Northern College, Manchester and Greenwood Lecturer in New Testament Studies at the University of Manchester. He is a member of the Tyndale Fellowship and has made an extensive study of archaeological and literary evidence relating to Philippi. His classical/historical work involves study on site and interaction with leading practitioners in the field. He is currently engaged in research on Rome and Pompeii for a book on Paul's letter to the Romans.

This book provides a case-study in modelling the social make-up of an early Christian community, including estimated figures for the various social groups in the model. It explains Philippians (the letter) by thinking about the lives of the Philippians (the people who received the letter). It also shows how much modelling can make an impact on the exegesis of a text. The result is a proposal for reading Philippians as a call for unity under economic suffering. In particular, the story of Christ in Philippians 2.6–11 is read as a reinforcement of this call in the specifically Roman context of Philippi.

The book begins with a discussion of archaeological and literary evidence about the development of the Roman colony of Philippi. It also includes discussion of the likely effects of suffering among various social groups in the church, exploration of Paul's and Christ's roles as models for the Philippians, and comparison of Paul's language about Christ with Imperial ideology.

PETER OAKES is Tutor in Biblical Studies at Northern College, Manchester and Greenwood Lecturer in New Testament Studies at the University of Manchester. He is a member of the Tyndale Fellowship and has made an extensive study of archaeological and literary evidence relating to Philippi. His classical/historical work involves study on site and interaction with leading practitioners in the field. He is currently engaged in research on Rome and Pompeii for a book on Paul's letter to the Romans.

SOCIETY FOR NEW TESTAMENT STUDIES

MONOGRAPH SERIES

General Editor: Richard Bauckham

110

PHILIPPIANS

Philippians

From people to letter

PETER OAKES

University of Manchester

CAMBRIDGE
UNIVERSITY PRESS

PUBLISHED BY THE PRESS SYNDICATE OF THE UNIVERSITY OF CAMBRIDGE
The Pitt Building, Trumpington Street, Cambridge, United Kingdom

CAMBRIDGE UNIVERSITY PRESS
The Edinburgh Building, Cambridge CB2 2RU, UK   www.cup.cam.ac.uk
40 West 20th Street, New York, NY 10011–4211, USA   www.cup.org
10 Stamford Road, Oakleigh, Melbourne 3166, Australia
Ruiz de Alarcón 13, 28014 Madrid, Spain

First published 2001

Printed in the United Kingdom at the University Press, Cambridge

Typeface 10/12 pt Times   *System* 3b2   [CE]

A catalogue record for this book is available from the British Library

ISBN 0 521 79046 8 hardback

In memory of my father,
STANLEY OAKES

CONTENTS

FIGURES

Photographs of Roman coins © Copyright The British Museum.
Other photographs © Copyright Janet Oakes.

Tables

PREFACE

How much explanatory power can there be in a study of the historical social context of a church to whom Paul wrote a letter? As I have sat reading archaeological reports, and stood looking at the ruined town in its wide, fertile plain, I have been surprised by how complete a framework the context seemed to provide for understanding Paul's letter to Philippi.

My study led me to two end-points, both of which go against a great deal of current scholarship on Philippians (but which have much in common with the approaches of Stephen Fowl and Wayne Meeks to the letter). The first is that the main thematic structure of the letter is a three-fold parallel between Christ, Paul and the Philippians, a parallel consistently directed towards affecting the attitudes and behaviour of the suffering Philippian church. The second is a reading of Philippians 2.6–11 as a carefully crafted piece of exhortation and encouragement, written specifically for the Philippian situation.

My method has been first to model the development of the town, then the social structure of the town, then the social structure of the church that one might typically expect in such a town. Particularly since this procedure is subject to such a wide range of uncertainty, the resulting model was then tested against the New Testament data about the church at Philippi. The strengths and weaknesses of the model were also compared with those of other possible models.

My next starting-point was a demonstration that the letter indicates that at least some Philippian Christians were suffering. I then used my model of the church and my model of the town to discuss what such suffering would be likely to have involved for the range of types of people in the church. I concluded that the primary long-term form of suffering would be economic.

In the letter, both Christ and Paul model a proper attitude to suffering. In both cases, the way of obedient suffering is seen to be the way of salvation. Paul calls the Philippians to this same way of salvation. This call is intertwined with an impassioned call to unity. The economic difficulties, which I think were the most likely primary content of Philippian suffering, provide a context which draws these things naturally together in a way that no other context for Philippians seems to do.

This leaves a question about Christ's exaltation in Philippians 2.9–11. Although it is bound to bring some message to the Philippian hearers that following Christ's way of willingness to lose status and to suffer carries a hope of salvation, it must also do more than this. Christ is not simply rewarded but is raised to the position of universal authority. My conclusion is that Paul presents a pattern in 2.9–11 and 3.20–1 in which Christ is compared with the Emperor, the head of Philippian colonial society. Christ is the one who, by his actions, showed himself to be the one who should be given an authority greater than that of the Emperor. This authority is the basis for his being able, at the End, to return and rescue his people. Such a portrayal of Christ makes his imperatives of unity supersede imperatives of the Philippian social order which would tend to break an economically suffering church apart.

Many scholars have argued that suffering usually promotes unity in groups such as small Christian communities. My study sees Philippians as a letter written at the point where, for this community, that outcome is in question. Will their suffering produce fragmentation or unity? Paul's letter is, I would argue, carefully put together to try to ensure that the outcome of their suffering is unity.

I have benefited from the support of many people during my work on Philippians, particularly Tom Wright, under whose supervision the core of this work formed an Oxford DPhil thesis which was examined in 1996. My examiners, Loveday Alexander and Robert Morgan, offered helpful corrections and advice. Also invaluable at Oxford was the encouragement of Chris Rowland and the members of the faculty and graduate seminars, particularly Crispin Fletcher-Louis and Sean Winter. Simon Price, Peter Pilhofer and Philip Esler generously responded to sections of my research and made suggestions for reading. Conrad Gempf has been a source of encouragement since the early days of my study. In Manchester, I have received steady support from David Peel, Martin Scott and my other colleagues at Luther King House and from George Brooke and other colleagues at the University.

This book rests on the work of many scholars of Philippians and of Philippi, particularly those of institutions such as the Ecole Française at Athens and the University of Thessaloniki who have excavated the site. I wish to thank the British Academy for funding much of my doctoral research. I also wish to thank the trustees of the British Museum for permission to reproduce photographs of their Roman coins.

I am grateful to Richard Bauckham for including my work in the SNTS monograph series and to Kevin Taylor and the other staff at Cambridge University Press for their work in preparing the book for publication.

I would have struggled to finish my doctoral thesis without the extended hospitality of Jane and Mark Smith. I would have struggled to start without the help of Janet.

1

PHILIPPI

In its introduction to Philippians, *The NIV Study Bible* has the following entry under the heading 'Recipients'.

> The city of Philippi was named after King Philip II of Macedon, father of Alexander the Great. It was a prosperous Roman colony, which meant that the citizens of Philippi were also citizens of the city of Rome itself. They prided themselves on being Romans (see Ac. 16.21), dressed like Romans and often spoke Latin. No doubt this was the background for Paul's reference to the believer's heavenly citizenship (3.20–21). Many of the Philippians were retired military men who had been given land in the vicinity and who in turn served as a military presence in this frontier city. That Philippi was a Roman colony may explain why there were not enough Jews there to permit the establishment of a synagogue and why Paul does not quote the OT in the Philippian letter.[1]

This description draws on a long history of scholarship on Philippians.[2] It uses a number of the major conclusions that can be drawn from the archaeological investigation of Philippi and from reading the key classical texts relevant to Philippi. The description provides a general impression of the Philippian Christians which will inform the reader's hearing of the text – an obvious example being the passage which it cites, Philippians 3.20–1. However, the impression given is false. It represents a radical misunderstanding

[1] *The NIV Study Bible* (London: Hodder & Stoughton, 1987 UK edn), p. 1767.
[2] E.g., J. B. Lightfoot, *St. Paul's Epistle to the Philippians* (London: Macmillan, 1885 edn), p. 52; Gerhard Friedrich, 'Der Brief an die Philipper', *Die kleineren Briefe des Apostels Paulus*, H. W. Beyer et al. (NTD (9th edn) VIII; Göttingen: Vandenhoeck & Ruprecht, 1962), p. 106; G. F. Hawthorne, *Philippians* (Waco: Word, 1983), pp. xxxiii–iv. After their first occurrence, commentaries on Philippians will be cited by name of author alone.

of the nature of a Roman colony like Philippi and of the kind of church likely to be found in such a setting.

To try to gain a reasonable impression of the nature of the Philippian church we need to build a model of the likely social make-up of that church. To do that, we need first to build a model of the social make-up of the town. To do that, we need first to model the development of the Roman colony of Philippi from its founding in 42 BC to the period, in the middle of the first century AD, when Philippians was written.

We will have to deal with estimating some figures. This seems strange when our aim is only 'to gain a reasonable impression'. However, it is unavoidable. The paragraph quoted above could be taken as being, in a literal sense, correct in stating that 'Many of the Philippians were retired military men'. I would estimate the number as being of the order of one hundred (see below). This is 'many' – but it is less that 1 per cent of the population. Without some consideration of numbers it is all too easy – and scholars have often done it – to slip from knowing that one has evidence of the existence of a particular type of person in a city to thinking that that type constituted a substantial proportion of the population. This tendency is greatly exacerbated in a case such as Philippi where the main thing that most scholars know about the city is that it was a Roman veteran colony.

Estimated figures may be subject to a wide range of uncertainty and yet still be useful. The factors in the estimate for veteran soldiers could vary a great deal yet still lead to the same conclusion about the veterans' numerical insignificance. Similarly, my estimate for the proportion of slaves in the population is 15–30 per cent. The upper figure is twice the lower one but the estimate is still useful for envisaging life in Philippi. If you lived in Philippi you would meet slaves every day. On the other hand they would not constitute a majority of the population. We can also then use our estimate for slaves as one component in a calculation of whether most Philippians were probably Roman citizens or not. The result of that calculation can then help in deciding whether Paul's news about heavenly citizenship was addressed primarily to those who already had an earthly citizenship or to those for most of whom citizenship of Philippi was an unattainable goal. In fact, even if we cannot decide on the answer to that question, the process of reflecting on the likely social composition of Philippi, and then of the church, will already have opened our eyes to the vital fact that there are two such groups, citizens and non-citizens, to be considered.

1. Looking at Philippi

To understand an ancient city such as Philippi we need to draw evidence both from the city itself and from further afield. Most of the features which are seen at Philippi are common to many Graeco-Roman cities. Evidence on the nature of such a feature (for example, the role of slaves) can, with caution, be drawn from many locations even though they are dispersed geographically and, to an extent, temporally. Some of Philippi's features are more specifically characteristic of Roman colonies. In fact, we need to be more specific than this because *colonia* covers a range of types of city including, from the first century AD onwards, a rapidly expanding group of cities which gained the title solely as an honour. Philippi has features characteristic of citizen colonies of the larger type which were set up during the late Republic and early Empire.[3] In some features, Philippi exceeds most other cities or colonies. The persistence of its Romanness is the best example. Finally, some features are special to it alone. These include its ethnic mix and its location, which has peculiarities in terms of agriculture, history and transport.

a. Archaeological investigation and reports

Philippi has undergone substantial archaeological investigation. Most of the recent attention has been on the Christian centre of the city, particularly under the auspices of the University of Thessaloniki. The early imperial period, with interest centred on the Antonine Forum area, has been the responsibility of the École Française at Athens. The main excavation here was carried out between the two World Wars and is summarised in Paul Collart's *Philippes, Ville de Macédoine: depuis ses origines jusqu'à la fin de l'époque romaine* (1937). Collart's work remains fundamental for any study of Philippi and all subsequent scholars on Philippi are in debt to him. His work has directed me to many of the primary sources which I have been able to consider in this study. Buildings

---

[3] See E. T. Salmon's tracing of types of colony founded at various times in his *Roman Colonization under the Republic* (London: Thames & Hudson, 1969).

of a later date among or near the early Roman ones are reported in Paul Lemerle's *Philippes et la Macédoine Orientale à l'époque chrétienne et byzantine* (1945), which also considers Paul's time in and contacts with Philippi. These two books gather data which was largely reported in more detail in various issues of the *Bulletin de Correspondance Hellénique*, which continues to publish articles and reports on studies of the forum and elsewhere by M. Sève, P. Weber and other scholars, who are mainly engaged in analytical work. Three important recent articles are on a revised plan of the forum (1982),[4] on a reconstruction of the way in which the north side of the forum was dominated by monumental buildings uphill from it (1986)[5] and on the discovery of a large monument from the Livia cult (1988).[6] Much of this recent work is gathered together in Sève's study on the development of the forum at Philippi, *Recherches sur les Places Publiques dans le monde Grec du Premier au Septième Siècle de Notre Ère: L'exemple de Philippes* (1989, 1990).

At the time of Collart and Lemerle's books, formal publication of the inscriptions from Philippi was announced as fairly imminent. In fact, the first volume, covering the unique mass of reliefs carved into the hill at the base of which Philippi was built, did not appear until 1975[7] and the remaining volumes are still awaited. Peter Pilhofer has provided substantial interim help with this in his *Habilitationsschrift* for which he gathered all the inscriptions available. His first published volume, *Philippi I: Die erste christliche Gemeinde Europas* (1995), gives his historical and exegetical results. The second volume will be a catalogue of the inscriptions from Philippi. Two other scholars who have done substantial work on Philippi are D. Lazarides, in particular in his 1973 book, Φίλιπποι-Ρωμαϊκή ἀποικία, and Fanoula Papazoglou, especially her 1988 *Les Villes de Macédoine à l'époque Romaine*. More recently, Chaido Koukouli-Chrysantaki has gathered material on the colony in his paper for a 1993 symposium on Paul and Philippi.[8] Among the

[4] M. Sève, 'Philippes', *BCH* 106 (1982), pp. 651–3.

[5] M. Sève and P. Weber, 'Le côté Nord du forum de Philippes', *BCH* 110 (1986), pp. 531–81.

[6] M. Sève and P. Weber, 'Un monument honorifique au forum de Philippes', *BCH* 112 (1988), pp. 467–79.

[7] Paul Collart and Pierre Ducrey, *Philippes I: Les Reliefs Rupestres* (BCH Supp. II; Paris, 1975).

[8] Chaido Koukouli-Chrysantaki, 'Colonia Iulia Augusta Philippensis', in C. Bakirtzis and H. Koester, eds., *Philippi at the Time of Paul and after His Death* (Harrisburg: Trinity Press International, 1998).

various Biblically oriented guides to Philippi, the most substantial is Winfried Elliger's *Paulus in Griechenland: Philippi, Thessaloniki, Athen, Korinth* (1978, 1987). Lilian Portefaix's book, *Sisters Rejoice: Paul's Letter to the Philippians & Luke-Acts as Received by First-century Philippian Women* (1988) also discusses Philippi in some detail, especially the rock reliefs, in which she follows the work of Valerie Abrahamsen.[9] Lukas Bormann, in *Philippi: Stadt und Christengemeinde zur Zeit des Paulus* (1995), discusses Philippi with particular reference the town's 'self-understanding'.

Two recent books which are not on Philippi help to put into perspective the evidence from there and the issues involved in employing it. Susan Alcock's book, *Graecia Capta: The Landscapes of Roman Greece* (1993), considers the experience of Greeks in Achaia under the early Empire. It particularly brings together and assesses the implications of the results of the technique of 'pedestrian surface survey' (a very controlled survey of a district looking for fragments of pottery, etc., of various dates in order to spot settlements and other sites which may not have left standing remains of buildings). These have been applied in the 1980s for the first time to a number of areas of Achaia and enable a rough picture to be drawn of changes in the pattern of occupation of the countryside (and also of large urban areas). Another book which helps give an idea of the issues involved in using archaeological evidence is Philippe Leveau's monumental study *Caesarea de Maurétanie: Une Ville Romaine et ses Campagnes* (1984). The main part of this study is a field survey of a wide area around Caesarea, looking at evidence of buildings, etc., that are still visible. A picture is built up of how various types of settlement were distributed in the city's hinterland. The study also considers issues concerning the use of evidence from epitaphs.

b. Overview of the geography and history of Philippi

The city lies 13 km north-west of Kavala, the ancient port of Neapolis. As it has always been, the site is bisected by the main road from there to Drama.[10] The road, which otherwise crosses a

---

[9] V. Abrahamsen, *The Rock Reliefs and the Cult of Diana at Philippi* (Diss. Harvard Univ.; Ann Arbor: University Microfilms, 1986).
[10] Any bus to Drama therefore visits the site, which is called Αρχαία Φίλιπποι – *not* simply Φίλιπποι, which is a modern village some kilometres to the east and on a different bus route!

Figure 1   View SW from acropolis of Philippi. The town lies in the lower half of the picture, occupying the space between the hill and marshland (now drained). The hills of the Pangaion are to the right in the distance.

Figure 2   View SE from acropolis. The line of the Via Egnatia can be seen running towards Neapolis, which lies behind the Symbolon, the low range of hills in the background.

Figure 3   View W from acropolis, showing the battlefield of Philippi and the wide expanse of agricultural land. The marsh and the Pangaion are to the left.

Figure 4   The Antonine forum at Philippi. Beyond lies the gymnasium and the market (largely covered by remains of a church).

fertile plain, must go through the city because the western end of a range of steep hills falls almost into the eastern end of what was until this century a great marsh. The city walls form roughly a rectangle 1 km x 700m (with the longer sides running NNW–SSE). At the northern corner is the citadel of the acropolis. The southern corner meets the marsh. Building is most feasible in roughly the area south of a line joining the north-west to the south-east corner.[11] Elsewhere, building seems not to have taken place, on account of the steepness of the hill, except in limited areas such as around the theatre. The Via Egnatia follows the base of the hill. The hills provide both abundant springs (the settlement was originally called *Krenides*, 'springs') and mineral deposits, particularly gold (exhausted by Roman times). Beyond the marsh lie the hills of the Pangaion, another, richer gold- and silver-mining area.

The extent of the colony's territory is at various points attested by inscriptions and has been estimated at 1900 sq. km (730 sq. miles).[12] This seems to put it at the upper end of the normal range: Barbara Levick cites Pisidian Antioch as 1400 sq. km and at the lower end.[13] The territory includes the Pangaion, the extensive plain surrounding it, and, beyond the low range of the Symbolon, the valuable port of Neapolis. The eastern edge forms a border with Thrace.

The various social groups in the area of the colony arrived in a fairly clear order. Before 360 BC, the inhabitants were various tribes, mainly Pieri and Edoni.[14] I will call them Thracians, as Collart does. Papazoglou reasonably objects that they ought really to be distinguished from Thracians:[15] those who migrated came from the west, ejected from west of Thessalonika and from Mygdonia,[16] rather than from Thrace in the east. However, I will persist with calling them Thracian because their religious affinities are with the Thracians, their names sound Thracian and, like the

[11] Of the walled area of 67.8 Ha about 45 Ha appear easy to build upon. Cf. Peter Pilhofer, *Philippi I: Die erste christliche Gemeinde Europas* (Tübingen: J. C. B. Mohr, 1995), p. 74.

[12] See below, pp. 45f.

[13] 540 sq. miles: Barbara Levick, *Roman Colonies in Southern Asia Minor* (Oxford: Clarendon Press, 1967), p. 45.

[14] Fanoula Papazoglou, *Les Villes de Macédoine à l'époque Romaine* (BCH Supp. XVI; Paris: École Française d'Athènes, 1988), pp. 385f.; Paul Collart, *Philippes, Ville de Macédoine: depuis ses origines jusqu'à la fin de l'époque romaine* (École Française d'Athènes: Travaux et Mémoires, Fascicule V; Paris, 1937), p. 55.

[15] Papazoglou, *Villes*, p. 342 n. 2.

[16] Collart, *Philippes*, p. 56; Papazoglou, *Villes*, pp. 385f.

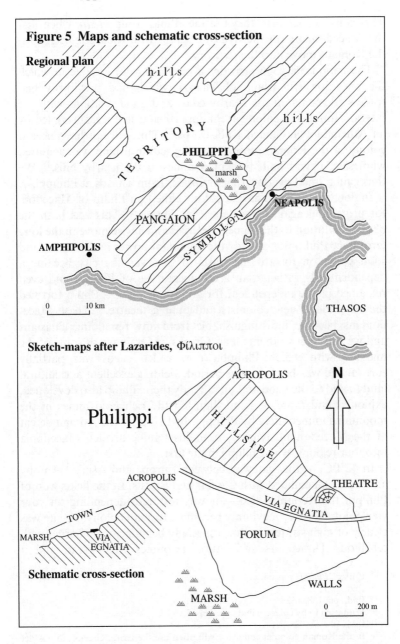

Figure 5 Maps and schematic cross-section

Regional plan

hills

TERRITORY

hills

PHILIPPI

marsh

NEAPOLIS

PANGAION

SYMBOLON

AMPHIPOLIS

0   10 km

THASOS

Sketch-maps after Lazarides, Φίλιπποι

ACROPOLIS

N

Philippi

HILLSIDE

ACROPOLIS

THEATRE

TOWN

VIA EGNATIA

MARSH

VIA EGNATIA

FORUM

Schematic cross-section

MARSH

WALLS

0   200 m

Thracians further east, they are the ethnic group *in situ* when first the Macedonians (in the dynastic sense, with their subjects) then the Romans move into the territory.

The period 360–356 provides a brief but vital episode in which the once-powerful island of Thasos, which had previously had trade-settlements on the nearby coast and good relations with the interior, founded a colony at Philippi (then called Krenides), led by an Athenian exile named Kallistratos.[17] This will not have been a colony in the Roman sense, where agricultural land was acquired wholesale. It was built to exploit mines in the nearby hills.[18] We thus gain a small overlayering of Greeks from Thasos at Philippi.

In 356, the young Thasian colony called on Philip of Macedon, for protection against invaders from Thrace.[19] This was both the obvious solution to the immediate crisis and a wise move in the long term since Philip was already the dominant power in the region and soon swept on toward the East. In this way the city became a dependent ally rather than a conquered foe of Philip's and even remained partly independent for about ten years.[20] Philip fortified the city, added new colonists and built a theatre.[21] These Macedonians become indistinguishable from any remaining Thasians and we will refer to them all as 'Greeks'.[22] Drainage of some of the marshes with which Philippi (now called such) was partially surrounded was begun in this period, yielding excellent agricultural land to add to the good amount already there. Philip also developed, exploited and more or less exhausted the rich gold mines in the mountains immediately by Philippi. In 167, after the Roman defeat of the Macedonian dynasty, Aemilius Paulus divided Macedonia into four regions, with Philippi in the first.

In 42 BC, at the 'gateway between Europe and Asia',[23] Antony and Octavian collided with Cassius and Brutus. In the fields west of Philippi the Republic died – or was restored, depending on your viewpoint. The city inevitably became a Roman colony. Its site was clearly of high strategic value, especially being near the border with rebellious Thrace, its agricultural resources were great, and it

---

[17] Collart, *Philippes*, p. 54.
[18] Ibid., p. 135.
[19] Ibid., pp. 138, 152.
[20] Witnessed to by coinage, ibid., pp. 162–5.
[21] Ibid., p. 177.
[22] In the Roman colonial context, I will often use the term, 'Greeks', in a wider sense to denote all non-Romans in the colony.
[23] Appian, *B. Civ.* IV, 106.

formed a memorial to the great battle which 'saved' the Roman people. It was also to hand when a large number of soldiers needed demobilising! The colony was founded almost immediately. Two altars celebrating the victory were set up on the battlefield and became famous monuments. They are reported to have burst spontaneously into flame when Tiberius approached the city.[24] The colony was also initially named after the battle: *Colonia Victrix Philippensium*.[25] Collart and others have also argued that, as a further commemorative act, the *pomerium*, the sacred boundary of a city, was uniquely extended 2 km to the west of the walls to include the battlefield.[26] However, Paul Lemerle expressed doubts about the extended *pomerium*, on account of discoveries of some sarcophagi in this area supposed to be free of burials and on account of the strange shape of Collart's *pomerium*.[27] These doubts have been verified by later discoveries. Pilhofer suggests that the cemetery west of Philippi is probably as extensive as that to the east. Pilhofer also notes that the objection to the account in Acts 16 based on Collart's *pomerium* – an area in which Jewish worship would have been forbidden – no longer holds.[28]

In 30 BC, after Actium, Octavian refounded the colony in his own name, adding a large influx of colonists. These included a cohort of Praetorians and civilian supporters of Antony. From 27 BC, the colony took the name *Colonia Iulia Augusta Philippensis*.[29]

[24] Suetonius, *Tiberius*, XIV, 3; Dio Cass. LIV, 9.6.

[25] Collart, *Philippes*, p. 227.

[26] Ibid., pp. 323ff.; D. Lazarides, Φίλιπποι-Ρωμαϊκή ἀποικία (Ancient Greek Cities 20; Athens, 1973), pp. 30, 37; Lilian Portefaix, *Sisters Rejoice: Paul's letter to the Philippians and Luke-Acts as received by First Century Philippian Women* (Coniectanea Biblica, NT Series 20; Uppsala/Stockholm: Almqvist & Wiksell International, 1988), pp. 62ff.; H. Conzelmann, *Acts of the Apostles* (Hermeneia; Philadelphia: Fortress Press, 1987), on 16.13; Winfried Elliger, *Paulus in Griechenland: Philippi, Thessaloniki, Athen, Korinth* (Stuttgarter Bibel-Studien; Stuttgart: Verlag Katholisches Bibelwerk, 1978), pp. 49f. Collart argues from the absence of buildings in the area and from the existence of what he calls a 'colonial' arch at the point where the Via Egnatia would cut the *pomerium*.

[27] Paul Lemerle, *Philippes et la Macédoine Orientale à l'époque chrétienne et byzantine: Recherches d'histoire et d'archéologie* (Bibliothèque des Écoles Françaises d'Athènes et de Rome 158; Paris: Boccard, 1945), pp. 26f., esp. p. 27 n. 1.

[28] Pilhofer, *Philippi*, pp. 26ff. Pilhofer also reports the discovery of the foundations of a bridge on the Via Egnatia a short distance beyond the town's western wall (p. 28).

[29] Pilhofer (*Philippi*, p. 47), firmly dismisses the suggestion that the colony is named after Augustus' daughter. P. A. Brunt, *Italian Manpower: 225BC–AD14* (Oxford: Oxford University Press, 1971, 1987), pp. 234f., explains how colonies took the names *Iulia* and/or *Augusta* in honour of Julius Caesar and/or Augustus as founders or benefactors.

One other influx of people probably began before the Romans arrived and certainly continued, and flourished, under them. Philippi, standing near the coast on the Via Egnatia, will have seen a fair amount of trade. This brought both traders and migrant workers, some of whom no doubt settled permanently, and an inflow of ideas and beliefs, such as the cult of Isis.[30] Another, unwilling, form of immigrant workers were slaves.

After a few decades in which there were occasional raids from Thrace, the colony developed steadily, its Roman monuments reaching a peak under the Antonines. In the fourth century, Philippi became an important bishopric.

2.   A model of the development of society in the area of Philippi

There is insufficient archaeological or literary evidence from the town in the middle of the first century AD for us to jump straight to a worthwhile estimate of its social composition. In particular, we lack a substantial collection of epitaphs from graveyards in use by the general population. There is, however, evidence indicating the process of development of the town. By considering various elements of that process, and the effects which such elements tended to have in similar contexts, we can build a model of the process of development and hence arrive at a model of the pattern which Philippian society is likely to have reached in the middle of the first century, a model which seems likely to be sufficiently accurate to give a good indication of the range of types of people who formed the great majority of those originally hearing the letter.

a.   The type of model

Thomas Carney and Bruce Malina discuss what is meant by the term 'model'. Carney has a tighter definition of 'model' than does Malina. Malina writes, 'Models are abstract, simplified representations of more complex real world objects and interactions'.[31] Carney would add that as many of the model's assumptions and limitations as possible must be specified in order for it to be a

---

[30] Paul Collart, 'Sanctuaire des dieux égyptiens', *BCH* 53 (1929), pp. 99f.

[31] Bruce J. Malina, *The New Testament World: Insights from Cultural Anthropology* (London: SCM, 1983 (page refs. unless noted); Louisville: Westminster/John Knox, 1993 edn), p. 17.

model rather than merely an analogy.[32] I think we should say that a description of something becomes a model when we turn round and look at it, prepared to ask questions about its presuppositions and limitations. It is at this point that we realise that it is indeed a model rather than simply a statement of how things are.

My model is shown graphically in figures 6 to 9. Like the model which Richard Rohrbaugh uses for the urban system of a pre-industrial city ('urban system' covers the town plus its dependent countryside),[33] my model shows the distribution of social groups between town and countryside. Rohrbaugh then adds arrows showing economic relationships between the groups. My interest is in the physical location of groups, since our objective is to estimate who was in the town in the middle of the first century AD. I have therefore simplified the model by removing the arrows, then made it more complex by giving it a stronger spatial dimension and by giving some detail on the variety of groups at any location.

The spatial dimension works in two ways. The size of each circle indicates the population of a settlement. The distance of a circle from the city of Philippi (the largest circle in each diagram) indicates the distance of the settlement from the city. The 'city of Philippi' in the model will include everybody living either within Philippi's walls or in areas of housing within a couple of kilometres of them. In particular, there is evidence, in the Imperial period, of a substantial area of accommodation around the Via Egnatia between the East Gate and the settlement of Dikili-Tash to the south-east.[34] Absolute numbers and sizes of circles are not signifi-cant. What matters are the changes in number and size and the indications of which settlements are larger or more numerous. The settlements indicated as being the very furthest from the city are in marginal agricultural land (hillsides and high valleys). Other settle-ments are assumed to be on land of a common, fertile standard.

The population within each settlement is shown in the minimum detail needed to indicate the kinds of trends which seem likely to have happened to significant groups. Relative proportions of the various social groups are very approximate. Neither slaves (other

[32] T. F. Carney, *The Shape of the Past: Models and Antiquity* (Lawrence, Kans.: Coronado Press, 1975), pp. 11ff.
[33] Richard L. Rohrbaugh, 'The Pre-Industrial city in Luke-Acts: Urban Social Relations', in J. H. Neyrey, ed., *The Social World of Luke-Acts* (Peabody: Hen-drickson, 1991), pp. 130–2.
[34] Lazarides, Φίλιπποι, pp. 31, 45f.

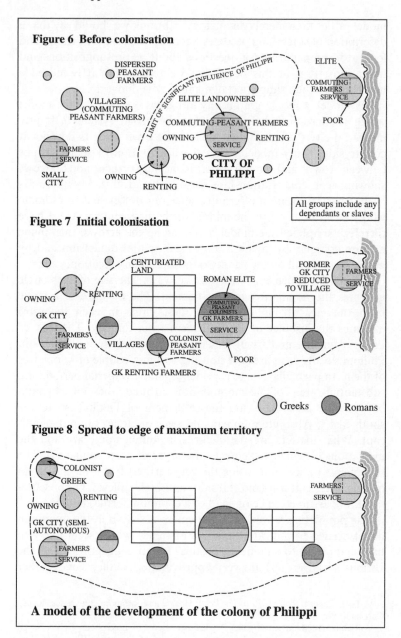

Figure 6 Before colonisation

DISPERSED PEASANT FARMERS

VILLAGES (COMMUTING PEASANT FARMERS)

FARMERS
SERVICE

SMALL CITY

OWNING

RENTING

LIMIT OF SIGNIFICANT INFLUENCE OF PHILIPPI

ELITE LANDOWNERS

COMMUTING-PEASANT FARMERS

OWNING   RENTING
        SERVICE
    POOR
CITY OF PHILIPPI

ELITE

COMMUTING FARMERS
SERVICE

POOR

All groups include any dependants or slaves

Figure 7 Initial colonisation

CENTURIATED LAND

ROMAN ELITE

OWNING   RENTING

GK CITY

FARMERS
SERVICE

VILLAGES   COLONIST PEASANT FARMERS

GK RENTING FARMERS

COMMUTING PEASANT COLONISTS
GK FARMERS
SERVICE

POOR

FORMER GK CITY REDUCED TO VILLAGE

FARMERS
SERVICE

⬤ Greeks   ⬤ Romans

Figure 8 Spread to edge of maximum territory

COLONIST
GREEK

OWNING   RENTING

GK CITY (SEMI-AUTONOMOUS)

FARMERS
SERVICE

FARMERS
SERVICE

A model of the development of the colony of Philippi

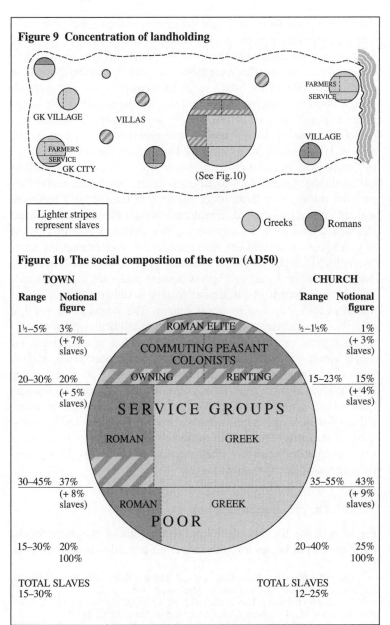

Figure 9 Concentration of landholding

FARMERS
SERVICE

GK VILLAGE   VILLAS

FARMERS
SERVICE
GK CITY   (See Fig.10)

VILLAGE

Lighter stripes
represent slaves

Greeks   Romans

Figure 10 The social composition of the town (AD50)

	TOWN			CHURCH	
Range	Notional figure			Range	Notional figure
1½–5%	3% (+ 7% slaves)	ROMAN ELITE		½–1½%	1% (+ 3% slaves)
		COMMUTING PEASANT COLONISTS			
20–30%	20% (+ 5% slaves)	OWNING	RENTING	15–23%	15% (+ 4% slaves)
		SERVICE GROUPS			
		ROMAN	GREEK		
30–45%	37% (+ 8% slaves)			35–55%	43% (+ 9% slaves)
		ROMAN	GREEK		
		POOR			
15–30%	20% 100%			20–40%	25% 100%
TOTAL SLAVES 15–30%				TOTAL SLAVES 12–25%	

than those on villa estates) nor freedmen/women have been indicated as separate groups. Slaves formed part of the *familia* of all
Roman households except those rather poorly off (the term *familia*
could include slaves who were domestic staff, labourers bought to
help a craft-producing family with their work,[35] or even agricultural labourers living on an estate, far from the actual family of the
Roman involved – this last usage was in fact a particularly
prominent one[36]). In my model, the slaves are indicated in the
enlarged diagram of the city (figure 10), and on the country estates,
by Greek stripes (although the slaves could, of course, be of various
nationalities). Greeks too might own slaves, but I have not differentiated those slaves from other 'Greeks' in the model. Freedmen/
women (*liberti*) are not differentiated from other Roman citizens
but would tend to be mainly among the service community of the
city. All Roman citizens are subsumed in the model under the term,
'Roman'. Similarly, all Greek-speaking groups, whether 'Thracian',
'Macedonian' or Asian, etc., are subsumed under the term, 'Greek'.

The development of Philippian society is shown by drawing the
model at four stages of its development. The stages in figures 7, 8
and 9 are separated on essentially an analytical rather than a
chronological basis. Philippian colonists ended up occupying far
more widely scattered land than could be accounted for on the
basis of the normal process of establishment of a Roman colony.
Landholding also became rather concentrated – certain landowners
held a large amount of land. We do not know the pace at which
either of these developments came about. In order to make fruitful
deductions from each, and to make my argument clearer, it seems
best to separate the two.[37] They are thus presented as though they
were chronologically distinct stages.

b.   The pre-colonial situation

Figure 6 shows the city of Philippi to the right of the centre of the
diagram and indicates a rough suggested breakdown of its popula-

---

[35] On such slaves, see Peter Garnsey and Richard Saller, *The Roman Empire: Economy, Society and Culture* (London: Duckworth, 1987), p. 52.

[36] F. M. Heichelheim, 'Latifundia', *Oxford Classical Dictionary*, ed. N. G. L. Hammond and H. H. Scullard (Oxford: Clarendon Press, 1980²), p. 579.

[37] This can only be done if the two processes are independent of each other. This is in fact unlikely. However, particularly since our interest is in the city, the level of dependence between the results of the two processes seems low enough for us to be able to consider them separately.

tion. Those who farm land near the city but who do not live in it are indicated as dispersed peasant farmers. The line of dashes indicates the limit of the countryside dependent on Philippi. Beyond that point, the smaller cities shown on the diagram are independent of Philippi. Near the small cities on the diagram are some villages dependent on them and some dispersed peasant farmers. No doubt there were several villages dependent on Philippi too, but our diagram is only very schematic. All the inhabitants of the area are taken to be 'Greek'.

In 42 BC, Philippi seems to have been a small, out-of-the-way Greek city. New Testament scholars sometimes feel that they need to give particular reasons for Amphipolis having been chosen as the principal city of the first district of Macedonia but the truth was probably that, in 167 BC, Philippi was a much less important town than Amphipolis. Philippi is not mentioned at all in connection with Aemilius Paulus' action at that time.[38] Strabo described it as κατοικία μικρά (VII, frag. 41) and Collart sums it up as 'Bourgade médiocre du premier district de la Macédoine'.[39] As Papazoglou has argued, Philippi cannot have had influence over the wide area which later became the territory of the Roman colony.[40] Other cities which were autonomous (within the Macedonian Roman context) and other villages unconnected with Philippi were spread around the area, the most prominent example of a city being Neapolis.

We must not, however, get carried away with the insignificance of pre-colonial Philippi. Contrary to the views of various scholars such as Lukas Bormann,[41] the population of the pre-colonial city and its surrounding area was probably quite substantial: substantial enough, first, for colonisation to involve large-scale dispossession of Greeks and, second, for the proportion of Greeks in the Roman city to be high. This last point requires an additional argument to the effect that there would have been strong attractions for dispossessed Greeks in the town to remain there and for dispossessed Greeks in the countryside to move into the town.

The city stood at the centre of what was for Greece, which has

[38] Collart, *Philippes*, pp. 189f.
[39] Ibid., p. 190.
[40] Papazoglou, *Villes*, p. 412.
[41] Lukas Bormann, *Philippi: Stadt und Christengemeinde zur Zeit des Paulus* (NovT Supp. 78; Leiden: Brill, 1995), p. 20.

only 18 per cent arable land,[42] a very large fertile plain. Even allowing for depopulation due to economic decline and due to contributions to, and harassment by, the forces involved in the Roman civil wars,[43] such land would still have been fairly thoroughly farmed. Susan Alcock's work shows that the effect of depopulation on farming would generally be to reduce the use of marginal land rather than to produce a blanket reduction in agriculture affecting all types of land fairly equally.[44] The land around Philippi was of high quality and we would expect, therefore, that it was still farmed. Given the continued agricultural vitality of the area, the long-established, substantially built city of Philippi is bound to have still acted as an important centre, both for services such as markets, theatre and religion, and for accommodation of farmers who commuted to their fields. Moreover, the pre-colonial population of the wider area that became the Roman colony's 'territory' must have been quite large and, as I will argue below, when patterns of landholding in the area changed, many of these people will have been attracted towards the city.

As well as the economic arguments for the city's continuing existence, from the fourth century BC to the time of colonisation there are various inscriptions attesting it. At Delphi, there are a fourth-century inscription about a *proxenos* (public guest) and a list of *theorodokoi* (officials receiving religious delegates) which refer to Philippi.[45] Of similar period are a list of subscribers at Argos and a list of mercenaries at Athens.[46] A third- or second-century BC list of *proxenoi* at Thebes also mentions Philippi.[47] A further inscription from Cos, dated to 242 BC, shows that Philippi was at that time sufficiently important for religious delegates from the island,

---

[42] Robert Browning, 'Prologue: Land and People', in R. Browning, ed., *The Greeks* (London: Thames & Hudson, 1985; Portland House, 1989), p. 25.

[43] Collart, *Philippes*, p. 229. Susan E. Alcock, *Graecia Capta: The Landscapes of Roman Greece* (Cambridge: Cambridge University Press, 1993), p. 14. However, she argues that, for the theatre of war generally, the effects of the depredations of armies will not have been as great as is often stated. She also argues that the continuation of low rural site numbers through the peaceful period of the early Empire shows that the link between military activity and depopulation is not as strong as some have supposed (p. 90).

[44] Alcock, *Graecia Capta*, p. 83.

[45] P. Perdrizet, 'Voyage dans La Macédoine Première', *BCH* 21 (1897), pp. 108ff.; Papazoglou, *Villes*, p. 407.

[46] *IG* IV, 617; *IG* II, 2, 963.

[47] *IG* VII, 2433.

announcing asylum at a sanctuary there, to visit the city and to record the visit (in some detail) back at home.[48] An inscription from the end of the second century mentions Philippi in a list of *mystai* at Samothrace.[49] Inscriptions discovered at Philippi itself are, however, very sparse. The latest pre-colonial one cited by Collart is an incription honouring a second-century BC benefactor who lent money to the city.[50]

An early literary reference to the city (300 BC) comes from Theophrastus, who shows detailed knowledge of the area, including the drainage of marshland and the development of agriculture.[51] The gold- and other mines near Philippi provided a great financial strength for Philip II.[52] However, where one might have expected literary references in Titus Livius' and Diodorus' discussions of the mines of Macedonia under Philip V (238–179) and Perseus (179–168), Philippi is not mentioned. Collart seems correct in suggesting that its mines were probably long exhausted.[53] There is testimony to the existence of Philippi in the first century BC in accounts of the Mithridatic wars. Granius Licinianus records the occupation of Philippi by Flaccus and Fimbria,[54] while Plutarch notes that Sulla received Archelaeus at Philippi.[55]

Appian writes about the town in *Civil Wars,* IV, 105–6. This includes his description of the place as, Δίοδος . . . ἐς τὴν Ἀσίαν τε καὶ Εὐρώπην καθάπηρ πύλαι ('A way through . . . to Asia and to Europe like a gateway'). He describes the town as a fortified πόλις on a hill and τοσαύτη τὸ μέγεθος, ὅσον ἐστι τοῦ λόφου τὸ εὖρος ('of the same extent as the width of the hill'). Philippi does somewhat fit the hill: the town's topographical *raison d'être* is the fact that the hill on which its acropolis stands ends in a low shelf sloping down to the marsh. The town occupies the shelf and a small section of the plain below. We may, however, doubt whether Appian visited Philippi since he also seems to envisage the marsh meeting the sea, whereas there is a range of hills in between.

[48] Papazoglou, *Villes*, pp. 406f.; Collart, *Philippes*, p. 181.
[49] *IG* XII, 8, 209.
[50] Collart, *Philippes*, p. 180. An earlier Philippian inscription of great interest is Alexander's decree concerning agricultural land and drainage of marshland (ibid., p. 179).
[51] Theophrastus, *Caus. Plant.* V, 14.5–6.
[52] Collart, *Philippes*, p. 167.
[53] Ibid., p. 189.
[54] Granius Licinianus, *Reliqueae*, XXXV.70; Collart, *Philippes*, p. 190 n. 2.
[55] Plutarch, *Sulla*, 23.5.

Strabo writes,

> οἱ δὲ Φίλιπποι Κρηνίδες ἐκαλοῦντο πρότερον, κατοικία
> μικρά· ηὐξήθη δὲ μετὰ τὴν περὶ Βροῦτον καὶ Κάσσιον
> ἧτταν.

> Philippi was called Krenides earlier, a small settlement; but
> it grew after the defeat of Brutus and Cassius.[56]

Reading this, we might think that the town was extremely small.
However, Strabo's grasp of the geography and history of the region
is rather thin. At the time when he is writing, Philippi, as he notes,
has been augmented by colonists. It is thus not now κατοικία
μικρά. When was it κατοικία μικρά? The sentence implies,
πρότερον, when it was also called Krenides. However, it changed
its name from Krenides to Philippi in 356 BC, not 42 BC. Strabo's
information seems somewhat confused. More seriously, he also
thinks that there is still gold-mining at Philippi:

> There are very many gold mines in Crenides, where the city
> Philippi now is situated, near Mt. Pangaeum. And Mt.
> Pangaeum as well has gold and silver mines, as also the
> country across, and the country this side, the Strymon
> River as far as Paeonia. And it is further said that the
> people who plough the Paeonian land find nuggets of
> gold.[57]

The critical error is that he sees gold production at Philippi in
distinction to the Pangaion. The only possible contemporary sense
in which Philippi could have been said to have had gold mines was
that of having control over working mines in the Pangaion. The
name Krenides looks likely to indicate that Strabo is drawing from
an old source and falling into anachronism.[58] The final sentence of
the fragment suggests a source with a folk-tale element to it.
Fragment 36 also seems to have a folk-tale element:

> Along the seaboard of the Strymon and the Dateni are,
> not only the city Neapolis, but also [Daton] itself, with its
> fruitful plains, lake, rivers, dock-yards, and profitable

---

[56] Strabo, *The Geography*, VII, frag. 41, my tr.

[57] Ibid., frag. 34, tr. H. L. Jones, p. 355.

[58] Papazoglou, *Villes*, p. 21, argues that this is the key difficulty with Strabo in
general.

gold mines; and hence the proverb, 'a [Daton] of good things' . . .[59]

The identity of Daton is unclear. Appian sees it as a name which Philippi held after being called Krenides,

οἱ δὲ Φίλιπποι πόλις ἐστίν, ἣ Δάτος ὠνομάζετο πάλαι καὶ Κρηνίδες ἔτι πρὸ Δάτου.

Philippi is a city, which was formerly called Daton – and Krenides before Daton.[60]

The name could also have originally referred to a place near Philippi or a broader area including Philippi.[61] Strabo's description, however, especially as he excludes Neapolis, gives Daton a combination of assets which are not geographically plausible. The incoherence is heightened by the lack of mention of Philippi. All this casts doubt on the reliability of Strabo's description of Philippi as κατοικία μικρά. One wonders whether his description might come from an ancient source which really is describing Krenides, before the city was built.

If we do take Strabo's assessment as reliable, we should note there are two other settlements that he describes as κατοικία μικρά. They are Achilleion, reputed site of Achilles' tomb (XIII, 1.39.8), which does seem to have been an insignificant settlement, and Abydus. For Abydus, the function of the expression is to contrast its modest present with its illustrious past,

ἔοικε δὲ ὑπάρξαι ποτὲ ἡ Ἄβυδος πόλις μεγάλη, δευτερ-
εύουσα μετὰ τὰς Φήβας, νυνὶ δ' ἐστὶ κατοικία μικρά . . .

Abydus appears once to have been a great city, second only to Thebes, but it is now only a small settlement . . .[62]

Assessment of the size of Abydus in Strabo's time is not easy, because its site has not been accessible for most of this century. However, it was an important toll station under the Empire and provides abundant finds of coinage right through to the third

---

[59] Strabo, *Geography*, VII, frag. 36, tr. H. L. Jones, p. 359. I have put the Greek form, *Daton*, in place of Jones' translation, 'Datum'.

[60] Appian, *B. Civ.* IV, my tr.

[61] Collart, *Philippes*, pp. 43f.

[62] Strabo, *Geography*, XVII, 1.42.14, tr. H. L. Jones. Strabo's other qualified uses of κατοικία are κατοικία μετρία (V, 1.6.16; XII, 3.17.12; XVI, 2.6.2.) and κατοικία μεγάλα (V, 3.6.43).

century AD,[63] so Strabo's description need not correspond to a town which had more or less disappeared. In the case of Philippi too, the function of the μικρά seems likely to be a comparative one, this time with ηὐξήθη. As I will argue below, ηὐξήθη is correct, and it will have come about by a number of mechanisms. We ought not, however, to infer from the term μικρά that the creation of the colonial city came about more or less *ex nihilo*.

One final piece of literary evidence which has particular bearing on our period is the existence of the substantial Greek writer, Marsyas of Philippi. He wrote multi-volume works on Μακεδονικά and Ἀρχαιολογία, which have not survived but seem to have been widely read. They are first cited by Pliny and by Athenaeus (who notes that Marsyas was a priest of Heracles).[64] This gives Marsyas a latest date of the first century AD. Laqueur argues that an earliest date is provided by Didymus' (80–10 BC) failing to distinguish Marsyas of Pella as 'the elder', as later became customary to avoid confusing him with his namesake from Philippi.[65] If Laqueur is correct, Marsyas of Philippi appears to date somewhere from the late first century BC to the first century AD. This is interesting whether he flourished before or after colonisation (the latter seems more likely). Either immediately pre-colonial Philippi could produce a substantial Greek writer, or the Greek community of colonial Philippi could. One cannot infer much from an individual case but it does lend weight to the Greek community's being a reasonably substantial one.

c.   The development of the colony

Figure 7: Initial colonisation. The city of Philippi has grown through the addition of Romans but has lost some Greeks, while others have moved from the farming to the service community. Some Greeks have moved in from other places such as the former Greek city on the diagram which has come within Philippi's authority and been downgraded. Most of the colonists[66] farming

---

[63] G. E. Bean, 'Abydos', *Princeton Encyclopedia of Classical Sites*, ed. R. Stillwell (Princeton: Princeton University Press, 1976).

[64] E. H. Bunbury, 'Marsyas (2)', *Dictionary of Greek and Roman Biography and Mythology*, ed. W. Smith (London: Taylor & Walton, 1846).

[65] Laqueur, 'Marsyas (9)', in G. Wissowa and W. Kroll, eds., *Pauly XIV (2)* (Stuttgart: Metzler, 1930), pp. 1998–9.

[66] The Latin word *colonus* holds a trap for the unwary. It has two distinct meanings, either 'colonist' or 'small renting farmer', whether the latter is a colonist

the 'centuriated' land live in the city but some live in villages nearby.

There is coin evidence of both the founding of the colony in 42 BC by Antony and its 'refounding' by Octavian after 30 BC. One type of coin refers to the ritual marking out of the boundary of the town by the use of a plough pulled by a bull and a cow[67] (not that the ceremony will have actually marked out the walls – they were built by Philip, long before: the ceremony marked the limit for taking town auspices[68]). The second type probably shows the colony's founding magistrate studying a register and supervising the process of drawing of lots for land.[69] These lots were mainly (or wholly) for parcels of land which had been *centuriated*, divided into a grid.[70] A grid of appropriate size will have been marked out on agricultural land close to the city. The size of each colonist's share varied from colony to colony and, within a colony, according to ground conditions and rank, etc.[71] This first allocation was for a body of Antony's legionaries who were retired immediately after the battle of Philippi. After Antony himself had been defeated at Actium, twelve years later, Octavian performed his 'refoundation' by settling a cohort of Praetorians (probably a thousand[72]) and a substantial number of Antony's supporters from Italy who were moved from their Italian homes to make way for Octavian's supporters.[73] Further grids must have been drawn, extending further from Philippi, eating further into the plain.

or not. See A. H. M. Jones, 'Colonus', *Oxford Classical Dictionary*, ed. N. G. L. Hammond and H. H. Scullard (Oxford: Clarendon Press, 1970²), p. 266. I will use the term 'colonist' to refer either to the colonial settlers or to citizens of the colony.

[67] *Roman Provincial Coinage, Vol. I* (44 BC–AD69), Pts. I and II, ed. A. M. Burnett, M. Amandry and P. P. Ripollès (London: British Museum Press, 1992), no. 1646: Antony/Q Paquius Ruf(us) C D LEG, man ploughing; no. 1648: A I C V P/Q Paq. Ruf, plough; nos. 1656–60 (probably Philippi): Augustus, Tiberius, Drusus or Claudius/two priests ploughing.

[68] I. A. Richmond and J. North, 'Pomerium', *Oxford Classical Dictionary*, ed. N. G. L. Hammond and H. H. Scullard (Oxford: Clarendon Press, 1970²), p. 856.

[69] *RPC, I*, no. 1647, cf. no. 1649.

[70] Collart, *Philippes*, p. 226. For a full description of the process, see Salmon, *Colonization*, pp. 29ff. For examples of traces of centuriation ('cadastral organisation') in Achaia, see Alcock, *Graecia Capta*, pp. 137f.

[71] Allotments could be of all sorts of sizes up to 37 Ha (62.5 acres) or, occasionally, 74 Ha: Salmon, *Colonization*, pp. 18, 25.

[72] Bormann, *Philippi*, p. 22 n. 67.

[73] Dio Cass, *Rom. Hist.* LI, 4.6. J. C. Mann, noting the work of M. Grant (*From Imperium to Auctoritas* (Cambridge: Cambridge University Press, 1969), p. 275), separates the settling of the Praetorians from that of the Antonian farmers by dating the former at 'shortly after 27BC': Mann, *Legionary Recruitment and Veteran*

'. . . les colons romains d'Antoine et d'Octavien s'étaient partagés leurs terres . . .' ('. . . The Roman colonists of Antony and Octavian divided up their land . . .')[74] – but whose '*terres*'? Allocation of land is almost certain to have started near the town.[75] This points to the land having belonged to Greek commuting farmers and élite landowners living in the town. Their land within the centuriated area was probably simply expropriated. Salmon comments that, during the civil war,

> [C]olonization took on the aspect of pragmatic improvisation and vindictiveness that it had worn under Sulla . . . To strengthen their position, the Triumvirs enriched their supporters, took vengeance on their enemies, and victimised the innocent. They were completely ruthless in their methods of procuring the land they needed for their ventures, callously seizing it wherever it seemed suitable . . .
>
> Presumably he [sc. Octavian] was also just as unscrupulous as his triumviral colleagues in obtaining land for colonies. The *Eclogues* of Vergil make it clear that he did not hesitate to confiscate it, and the later insistence of his official autobiography that he was the first to buy land for distribution to settlers, a claim that has reference in the main to the period after Actium, suggests that, as Augustus, he had considerable difficulty in living down the misdeeds he had perpetrated as Octavian.[76]

Octavian and Antony's behaviour in settling colonists in Macedonia is likely to have been more ruthless than it was in Italy, about which Appian writes,

> The task of assigning the soldiers to their colonies and dividing the land was one of exceeding difficulty. For the

---

Settlement During the Principate, ed. M. M. Roxan (Occasional Publication No. 7; London: Institute of Archaeology, 1983), p. 9. Whether or not this is correct, I will leave this grouped with the 30 BC settlement. The common Philippian coins marked, VIC AUG/COHOR PRAE PHIL, 3 standards (*RPC, I*, no. 1651), are now regarded as Claudian or Neronian (because they are copper) rather than Augustan, as was previously thought.

[74] Collart, *Philippes*, p. 296, my tr.

[75] Centuriation usually began at the town wall: Salmon, *Colonization*, p. 22.

[76] Ibid., pp. 137f. Collart applies the argument about Augustus not buying provincial land in his early career (before 14 BC) specifically to Philippi, *Philippes*, p. 229.

soldiers demanded the cities which had been selected for them before the war as prizes for their valour, and the cities demanded that the whole of Italy should share the burden, or that the cities should cast lots with other cities, and that those who gave the land should be paid the value of it: and there was no money. They came to Rome in crowds, young and old, women and children, to the forum and the temples, uttering lamentations, saying that they had done no wrong for which they, Italians, should be driven from their fields and their hearthstones, like people conquered in war.[77]

Legally, Octavian and Antony were on solid ground in allocating Philippian land because provincial soil 'was regarded as land won by conquest and therefore readily available'.[78] J. C. Mann writes, '[N]ewly acquired provincial land would presumably cease to be available for veteran settlement, only if and when it was assigned to recognized provincial communities by a *lex provinciae* or similar enactment. Otherwise it remained public, and at the disposal of the government, for military or other purposes.'[79] The first effect on the city was therefore probably the replacement of Greek commuting farmers and élite landowners by commuting peasant colonists and colonial élite landowners.

We might have expected a noticeable group of Greek élite landowners to maintain a high position in the town. The general Roman strategy in the Greek East involved bolstering local élites and using them as a vehicle for government.[80] A number of the native élite were sometimes incorporated into the body of Roman citizens at a colony's foundation.[81] However, in Philippi there is no evidence of the persistence of any town-based Greek élite. (The kind of evidence would be effects on some epigraphy and maybe some tendency towards Hellenisation in the élite as a whole – as happened at Corinth, for example.)[82] Since their wealth will have

[77] Appian, *B. Civ.* V, 12, tr. H. White.

[78] Salmon, *Colonization*, p. 148.

[79] Mann, *Veteran Settlement*, p. 7.

[80] G. W. Bowersock, *Augustus and the Greek World* (Oxford: Clarendon Press, 1965), *passim*.

[81] See Adrian N. Sherwin-White's discussion of Claudius' Lyons oration: *The Roman Citizenship* (Oxford: Clarendon Press, 1973[2]), pp. 237–49, 352; Levick, *Colonies*, pp. 68–76.

[82] It is unfortunate that Corinth, about which we know a great deal and which is hence potentially a useful example, has special factors which actually make it rather

been land-based, they may simply have lost their status. Alternatively they may have moved to other cities, Amphipolis and Thessalonika being two attractive possibilities. They may also have retreated to land held at the periphery of the colony, as Collart argues was the case for certain farmers.[83] Greek peasant farmers too, having lost their land, could move and seek to rent Greek-owned land elsewhere. Alternatively they could stay in Philippi and try, for example, to rent land from Romans.

Staying in Philippi was a particularly likely option for those who had lost their land. As Alcock has argued at length, increased nucleation – people moving to settlements, particularly to large ones – often accompanied peasant land loss in this period, and was a logical consequence of it.[84] The village, town or, especially, the city provided both alternative employment, if some or all of a family's income needs could not be met by farming, and various further ways of seeking support, either through a network of people of similar social level who could help absorb economic shocks or through seeking help from those of higher status. A further factor was that the loss of a self-sufficient peasant lifestyle, together with any taxation demands not taken in kind, raised a need for cash which again increased the advantage of diversifying one's employment beyond agriculture. More generally, taxation encouraged cash-cropping and hence specialisation and further concentration of land ownership. In the case of Philippi, there would also have been the immediate attraction of the need for a substantially increased service community to provide for the needs of the Romans, both those in the town and those dispersed in the countryside. Even those Romans some distance from the town would, in the colonial situation, have been tied to Philippi as a service centre. This is in marked contrast to the previous Greek situation with more diversity of centres.

Collart argues that most colonists will have lived scattered across the colony's territory.[85] Eventually, this looks correct. However, it

atypical. It was seen by the Romans as being of great historic significance as a Greek city and this affected behaviour towards the city, particularly by Hadrian. With regard to Hellenisation at Corinth, the waters are, therefore, seriously muddied. However, I imagine that the rate of Hellenisation at Corinth does also reflect the presence of a substantial number of influential Greeks.

[83] Collart, *Philippes*, p. 296.
[84] Alcock, *Graecia Capta*, pp. 106–15.
[85] Paul Collart, 'Philippes', *Dictionnaire d'Archéologie Chrétienne et de Liturgie*

seems likely that most colonists would initially live in the town, given the probable proximity of the centuriated land and the various attractions of the town itself. A particular attraction in the early period would have been security, both in numbers and in what town defences there were at that time, against Thracian raids which troubled the area during the first few decades of the colony.[86] Some colonists, on the other hand, no doubt lived from the beginning in settlements away from the town, either creating fresh villages or expanding existing ones.

Figure 8: Spread to edge of maximum territory. The limit of the city's authority moves to the maximum distance that it reached. Some colonists move into Greek villages towards the periphery of the territory. Increasing numbers of Greek peasants lose ownership of their land. In Philippi itself, the situation stays the same, apart from some further drift of Greeks from the territory into the city.

No doubt the land owned by colonists extended beyond the centuriated grid from the very beginning. Some of the colonists, whether military or civilian, must have arrived at Philippi with surplus wealth and, in line with general contemporary habits,[87] will have wanted to invest that money in land. Some land was probably traded among the Romans but the bulk of acquired land must have been taken from Greeks, either by forceable or voluntary sale, or by seizure. While individual Romans would not have had the legal right to seizure that a leader acting in the name of the Roman People had, seizure by direct violence or by economic pressure has generally been a feature of the treatment of politically and economically subjugated peoples and, as Ramsay MacMullen argues, was no doubt a common feature of relations between town-based élites and peasants in the countryside of the Roman Empire.[88]

I would thus want to disagree with Winfried Elliger's assessment that,

> Die alten Einwohner behielten zwar meistens ihre Häuser und Felder, bildeten aber die unterprivilegierte Klasse.

XIV:1, ed. F. Cabrol and H. Leclerq (Paris: Librairie Letouzy et Ané, 1939), col. 719.

[86] Collart, *Philippes*, pp. 249ff.

[87] Ramsay MacMullen, *Roman Social Relations: 50BC to AD284* (New Haven: Yale University Press, 1974), pp. 48ff.

[88] Ibid., pp. 5–16.

The old inhabitants no doubt mostly retained their houses and fields, but constituted the underprivileged class.[89]

With such a large territory as that of Philippi, it is difficult to assess what proportion of Greeks lost their land, and what proportion remained as peasant small-holders or larger landowners. However, Collart comments that 'c'est par centaines que les inscriptions relatives aux colons y [sc. right to the edges of the territory] ont été retrouvés' ('Inscriptions about the colonists have been found there in their hundreds') and 'peut-être n'est-il pas, dans toute la plaine, un seul village qui n'ait conservé quelque trace de l'établissement des colons' ('it may perhaps be that there is no village in the entire plain that has not preserved some trace of the establishment of the colonists').[90] In that case it seems very unlikely that the Greeks 'mostly' retained their land. No doubt some did, but I would think that in the Philippian context they were unusually fortunate.

One wonders whether specific occasions for the seizure of Greek land were provided by the Thracian incursions into Macedonia. Since many of the Greeks in the territory of Philippi were religiously and linguistically 'Thracian', either real or imagined support for, or acquiescence in, the rebellious invasions could become a pretext for further confiscation and appropriation of land.[91] Such a scenario could certainly have brought about extension of the colony's political control, both in terms of distance and in terms of reduction in status of Greek cities within the territory.

'City' is a term which can cover fairly small towns or even groups of villages.[92] Its significance is in the settlement being autonomous to the extent of being under only regional government rather than the government of a neighbouring city. One would expect any city, once it was within the territory, to have been reduced to the status of village, i.e., a community with very limited autonomy,[93] politically dependent on Philippi. Matters are complicated, however, by the discovery of a block re-used in a Byzantine gateway at Philippi and by investigation of a site about a dozen kilometres north of the

[89] Elliger, *Paulus in Griechenland*, p. 44, my tr.

[90] Collart, *Philippes*, pp. 290, 286.

[91] For an example of a similar phenomenon see Philippe Leveau's account of a Roman land seizure in Mauretania: *Caesarea de Maurétanie: Une Ville Romaine et ses Campagnes* (Collection de l'école française de Rome 70; Rome: École Française, 1984), p. 148.

[92] Papazoglou, *Villes*, p. 51.

[93] An example of the kind of autonomy remaining is given by an inscription from a village which regulates the wine trade in its area. Collart, *Philippes*, pp. 287f.

city. The block dates from AD 202, near the peak of the colony's 'Romanness'. It commemorates a sacrifice offered to Septimius Severus, Caracalla and Julia Domna.

Αὐτοκράτορι Καίσαρι Σε[β]αστῷ . . .
. . . οἱ Πενταπολεῖται, [   ]οι,
Ἀδριανοπολεῖται, [Β]έ[ρ]γκοι,
Σκιμβέρτιοι, Γαζώριαι, τὴν θυσίαν[94]

Of the five cities, only Gazoros and Berga were known in 1938, when the inscription was published, and they were vaguely located in, and just beyond, the far western edge of the colony's territory, about 40 km away. Recently, however, Demetrios Samsaris has argued that Hadrianoupolis is to be identified with a site at the village of Edirnedzik, not far north from Philippi. The well-known Hadrianoupolis in Thrace has the Turkish name Edirne. Our village's name means 'Little Edirne', or 'Little Hadrianopolis'.[95] Samsaris has surveyed the area and, on the basis of pottery finds, has been able to establish that there was there an archaic Thracian town, abandoned by the classical period, and then another town, 1.5 km to the south-east, founded during the Roman period.[96] He suggests for the latter a majority Thracian population with a reasonable number of colonists, and either foundation at the same time as the colony, with substantial augmentation under Hadrian, or foundation under Hadrian.[97]

The existence of a Greek-speaking *polis*, just north of Philippi, at the height of Roman dominance there, is very interesting, especially in view of its union with other towns across and outside the colony. As Roger comments, the towns need not be politically independent of the colony.[98] Independence would be highly unlikely, so one probably ought technically to describe those in Philippi's territory as *vici* (villages) of Philippi (although substantial communities probably had more legislative scope than the villages proper:

[94] J. Roger, 'L'enceinte Basse de Philippes', *BCH* 62 (1938), pp. 37f. The entire inscription is lengthy because it includes a long list of Imperial family members. The titulature of the various members dates the inscription to between AD 201 and 209 (p. 38). At the specific occasion of the inscription, representatives of these towns probably met the Emperor. This was most likely early in 202 (p. 41).

[95] D. Samsaris, 'Τοπογραφικα Προβληματα της Επικρατειας της Ρωμαικης Αποικιας των Φιλιππων: τα Πολισματα Αγγιτης και Αδριανουπολη', *Ancient Macedonia, IV*, (Thessaloniki: Institute for Balkan Studies, 1986), p. 546.

[96] Ibid., pp. 546f.

[97] Ibid., pp. 546ff.

[98] Roger, 'L'enceinte Basse', p. 41.

Papazoglou points out the particularly obvious case of Neapolis[99]). However, they regarded themselves as πόλεις and were allowed to set up an inscription in Philippi using the term and also describing their κοινόν, despite its crossing the territorial boundary. Roger notes that the *koinon* would have no longer held any political significance.[100] This is presumably true in a legislative sense. However, it does mean that Greek towns in the colony could have a reference group and a source of status outside the colony. Similarly, in using the term πόλις, they would be asserting a claim to status as a community in their own right. Concretely, there must also have been a fairly substantial, mainly Greek, population. This supports our earlier arguments for the territory's having quite a large, Greek population before the arrival of the colonists.

Philippi is the only city in Macedonia for which we have inscriptional evidence of villages dependent on it. We know fifteen names. Fourteen of these names are Thracian, one is Latin. Six inscriptions (of six villages) are in Greek lettering, eight inscriptions (of ten villages) are in Latin lettering. One village has inscriptions in each lettering. Since various of the inscriptions relate to colonists,[101] those villages would seem to be pre-existing Thracian ones which colonists have joined. Only the one Latin name, *Mediani*, suggests a settlement founded by colonists.[102]

Three factors will have given extra impetus to the spread of the colonists' land ownership. One is the gradual flow of further individual colonists into the colony. Notable are a number of veteran soldiers. A second is the economic success of some colonists leading to an extension in demand for landholding. In contrast, a third factor would be that, one way or another, some colonists would lose their land. Although, as noted above, the strongest attraction would probably then be towards seeking a living in the town, one alternative would be to attempt to gain land beyond the limits of the original settlement. The second and third factors are facets of the process of concentration of landholding – showing one limit on our ability to separate the various parts of the colony's development.

[99] Papazoglou, *Villes*, p. 412.
[100] Roger, 'L'enceinte Basse', p. 41; cf. Samsaris, 'Τοπογραφικα Προβληματα', p. 545.
[101] See particularly Collart, *Philippes*, p. 287 n. 5. The texts of the various inscriptions are given in Collart's notes to pp. 286f. There are also texts relating to colonists found at various villages but not naming the village.
[102] Papazoglou, *Villes*, p. 411.

Figure 9: Concentration of landholding.[103] Much of the pattern of
small-holding on the centuriated land has been replaced by larger
farms. Some of these are farmed as villa estates. Many of the
descendants of the original settlers have lost ownership of the land.
There are now some Roman poor in the city, the population of
which has continued to grow.

There are maybe three main phenomena involved in concentration of landholding at Philippi. One is that many peasant colonists
must have partly or wholly lost ownership of their land. Another is
that the town's élite will have grown more wealthy and a little more
numerous. A third is that estates run by agents on behalf of
absentee élite landlords appeared.

These agents, *actores*, πραγματευταί, are the main evidence of
land concentration. Six epitaphs relating to them have been
found.[104] Given the small percentage of inscriptions from any place
which survive and given the paucity of inscriptions relating to other
professions, this suggests that estate-farming must have become a
major factor in the Philippian countryside. One particular bonus is
that we have inscriptions for two *actores* of the same landowner,
Caesius Victor. They are located 38 km apart, one of them being
almost at the colony's most distant point from the town.[105]

For the peasant colonist farmers who lost the ownership of their
land there were two main ways forward. One was where the new
landowner allowed the farmer to rent the land and continue to
work it. This could be done on a variety of financial bases.[106] The
second was to move to the town and seek a partially or totally
service-based income and to hope for benefaction – which was
more likely for a Roman citizen than for a Greek, the Roman being
both more likely to benefit from civic handouts and more able to
attempt to form a standard client–patron relationship. A further
factor swelling the Roman service community would be the freeing
of slaves.

The increase in wealth of the town's élite, attested not only by the
existence of stewards but also by monumental and other luxury
construction, would (together with the increase in the town's

[103] Cf. Douglas E. Oakman, 'The Countryside in Luke-Acts', in J. H. Neyrey, ed.,
The Social World of Luke-Acts (Peabody: Hendrickson, 1991), pp. 157f., who gives a
general model of concentration of landholding, centred on debt and foreclosure.
[104] Collart, *Philippes*, p. 289.
[105] Ibid.
[106] Leveau, *Caesarea*, p. 475.

dependent territory, noted above) strengthen the 'demand' side of the town's service economy. This is most visible during the Antonine period when large numbers must have been involved in local marble-quarrying and construction. Such luxury and monumental demand must, however, also have been a significant factor in first-century Philippian life. For example, the town's first proper forum was built under Claudius and, although not as elaborate as the Antonine one, it was of the same size and must have involved considerable work.[107] One effect of this demand, particularly in the area of specialist luxury goods such as purple, was the drawing in of further merchants and craftspeople from other regions, in particular Asia. Further indigenous Greeks, too, would have been drawn into town from the countryside, bolstering the service community.

The inscriptions relating to stewards are evidence of estates with absentee landlords. These must have had an element of slave agricultural labour but they may also have involved land rented out to Romans or Greeks. Discerning whether slave-based or tenant-based land-use was predominant in an area at this period is a particularly difficult issue. The majority of owners would be likely at best to have a temporary residence on the estate, arriving, say, to supervise the harvest.[108] Evidence for a landowner living on an estate fairly permanently is provided by any presence of monumental epitaphs at the site.[109] There are enough of these to indicate a fair level of élite residence in the countryside, but other considerations (see below) suggest that most would live in the town.[110]

Our model of the development of Philippian society has considered three processes which we know to have happened at Philippi: initial occupation of land by the colonists; spread of colonial land to distant parts of the territory; concentration of land ownership. In the first two processes the interests of the colonists compete with those of the Greeks; in the third, the interests of the élite compete

---

[107] Michel Sève, *Recherches sur les Places Publiques dans le Monde Grec du Premier au Septième Siècle de Notre Ère: L'Exemple de Philippes* (Microfiche; Lille: Lille-Thèses, 1989, 1990).

[108] See Leveau, *Caesarea*, pp. 406, 417, 476f., for a range of types of ownership and residence.

[109] Ibid., p. 417.

[110] Collart, *Philippes*, p. 472. For *decuriones* (members of the municipal senate), for example, Collart's list of inscriptions (of all types, not just epitaphs) includes eight from the territory and twelve from the city (pp. 266f.). The city, of course, has been far more closely investigated and includes purely honorific monuments, which would be very rare in the countryside.

with those of everyone else. We have followed Alcock in seeing a substantial consequence of land-loss as being movement to the city. This movement then involves a further competition of interest because the interests of those arriving in the town and seeking service work or benefactions will compete with the interests of those already enjoying them. A consequence of this is that service and poor communities in the town were almost certain to have become, and remained, over-enlarged (from a functional point of view) throughout our period. This problem will have been partially alleviated by the increase in expenditure by the élite, although the most prominent forms of élite expenditure, on luxury goods, will have tended to favour specialists, who would often be migrant workers rather than indigenous peasants who had lost their land.

d. Checking the model's main implication

Before moving on to try estimating ranges of numbers for the various social groups in the town, it would be as well to ask whether the general position in which our model of the colony's development leaves the colony fits what evidence we do have about its social composition in the middle of the first century. The critical question is whether we have placed too many Greeks in the town for the number of Greek inscriptions found there.

This leads us to a sharp scholarly disagreement between Paul Lemerle and Paul Collart. At the end of an article describing three monumental, eleven honorific and seven funerary inscriptions, Collart pointed out that only two were in Greek (both were epitaphs) and that this indicated that

> le grec ne s'était guère maintenu, à Philippes même, devant le latin . . .
>
> Greek scarcely persisted, in Philippi itself, in the face of Latin . . .[111]

Lemerle responded that Collart underestimated the role of Greek in the Roman period because his digging had been almost solely in places where one would expect Roman inscriptions.[112] The collection in Collart's article is indicative of the issue. Two out of twenty-one inscriptions overall – just under 10 per cent – are in Greek.

[111] Paul Collart, 'Inscriptions de Philippes', *BCH* 56 (1932), p. 231, my tr.
[112] Lemerle, *Philippes*, p. 13 n. 1.

However, the language of inscriptions such as honorific ones will reflect political, rather than numerical factors. If we consider only the funerary inscriptions, the proportion of Greek inscriptions is two out of seven – just under 30 per cent. The really relevant figure would be that for first-century, non-élite epitaphs. Collart does not discuss dates, and the only status-indicators which look clear to me are that no. 20 is of a *libertus* and that no. 21, which is in Greek, seems elaborate enough to suggest high status. We cannot deduce anything worthwhile from this set but they do highlight the problem of the fairly inevitable selectivity of digging.

Pilhofer, in cataloguing the Philippian inscriptions as a whole, including those published in the fifty years since Collart, has been able to gain as broad a view of the inscriptional evidence as is currently possible. His impression is that the Greek element of the population was the most important factor in the overall history of the town.[113] Even on the markedly Roman period of the town's life he concludes:

> Gewiß waren die Römer zahlenmäßig nicht in der Mehrheit, wie es das römische Gepräge der Stadt vermuten lassen könnte, aber das Lebensgefühl war durch und durch römisch.

> Certainly the Romans were not numerically in the majority, as the Roman impression given by the town might lead one to surmise, but life there felt Roman through and through.[114]

Collart (and others) basically dug up the Roman forum, the Roman market, the Roman gymnasium and the Roman baths. It is actually very significant that the Roman inscriptions there are all in Latin because that was not the case in most Eastern colonies after they had been running for some time. In Corinth, despite a firmly Roman colonial foundation, by the second century the Romans were using the Greek language.[115] Something similar could be said of another Peloponnesian colony, Patrai.[116] Barbara Levick, too, contrasts the persistence of Latin in Roman inscriptions at Philippi with its decline in colonies in southern Asia Minor.[117] J. Coupry

---

[113] Pilhofer, *Philippi*, p. 90.
[114] Ibid., p. 92, my tr.
[115] Alcock, *Graecia Capta*, p. 169. But see note 82 on Corinth, above.
[116] Ibid., p. 144.
[117] Levick, *Colonies*, pp. 161f.

and M. Feyel, in an article publishing a variety of Greek inscriptions from Philippi, commented,

> [N]ous ne contredirons pas ici l'opinion reçue, selon laquelle c'est surtout après la fin des Antonins que le grec remplaça le latin, à Philippes, dans les documents *romains* [their emph.].

> [W]e will not contradict here the received opinion, according to which it is above all after the end of the Antonines that Greek replaced Latin, at Philippi, in *Roman* documents.[118]

It is very important in understanding Philippi to notice that the Romans remained very Roman for more than two-and-a-half centuries. Collart writes,

> [D]e ses trois éléments constitutifs, thrace, grec et latin, le dernier avait pu rester, pendant plus de trois siècles, préponderant. Là resident l'originalité de son histoire et l'intérêt de son développement.

> [O]f its three constituent elements, Thracian, Greek and Latin, the last of these was able to remain dominant for more than three centuries. In this lies the originality of its history and the interest of its development.[119]

However, being 'préponderant' in controlling the colony, controlling the land, controlling the wealth, and hence in putting up the great majority of prominent inscriptions, does not necessarily mean being in a majority in the population. The Roman Imperial cult temple in the forum actually contains quite a number of Greek inscriptions. They are on the joined faces of the sections of the columns – Greek letters used by the builders as marks to match up the pieces.[120] Similarly, Pilhofer notes examples of Greek units of measurement in use in Philippi.[121] If we consider priestly inscriptions found within Philippi's walls and reported by Collart in his book, Greek inscriptions are in the majority. Although there is one Latin inscription on the way to the sanctuary of the Egyptian gods,

---

[118] J. Coupry and M. Feyel, 'Inscriptions de Philippes III (I)', *BCH* 60 (1936), p. 46, my tr.
[119] Collart, *Philippes*, pp. 315f., my tr.
[120] Ibid., p. 305.
[121] Pilhofer, *Philippi*, p. 86.

for *L. Titonius Suavis, sac. Isidis*,[122] the three priestly inscriptions in the sanctuary itself are in Greek, two for a ἱερεὺς τῆς Εἴσιδος καὶ Σαράπιδος and one for Κάστωρ Ἀρτεμιδώρου ἱερητεύσας.[123] Similarly, the three priestly inscriptions in the theatre are for a ἱερεὺς Νεμέσεως,[124] while back near the centre of the city there is the inscription which includes the words,

> . . . τοῦ κρα., γυμνασιάρχου κα[ὶ] ἀρχιερέως, οἱ θρησ-
> κευτὲ (του Σεράπιδος) . . .

> . . . of the most excellent gymnasiarch and high priest, the
> devotees (of Serapis) . . .[125]

Here, the priest in the inscription is probably a priest of the Imperial cult and is the father of a Roman benefactor (and is himself a benefactor) of the Serapis cult, adherents of which have put up the inscription.[126] In the forum there are three Latin inscriptions for *flamines* of the Imperial cult.[127] On the hillside there is the long Latin inscription for the *cultores* of Silvanus which includes five priests[128] (although this inscription does also include six Greek slave names and some other people with Greek *cognomina*[129]). Seven Greek inscriptions, five Latin.

However, hardly any of these inscriptions are first-century (Bormann notes that one of the Isis inscriptions could be from the end of the first century – but he prefers to follow Collart in a second-century date[130] – and I imagine that one or two of the *flamines* might be first-century). Furthermore, there is likely to be a systematic skewing of the evidence. Undated Greek inscriptions are more likely to be from the third century onwards when dated inscriptions are usually in Greek. Undated Latin inscriptions are likely to be before then. However, some of the Greek inscriptions are from the second century, a period when Latin in the colony was still overwhelmingly predominant in civic inscriptions. They thus testify to the presence of Greek-speakers in such a context and

[122] Collart, *Philippes*, p. 266. The same man has another inscription at the village of Angista.
[123] Ibid.
[124] Ibid.
[125] Ibid., my tr.
[126] Bormann, *Philippi*, p. 60.
[127] Collart, *Philippes*, p. 265.
[128] Ibid., p. 266.
[129] Pilhofer, *Philippi*, p. 109.
[130] Bormann, *Philippi*, p. 67.

hence give some support to the idea that the same was likely to have been true in the first century.

For the first century we seem to have very little evidence either way. What matters for population estimates is non-élite evidence, and there is very little that can be dated to this period. The best we can do is probably to consider the situation for second-century inscriptions and assume that not too much will have changed. For that period, as we have noted, there are some Greek cult inscriptions and some Greek labourers' inscriptions. In our model, these are kinds of inscriptions that we would expect to find. We would also expect epitaphs from Greeks who were in the service sector and could afford such things, but I am not aware of any substantial work done on Philippian graveyards.

Our sample of inscriptions is very small. Writing on Rome, P. Huttunen, with what seems excessive caution, gives, as his first argument against H. Solin's assertion that he had proved a link between Greek *cognomina* at Rome and servile birth, the fact of the small quantity of epitaph material preserved.[131] Solin's study covered more than 26,000 epitaphs. Huttunen might just wonder why we are bothering considering a list of twelve priestly inscriptions in a discussion on the town's overall population!

Yet it is worth while, because what we are doing is testing our model against the set of inscriptions we have. On the question of the number of Greeks in the town the inscriptions are not sufficiently numerous to offer positive support to our model. However, if places in which our model would expect to find Greek inscriptions, such as the temple of the Egyptian gods and the joints of columns, had yielded only Latin ones, this would have contradicted our model and would be a strong reason to go back and rebuild it. On the other hand, since our model puts almost all the power and wealth in the city in the hands of Romans, the model would also suggest that honorific inscriptions ought to appear in Latin only.

The honorific and similar inscriptions in town are actually a major source for the political aspect of our model (in particular for the lack of a significant Greek élite) and they offer positive support for it. For the population aspect of our model, the inscriptional evidence is such that it can only go as far as not negating it. That still constitutes an important test. Should study of Philippi reach

[131] Pertti Huttunen, *The Social Strata in the Imperial City of Rome: A Quantitative Study of the Social Representation in the Epitaphs published in the Corpus Inscriptionum Latinarum Volumen VI* (Oulu: University of Oulu, 1974), pp. 195f.

the stage when we have available a classified collection of a substantial number of epitaphs covering a wide social spectrum then this test will have to be redone and we may also be able to draw positive inferences about the population.

3.   A model of the social composition of the town of Philippi

Figure 10 is an enlargement of the diagram of the city in figure 9. Particularly because of the concentration of landholding, the service groups and the poor now include Romans. Many of the peasant colonists no longer own their land.

We now need to ask questions about the relative proportions of the various social groups in the city. We will focus on the city itself rather than the colonial territory as a whole because it is mainly the city that is relevant for understanding the likely composition of the church.

Bruce Malina, in *The New Testament World*, applies a general model for pre-industrial cities to the first-century Mediterranean world as a whole:

> The preindustrial city contained no more than ten percent of the entire population under its direct and immediate control. And of this ten percent that constituted the preindustrial urban population, perhaps less than two percent belonged to the élite or high class . . . The majority of the urbanites (the remaining eight percent) were engaged in handicraft manufacturing . . .
>   . . . below the low-class urbanite stood the marginal group of beggars and slaves.[132]

The wider the range of cases covered by a model, the more useful it is, and it is certainly very useful to build categories, 'pre-industrial city' and 'industrial city', to bring out the many common features of cities prior to industrialisation and thus to provide a model by which those whose assumptions about cities are based on industrial ones can better interpret data from the other type of culture. In the NT field, there is, as well as Malina's work, Richard Rohrbaugh's useful application of this to the study of Luke-Acts.[133]

However, to construct a model which covers, say, Elizabethan

---

[132] Malina, *NT World*, pp. 72f.
[133] Rohrbaugh, 'Pre-Industrial City'.

Colchester and Roman Colchester requires a great deal of general-isation. The model can easily become too general to be useful for a particular interpretative purpose. Conversely, a model which is sufficiently specific to be useful for such a purpose may easily be insufficiently general to fit the range of cases which it is supposed to cover. In particular, the mis-match between the details of the model and the period in which the interpreter's interest lies may be so great as to hamper the usefulness of the model for helping the interpreter.[134] For the purpose of interpreting Paul's letters to first-century Achaia, Rome or Philippi, and probably for his other letters too, a model of the 'pre-industrial city', drawn to a level of detail such as Malina's, has too serious a mis-match with the likely context to be of great use. Various factors such as the peculiarly narrow élite base and the presence of slaves and of commuting farmers make it necessary to build a more specific and more complicated model than Malina's if it is to be useful for interpreting Pauline texts. We at least need a model for 'the Graeco-Roman city' rather than for 'the pre-industrial city' in general.[135] My own aim is the more limited one of building a useful model specifically for Philippi.

Malina's model for the city (as opposed to the countryside) consists of up to 20 per cent élite and 80 per cent craftspeople. As my pulling together of quotations from him shows, this leaves beggars and slaves in an anomalous position. I will argue, below, that the proportion of slaves in the population of Philippi was likely to be of the order of 20 per cent, so they certainly ought to have been built into his model if it was to be useful for a town of that kind. Beggars are a more uncertain group because there will have been a continuum of positions from craftspeople who could not quite make ends meet to destitute firewood sellers who also begged, then right through to those who simply begged. Malina's characterisation of the service community as solely involved in handicraft manufacturing sits uneasily with the inscriptions at

---

[134] This can happen through a parameter being considerably too loosely specified for the period of interest, and hence giving a false impression, as well as through details being incorrect. For example, if our model for a pre-industrial city contained the element, 'the proportion of slaves does not exceed 40 per cent', and we used the model to interpret texts directed at people from Elizabethan Colchester, then our model would be likely to lead us down various blind alleys, even though it was mathematically correct.

[135] In fact, two models are probably needed: one for the very large Graeco-Roman cities and one for the more typical ones.

Philippi where the jobs attested include cashier, hunter, town-crier, head of a troupe of actors, stage-manager, and doctor.[136] Such professions are more likely to leave inscriptions than craftspeople are, but they do indicate that, at a place like Philippi, a substantial percentage of the service community would not be engaged in handicrafts.

More important, however, is what for Philippi must be a very significant lacuna in Malina's model, namely the absence of commuting farmers. A particularly clear counter-example to the model is Koressos, a city in the province of Achaia which Alcock discusses. She argues that there were never more than 25 per cent of the population of the *polis* as a whole (town plus countryside) living away from the town.[137] Since the great majority of the population of the *polis* must have been involved in farming, commuting farmers, living in the town and travelling daily to their fields, must have been central to the population of the town itself. Under the Roman Empire in Achaia and Macedonia, commuting farmers must have been widespread.[138] This is especially so since, as Alcock argues, peasant loss of land ownership and the demands of cash taxation will have made residence in town, with its options for supplementing farming income, increasingly attractive for farmers.[139] Philippe Leveau has found evidence in the Roman period for one form of farming particularly suited to commuting, namely market-gardening, in the pattern of cisterns in the area around the edge of Caesarea in Mauretania.[140] Alcock notes that farmers are willing to commute far further than this fringe area.[141]

The only possibility for commuting farmers not being an important group at Philippi would be if almost all the land near the town was farmed by slaves. This, however, is unlikely in general in the Roman Empire[142] and is extremely unlikely at Philippi given its foundation as a Roman colony. Even with the land concentration for which I have argued above, a substantial number of Roman peasant farmers must still have owned their land in the middle of the first century. Furthermore, those who had lost ownership,

[136] Collart, *Philippes*, pp. 271ff.
[137] Alcock, *Graecia Capta*, p. 117.
[138] Garnsey and Saller, *Roman Empire*, p. 98.
[139] Alcock, *Graecia Capta*, ch. 3.
[140] Leveau, *Caesarea*, p. 466.
[141] Alcock, *Graecia Capta*, p. 82.
[142] Garnsey and Saller, *Roman Empire*, pp. 72, 111.

probably through debt,[143] would be likely to continue to rent some or all of their former land and to carry on farming it.

The most serious problem, however, in applying Malina's model to Roman cities is that it suggests the possibility of an implausible 20 per cent of a town's population being of élite status. The problem is generated by two factors. First, Malina's 'perhaps less than two percent' may be fair for the proportion of élite in pre-industrial societies as a whole, but Graeco-Roman society had a particularly narrow élite. MacMullen writes of 'the small number of officers in the army and the few decurions in cities. Perhaps that last proportion needs emphasis. It marked off the aristocracy from the masses in the most blatant fashion.'[144] Meeks concludes from MacMullen's suggested figures that the élite, those of the status of local councillor (decurion) or above, 'comprised considerably less than 1 percent of the population'.[145] Whether or not Meeks is justified in drawing the 'considerably' from MacMullen's figures, a model which was useful for Graeco-Roman society would seem to be better with the élite as 'perhaps less than one percent' rather than two.

This halves the suggested maximum proportion of élite. Our questioning of Malina's figure of 'no more than ten percent' of the total population of an area living in the town takes us further. Malina's figure has the effect of multiplying the concentration of élite in the town by ten, converting a 2 per cent figure for the élite overall to 20 per cent in the town.

Malina's assumption that all the élite live in the town is fairly reasonable. Those of decurial status probably had to have a house or large apartment in town.[146] Leveau observed that no inland rural villa in his survey of the hinterland of Caesarea showed signs of a substantial residential section and concluded that few landowners were likely to have done more than spend brief periods at the villas, inspecting agricultural work.[147] As noted above, he did, however, suggest that signs of tombs by villas would be an indication of a real link between a family and an area.[148] We do have

---

143 See Oakman, *Countryside*, pp. 157f.

144 MacMullen, *Social Relations*, p. 97.

145 Wayne A. Meeks, *The First Urban Christians: The Social World of the Apostle Paul* (New Haven: Yale University Press, 1983), p. 53, citing MacMullen, *Social Relations*, pp. 88–91.

146 Peter Garnsey, *Social Status and Legal Privilege in the Roman Empire* (Oxford: Clarendon Press, 1970), p. 244.

147 Leveau, *Caesarea*, p. 476.

148 Ibid., p. 417.

evidence of élite tombstones in the Philippian countryside so the élite may not have all lived in the town. However, the assumption that they did seems reasonable at the level of accuracy of a useful model.

Koressos, where the peak dispersion of population (which was in the classical period) saw 25 per cent in the countryside, shows that Malina's figure of at least 90 per cent (or, even more so, Rohrbaugh's figure of at least 93 per cent[149]) is far from applying everywhere in the Roman period. We can extend the observation elsewhere in Achaia. Alcock also cites Hyettos, with 30 per cent in the countryside.[150] A bloated city, such as Corinth, will also have had a low figure and Achaia generally was heavily urbanised. Italy is another region for which we can sometimes estimate worthwhile figures and Duncan-Jones' discussion of some of the best-known cases seems to suggest that Malina's figure is far from applying there either.[151] Garnsey and Saller adopt Hopkins' estimate that 68 per cent of the six million inhabitants of Italy lived in the countryside.[152] If we exclude Rome, with about one million inhabitants,[153] the figure rises to 80 per cent. This is much closer to Malina's but, if the percentage in the towns is 20 per cent instead of Malina's 10 per cent, then the proportion of élite in the towns will have again been halved. In fact, we cannot simply remove Rome from one side of the equation. We would need to take a few points off the countryside figure as well, so the percentage is not quite as close to Malina's as it appears. Two other spheres of Paul's action, Ephesus and Antioch, fall into a similar category to Corinth. For such overgrown cities, Malina's 90 per cent in the countryside cannot be used. In a variety of Pauline contexts at least, the figure of 90 per cent seems inappropriate. For Philippi, 90 per cent does not seem possible. Instead of a figure of 1:9, the city to country ratio seems more likely to be about 1:2.

Let us consider first the population of the city. My impression of the ground at Philippi is that about 45 Ha was likely to be built

[149] Rohrbaugh, 'Pre-Industrial city', p. 133. Rohrbaugh also uses a figure of up to 5–10 per cent élite in the total population.

[150] Alcock, *Graecia Capta*, p. 96.

[151] R. Duncan-Jones, *The Economy of the Roman Empire: Quantitative Studies* (Cambridge: Cambridge University Press, 1982²), pp. 259–77.

[152] Garnsey and Saller, *Roman Empire*, p. 6, following K. Hopkins, *Conquerors and Slaves* (Cambridge: Cambridge University Press, 1978), pp. 68f.

[153] Garnsey and Saller, *Roman Empire*, p. 6.

on.[154] If the population density equalled that of Pompeii,[155] which we know fairly well, Philippi would house 10,000. Adding, say, 5,000 for the suburb, we have 15,000. An alternative approach is that of Pilhofer. He follows Lazarides in using the size of the theatre as a means of estimating the population. This is a precarious method since theatre-size could reflect the hoped-for prestige of a city rather than its present population. This is particularly an issue at Philippi because the theatre was built in the fourth century BC by Philip II, not by the Romans. However, Pilhofer does have a somewhat reasonable argument because, by the second century AD, demand seems to have outstripped the supply of seats and the theatre was extended to a total capacity of 8,000. He suggests that this represents a population of 5–10,000.[156] This is of the same order as my estimate but a bit lower. I agree that he can use the second-century theatre extension as evidence for the first-century population but I would argue that a theatre extension is only evidence for a minimum figure for the population. With surplus demand you may extend your theatre, but the size of the extension seems likely to depend more on your financial situation and (in Philippi) the topography of the area around the theatre than on the maximum possible audience. A population figure somewhat higher than Pilhofer's seems quite possible – although we are, in any case, talking about the same class of town size.

Fanoula Papazoglou, in her study on the extent of the territory of Philippi, does not give a figure for its area. However, her deliberations,[157] when traced on a map, seem to leave it at about 1900 sq. km, the figure also used by Barbara Levick.[158] Papazoglou seems reasonable in being dubious about the contorted shape that the western arm of Philippi's territory takes if we construct it strictly by following inscriptions which relate to the colony. However, her specific case for amputating the arm seems to collapse since it centres on the argument that the independence of the town of Gazoros means its exclusion from the territory. As she herself indicates, Hadrianoupolis raises the same issues but cannot be excluded since it is right in the territory's heart.[159] Pilhofer's

---

[154] See note 11 above.
[155] Duncan-Jones, *Economy*, p. 276.
[156] Pilhofer, *Philippi*, p. 74.
[157] Papazoglou, *Villes*, pt 2, ch. IV.
[158] Levick, *Colonies*, p. 45.
[159] Papazoglou, *Villes*, p. 410. See pp. 30–2, above.

territory is similar to that of Papazoglou. The main difference is that the number of Latin inscriptions at Neapolis makes him confident of its inclusion[160] whereas Papazoglou omits it. Taking Philippi's territory as 1900 sq. km, assuming a population density comparable to Italy for this accessible and largely very fertile region, and then taking loosely from P. A. Brunt[161] a figure of 24 per sq. km for the population density of Italy, we arrive at about 46,000.

This places about one-third of the territory's total population in the town. Philippi probably overflowed its walls in our period. It is difficult, therefore, to reduce the population below about 10,000. This means that, for Malina's 90 per cent, the total population of the territory would need to be 100,000. This would require twice the population density estimated for Italy and does not seem plausible. Furthermore, of those living outside Philippi, many would have lived in substantial towns such as Neapolis, rather than in the countryside or small villages. Malina's model seems not to fit Philippi.

We can also critique Malina's figures from the point of view of their outcome. A Roman city with 20 per cent élite residents would not function. Its population would consist of little more than the élite and their domestic slaves. The figure also does not fit the likely developmental pattern of a Roman city. As well as craftspeople, whose existence a functional model would predict, providing services for the élite, the presence of the élite would draw in existing or would-be clients, the poor and, as argued above, far too many craftspeople for the jobs needed, producing the continuum of viable and non-viable workers already described. The population would thus be swollen into one with substantial (if low-value) economic activity at one or two removes from the élite. Again as noted above, Alcock describes the various forces driving increased nucleation under the early Empire.[162] At Philippi, there was also a substantial force of non-élite but economically viable colonist farmers.

Taking all these factors into account, I cannot envisage the proportion of élite (people of decurial status, including close relatives) in a town such as Philippi as being more than 5 per cent. This finds support in Lane Fox's general comment, 'The order of

---

[160] Pilhofer, *Philippi*, pp. 66–7.
[161] Brunt, *Italian Manpower*, p. 126. I have taken his upper figure then subtracted one-seventh to remove Rome.
[162] Alcock, *Graecia Capta*, ch. 3.

city councillors would cover 5 per cent, at most, of a city's adult male population'.[163] To estimate a lower limit for the proportion, we can start from an estimate of the percentage of élite in the total population. Taking MacMullen's kinds of figures, and bearing in mind that Philippi had a reasonable continuing supply of distinguished veterans, it must be at least half a per cent. At least about two-thirds of the population probably lived away from the city so, assuming all the élite lived in the city, this gives a minimum of 1.5 per cent élite in the city.

Within this range from 1.5 per cent to 5 per cent, 3 per cent seems a reasonable estimate. We can even support this figure, by various means – albeit highly approximate ones. First, if one-third of the territory's total population lived in the town, then there would be 3 per cent élite in the town if the proportion of élite in the total population was 1 per cent, a figure which does look reasonable, given the nature of Philippi. An alternative calculation, which is equally suspect but which gives a useful feel for some of the figures that are likely to be involved, starts from MacMullen's statement that towns with Italian charters typically had 100 decurions (local councillors) but that they were sometimes in short supply.[164] If Philippi managed 100 fairly exactly, and we add family members, we might have, say, 500 inhabitants of decurial status. Taking our tentative estimate of population of about 15,000, this would again give a figure of 3 per cent.

Let us now move from the top of Philippi's social structure to the bottom. The boundary-line between the service community and the poor would not be sharply visible if one lived in Philippi. The poor would range from those solely begging, through those selling marginal goods such as firewood, to those involved in mainstream service activities. What distinguishes the group is that their income is below subsistence level. MacMullen cites fourteenth- to fifteenth-century European evidence of one-third of the population being in habitual want. He argues that the figure for the Empire was unlikely to be lower.[165] Given the nature of Philippi, we should probably take a somewhat lower figure than the average: say, a range of 15–30 per cent, with a nominal estimate towards the bottom end: say, 20 per cent.

[163] Robin Lane Fox, *Pagans and Christians* (Harmondsworth: Viking, 1986), p. 57.

[164] MacMullen, *Social Relations*, p. 90.

[165] Ibid., p. 93.

It will be clear that I am not following Justin Meggitt in using Peter Garnsey's definition of the 'poor' as those at or near subsistence level.[166] This leads Meggitt to describe 99 per cent of Graeco-Roman society as poor.[167] I imagine it is right that almost all the non-élite lived near subsistence level. The peasant colonist farmers and service-providers in my model do not constitute a 'middle class' – although I imagine that a small proportion would be some way above subsistence. However, if I am going to paint a picture of Philippian society, I need an economic marker that indicates a smaller proportion of the population. I think that it is more useful to describe as poor those who are below a healthy subsistence level – those who are, in MacMullen's terms, in habitual want. This definition ought also to fit better with the perceptions of the Graeco-Roman non-élite. When Paul talks about 'remembering the poor' (Gal. 2.10), he would not see this as a term describing almost everybody.

Slaves are subsumed under each section of figure 10 except the poor, included with their owners. These are slaves living in town, who are likely either to be domestic servants or working alongside their owners at crafts.[168] Duncan-Jones discusses figures for proportions of slaves, such as Galen's figure of 22 per cent and Brunt's estimate of 40 per cent for Augustan Italy.[169] Garnsey and Saller see 30 per cent as a reasonable estimate for Rome.[170] MacMullen estimates 25 per cent for Italy and 10 per cent for the provinces.[171] Given Philippi's substantial Roman population, who would have owned most of the slaves, we probably ought to use a figure more like that for Italy than like that for the provinces. A range of 15–30 per cent, with a nominal figure of 20 per cent, again looks reasonable.

The size of the peasant farming community (owning or renting land) who commute from the town will have been fairly fixed since before colonisation because the amount of land within economic walking distance is fixed. They may have suffered a slight decline if

---

[166] P. Garnsey and G. Woolf, 'Patronage of the rural poor in the Roman world' in A. Wallace-Hadrill, ed., *Patronage in Ancient Society* (London: Routledge, 1990), p. 153.

[167] Justin J. Meggitt, *Paul, Poverty and Survival*, (Edinburgh: T&T Clark, 1998), p. 50.

[168] Garnsey and Saller, *Roman Empire*, p. 265.

[169] Duncan-Jones, *Economy*, p. 265.

[170] Garnsey and Saller, *Roman Empire*, p. 83.

[171] MacMullen, *Social Relations*, p. 92.

any estates farmed at least partly by slaves have appeared within this radius. The substantial growth which took place in the town will therefore be in the service and poor communities and among slaves. Also, as conditions for trade improved during the first-century peace, the number of those in the town engaged in external trade will have increased. In the model, these are included in the service sector. As argued above, the double land-loss involved in the early history of the colony – first by Greeks and then by many of the poorer Roman colonists – will also have swelled both the service groups[172] and the poor.

This growth in the service, poor and slave groups means that the proportion of colonist farmers in the town in the mid-first century cannot have been too high – say, above 30 per cent. On the other hand it cannot have dropped too far – say, below 20 per cent. I am inclined to put the figure at about the lower limit. This means about 3,000 people. Given the typical scale of Roman colonial settlements of the kind that happened at Philippi[173] this seems a reasonable number for colonists' descendants and their families who are still living in the town and primarily occupied in farming. Of course, many of these colonist farmers will have lost the ownership of part or all of their land and would be at least partially renting. In our model, we will represent this as a 50–50 split between those owning land and those renting.

If we use our nominal estimates and take the remainder as our figure for the service groups, then the population of the town in our model would consist of something like 37 per cent service groups, 20 per cent slaves, 20 per cent colonist farmers (10 per cent owning their land, 10 per cent renting), 20 per cent poor, 3 per cent élite. All these figures include any family members.

Since Philippi was an agricultural colony, the Roman settlers would all have been given land. The service community would, therefore, initially be almost wholly Greek. By the middle of the first century, Roman *liberti* and colonists who had lost their land must have shifted the balance, maybe to something like one-third Roman, two-thirds Greek. The poor must have been predominantly Greek, but there were various mechanisms by which either

---

[172] I have argued, above, that many in this sector will have also done some farming. In my model I have separated groups out as 'farmers' and 'service groups' – the titles represent their main activity.

[173] Brunt suggests 2,000–3,000 for the typical size of colonies of this period: *Italian Manpower*, p. 261.

Table 1. *The composition of the population model of the town of*
Philippi, under various scenarios

	Service	Slaves	Colonist farmers	Poor	Elite	Roman	Greek, etc.
Standard scenario	37	20	20	20	3	40	60
High slave	27	30	20	20	3	37	63
High poor	27	20	20	30	3	39	61
High colonist farmer	32	20	30	15	3	47	53

freed or freeborn Romans could fall into that situation and we
could use a figure such as one-quarter Roman, three-quarters
Greek, in our model. This leaves the model with 40 per cent Roman
citizens, 60 per cent 'Greeks' – or, more strictly, non-citizens who
were largely Greek-speakers.

Table 1 shows these figures. The top line gives the figures that we
will use. I have then put in a line of figures using the assumption
that the percentage of slaves was at its probable maximum and
have worked out what effect that would have on the proportions of
Romans and Greeks. I have then tried the same thing with the
maximum number of poor and the maximum number of colonist
farmers. I have assumed that an increase in the figure for either the
slaves or the poor would mean more service work being done by
those categories of people and so the percentage of free, economically viable service-providers would drop. An increase in the number
of colonist farmers is assumed to be at the expense of the service
groups and the poor.

4.   Veteran soldiers in Philippi in the middle of the first century AD

Since a number of scholars have made the exegetical assumption
that the bulk of the hearers of Philippians were veteran soldiers, we
must turn our attention briefly to an estimate of the number of
veterans likely to be in Philippi at the time of the letter.

It was now almost a century since the division of land at Philippi
among veterans and other colonists and that land would, of course,
have been passed on by inheritance rather than allocated to newly

arriving veterans. However, later veterans could choose to settle in Philippi. Some could be men from Philippi who had left to serve in the army, then returned. They would presumably buy land with the money they had at retirement, either from existing owners or from land which was still owned publicly. We have epigraphical evidence of a number of these later veteran settlers.[174]

In the early years of the century, when Macedonia was under threat from Thrace, it is just possible that there could have been some encouragement for veterans to settle in Philippi to strengthen a local reserve force.[175] However, Karl Bornhäuser is incorrect both in his assessment of the continuing military significance of Philippi and in his understanding of the nature of ongoing veteran settlement when he writes,

> Bei der strategischen Bedeutung der Stadt ist es selbstver-
> ständlich, daß sie immer wieder einmal einen Nachschub
> von Veteranen erhielt.

> With the strategic significance of the town it is self-evident
> that it would have again and again received a supply of
> veterans.[176]

By the middle of the first century, Philippi was far from any potential area of conflict and hence not of substantial military importance. Veterans tended to settle either back home or in the frontier districts where they served, where they 'were well placed to acquire land at little or no cost'[177] and were quite likely to have an unofficial wife and family. Mann writes, 'Most of the veterans known in the pre-Hadrianic colonies were probably men who had returned home. Such colonies also, and more especially those away from the military areas, must soon have become settled communities with little to offer a veteran who was not a native.'[178]

[174] Collart, *Philippes*, pp. 293f.
[175] Cf. Bowersock, *Augustus*, p. 70. However, Benjamin Isaac has argued strongly that veteran colonies would not have been used in this way: *The Limits of Empire: The Roman Army in the East* (Oxford: Clarendon Press, 1992 (revd)), pp. 315, 331f.
[176] D. Karl Bornhäuser, *Jesus imperator mundi (Phil 3, 17–21 u. 2, 5–12)* (Gütersloh: Bertelsmann, 1938), p. 10, my tr.
[177] Garnsey, *Legal Privilege*, p. 249. In n. 5 he cites H. Schmitz, *Stadt und Imperium: Köln in römischer Zeit* (Cologne, 1948) for the average amount of such land being 1 sq. km (100 Ha), which A. Mócsy, *Die Bevölkerung von Pannonien bis zu den Markomannenkriegen* (Budapest: Verlag der Ungarischen Akademie der Wissenschaften, 1959), p. 91, describes as the average holding for a decurion.
[178] Mann, *Veteran Settlement*, p. 18.

A legionary with his 12,000 sesterces *praemium*, or a praetorian with his 20,000 sesterces,[179] together with any booty or other savings, would be in a good position, if returning to relatives, to add to a family's landholdings in the territory. In contrast, although an isolated soldier could arrive and seek to acquire land which would make him the leading man in a village, such a plan would seem neither particularly easy nor particularly attractive. Of soldiers from Philippi, and hence potential returnees, there are 52 known out of about 250 soldiers from Macedonia as a whole[180] (although most of these actual soldiers are not potential returnees because we know of them from gravestones found elsewhere!). This is a high figure (the other high ones are 57 from Scupi and 36 from Thessalonika) and follows the general trends for the sons of veterans to be 'somehat less reluctant than Roman citizens in general to serve in the imperial army'.[181] Thus a noticeable percentage of mid-first-century colonist households (5 per cent? 10 per cent?) may have been headed by a veteran. Presumably, involvement in the army among the élite, as officers, would be substantially higher than this average. My estimate is that colonists (élite or farming) formed 23 per cent of the city population. Heads of household would, say, be one-quarter of that: 6 per cent. Ten per cent of heads of colonial households would thus be 0.6 per cent of the population. This looks a reasonable estimate for the number of veterans, a group whose families would be in, or a little beyond, the fringes of élite status.

At first glance, these conclusions seem strongly opposed to those of Lukas Bormann. In his recent book on Philippi, he argues for the continuing role of veteran soldiers in shaping the town's 'self-understanding' – especially its identification with Imperial policy.[182] However, there is no substantial disagreement. Unlike the original veteran settlement, quite a high proportion of the veterans who settled later, individually, are likely to have attained

[179] J. B. Campbell, *The Emperor and the Roman Army, 31BC–AD235* (Oxford: Clarendon Press, 1984), p. 162. A labourer in Rome earned 3–4 sesterces/day, a farm-labourer 2 sesterces/day. An average family needed 450 sesterces/year for wheat to survive (ibid., p. 177). The census requirement for a decurion (from second-century evidence) was 100,000 sesterces (Garnsey, *Legal Privilege*, p. 243).

[180] Théodore Chr. Sarikakis, 'Des Soldats Macédoniens dans l'Armée Romaine', *Ancient Macedonia, II* (Thessaloniki: Institute for Balkan Studies, 1977), p. 433.

[181] Salmon, *Colonization*, p. 150.

[182] Bormann, *Philippi*, p. 28.

decurial status,[183] and those who did not would have been at least able to be leading figures in villages. My estimate for decurions as a whole was 0.6 per cent of the town's population so, if, say, a quarter of veterans joined the decuriate, they would form a quarter of it – probably a particularly influential quarter. The important point for my thesis is that there was probably a negligible proportion of veterans among the hearers of the letter. The important point for Bormann's thesis is that there was probably a high proportion of veterans among the colony's authorities.

My conclusions about veteran soldiers demonstrate the importance of using numbers in modelling. Without numbers it is very difficult to combine different elements of an estimate – in this case the proportion of colonists, the proportion of heads of household and the proportion of veteran heads. If the elements are not properly combined then completely unrealistic impressions about the population may be maintained. Scholars may jump from the evidence for a fair number of veteran heads of colonist households to thinking that veterans would constitute a substantial percentage of the population in Paul's day – neglecting the two diluting factors. Scholars are properly wary about putting figures on things of which we have only vague knowledge. Our calculation is actually a clear case in point: all the figures are very vague estimates. However, there is a limit to their vagueness. Colonist farmers and landowners cannot exceed about 50 per cent of the city's population. The average size of households cannot be less than about four. The proportion of veterans as heads is very unlikely (in the middle of the first century AD) to be above 25 per cent. The calculation still gives a result of only 3 per cent veterans if we push the figures to their limit. The conclusion drawn from the calculation, that the proportion of veterans in the population was extremely small, is a secure one. If we slant these figures on account of social accessibility (see chapter 2, below), the maximum plausible percentage of veterans in the church becomes even lower. It is possible that an individual veteran in the church could have been an important figure in it. However, the exegetical assumption that a substantial group of the hearers were likely to have been veterans seems completely indefensible.

Some may still be doubtful of the value of spending time 'playing

---

[183] My arguments, above, suggest that most ordinary soldiers would not have found Philippi an attractive choice for retirement.

with numbers' when we could be devoting ourselves to the usual material of NT scholarship, about which we can be 'more certain'. Two quotations from P. A. Brunt are apposite.

> An eminent demographer [D. V. Glass] has written that 'for some purpose it may clearly be more useful to have an estimate subject to a 15 or 20 per cent error than no estimate at all'. For antiquity an even wider margin of error may have to be accepted, and the estimate still be better than nothing. It should be obvious that if we have no conception of the numbers of peoples about whom we write and read we cannot envisage them in their concrete reality. What does a statement about the Romans *mean*, if we do not know roughly how many Romans there were? Without such knowledge even politics and war cannot be understood.
>   . . . data are not lacking, and perhaps permit solutions not less convincing than for conundrums of political conduct and motivation which never cease to exercise the ingenuity of scholars.[184]

For the word 'political', various others, such as 'religious', could certainly be substituted.

The likely pattern of the development of Philippi means that the majority of the population of the town were probably not Romans and not citizens. As noted above, I will gather these together under the term, 'Greek'. Many were ethnically Greek and their predominant language would have been Greek. However, the scholars whose conclusions I am challenging are talking about the church, not the town. Might the church be predominantly Roman even though the town was predominantly Greek? Let us now consider the Philippian church.

---

[184] Brunt, *Italian Manpower*, pp. 3, 4.

2

THE PHILIPPIAN CHURCH

1. Approach

There are two starting-points that scholars tend to use when reflecting on the make-up of the Philippian church. The first is the New Testament evidence, either about individuals in the church or about the church's financial relationship with Paul. The second is general evidence about Philippi, such as its characterisation as a Roman veteran colony. Each starting-point is problematic.

Starting from the New Testament evidence about a very small number of individuals cannot take us far at all. Acts 16 gives us the professions of three people who might be members of the church when the letter is written. The letter itself gives us four names of Philippians and some slight clues about their status. These seven provide no route to characterising the church as a whole. Starting from the church's financial relationship with Paul is also of little help. The amount of money needed to provide worthwhile gifts to an itinerant missionary would not be a substantial burden on any church of a size large enough to have distinct ἐπίσκοποι καὶ διάκονοι (see below).

Starting from a general characterisation of Philippi as a Roman veteran colony is not viable either. The main reasons are those discussed in chapter 1, above. However, the scholars who use this starting-point do then take a methodologically useful approach. After their first step of deducing that Philippi was full of veteran soldiers, their next – unstated – step is to assume that the church will be made up of the kind of people in the town. This is a reasonable initial working assumption. It then needs testing (and modifying somewhat: see below). These scholars do then test their view against the data in the New Testament. They find that several points in the letter fit such recipients very well. They also see that their recipients would indeed be in a good position to support Paul financially.

Because these scholars are not consciously modelling, their testing goes astray. Instead of trying to write a list of the groups that might make up the whole Philippian church, they pick one group, veteran soldiers, look for evidence supporting that group's presence, then use that as the key group for their exegesis. They are unconsciously using a model of the church as largely consisting of veteran soldiers but, because they do not think of it as a model of the church, they do not test it against the New Testament data as a whole. If they tried to do so, their model would come to grief when faced with the evidence either about the nature of Pauline churches in general or about the named individuals likely to be in the church at Philippi. In the latter case the predominant group is Greek women and there is not a likely veteran soldier to be seen. The New Testament evidence about the Philippian Christians does not provide a viable starting-point for deciding the make-up of the church but it does provide a key test for any explicit or implicit model which is to be used as a basis for exegesis.

The general method of the second group of scholars seems reasonable. They start from the assumption that the church will be like the town then test this assumption against the New Testament data. A major caution is, however, clearly needed. The adherents of a particular religion in a town might be highly untypical of the town as a whole. Devotees of a particular cult in Philippi might all be immigrant workers from one village in Asia Minor.

The situation is not as desperate as this. Throughout the New Testament, evidence consistently indicates churches that were diverse, both ethnically and socially. This is illustrated most graphically in the list of Christians in Romans 16. To this we can add the fact that many possible eccentric models of the church at Philippi (for example, if all the members were thought to be slaves) would not test well against the specific New Testament data about that church. Furthermore, if the church had had a very eccentric composition, we might have expected clues in the letter as to such a composition. However, if the starting-point for the model of the church is the model of the town's social make-up, we do need to adjust our model to some extent to take account of the fact that some types of people in the town are much less likely than others to have joined the church.

Since the church at Philippi was a result of the Pauline mission,

Paul himself probably constitutes the best starting-point for assessing which groups were likely to have been under- or over-represented in the church. The assumption I will use is that the composition of the church will be slanted towards those more accessible to Paul (and, by extension, towards a somewhat similar group, who will be most accessible to Paul's converts).

Accessibility will have two definite dimensions and a third probable one. The first is spatial accessibility. If Paul arrives in the town and preaches there, he will not have access to farmers in distant valleys. Such farmers will come occasionally to the town, but if they only spend, say, 2 per cent of their time there, they will have little opportunity to come across Paul. Moreover, it may be only the farmer and a couple of relatives or slaves who come into town, leaving a dozen people at home, so the proportion of people from that area who may meet Paul is even lower. It seems safe to suggest that people a substantial distance from Philippi will be sharply under-represented in the church. We will use the assumption that the church will be composed of people living in the town of Philippi itself (or in the immediately neighbouring area which, in our model, is included in the population of the town). This, of course, fits with the impression gained from Acts and the Epistles about the general nature of the churches founded by Paul: that they both originate and meet in the towns.[1] This is significant because Philippi's *territorium* was very large and included many other villages and small towns. Most of the population within the colony's boundaries thus seem likely to have lived away from Philippi. The town had particular functions within the colony and these will have affected the composition of its population. As a result, a church centred on the town will not have a composition which mirrors that of the colony as a whole but one which mirrors the somewhat different composition of the town.

A second dimension of accessibility is social accessibility. The Book of Acts recounts a couple of stories of Paul encountering very senior members of the élite. However, the élite would not generally seem likely to be accessible to Paul without great difficulty. Without prior friendship or recommendation, and without a client–patron relationship, Paul seems unlikely to have often gained access to their homes. Even if some of his converts were clients of élite

---

[1] Cf. Meeks, *First Urban Christians*, pp. 9f.

patrons, that was a relationship in which an attempt by the client to proselytise would seem to fall outside what would be socially permissible. At the other extreme of accessibility would be those fixed in the town and committed to talking to strangers, namely the poor and the craftspeople and other small traders who would be sitting working and selling. If Paul wore one of his more habitual status 'hats', he would tend to socialise with craftspeople as someone on their level. Robin Lane Fox highlights social accessibility in responding to the approaches of Wayne Meeks and Edwin Judge:

> Much depended on how, if at all, the various groups encountered Christian preaching. If the first converts tended to be people of modest property, living in towns, the reason may lie, not in their particular view of their 'status' but in the fact that they happened to hear most about the faith from people to whom they could relate. The scarcity of converts in the highest or lowest classes may reflect on their lack of occasion to learn about Christianity from a teacher whom they could take seriously.[2]

Lane Fox seems basically correct, but I think that the main social factor would be about whether one heard at all, rather than about how one related to the speaker. His implied suggestion that the poor would not take seriously a teacher of slightly higher status than themselves seems doubtful. It fits with his arguments from evidence about the later Church, although being generally open, having some reluctance to accept those of lowest status, in particular, slaves.[3] My model does not include any reluctance to accept converts into the fledgling church and thus includes a higher proportion of poor than does Philippi overall.

One of Paul's alternative entrées was, of course, into the Jewish community and, in Acts 16, in a passage widely regarded as evidentially strong, he is reported as persuading a 'God-fearing' woman. Progress among 'God-fearers' seems unlikely to have been in itself of great numerical value to the Philippian church since both Acts 16 (in particular when the author notes only that they spoke

[2] Lane Fox, *Pagans and Christians*, p. 319.
[3] Ibid., p. 299, cf. pp. 324f.

to women) and the almost complete lack of archaeological testi-mony,[4] suggest that any Jewish community at Philippi was minute (which is rather a surprise given Philippi's good communications and hence trading links). However, Lydia and her household would also have represented a range of other social points of entry into the Philippian population: in her own case, among Asian migrant traders of reasonable wealth (see below). Also in Acts 16, in a passage whose evidential value is much more disputed, is the account of the conversion of a low-status Roman official, namely a gaoler, and his family. Low-status officials, while not obviously immediately accessible to Paul and his converts, would seem to be on an accessible social level.

A third, less clear form of accessibility would be what one could call 'religious accessibility'. Among the least accessible would be Roman members of the élite, who were likely to have a strong allegiance to traditional, civic religions.[5] Among the most accessible would be those already interested in Judaism. Another group which might be considered particularly open to 'oriental', personally oriented religions such as Christianity would be Asian and other migrants, whose typical religions might be regarded as somewhat of this kind. However, 'religious accessibility' seems unlikely to have very much effect on the composition of the church at Philippi. Jews seem to have been few and, for the élite and for migrants, factors of social accessibility seem likely to be much more important than religious ones.

The results of our assumptions – of a town-centred church, and of one slanted towards those most accessible to Paul and his early converts – will need to be checked against data in the letter and elsewhere in the New Testament. These data also give more specific indications about the situation of the Philippian Christians.

2. A model of the composition of the church at Philippi

For any social group, putting absolute figures on the degree of under- or over-representation in the church is not possible. What does seem worth while, however, is to rank the probable under-

---

[4] The only evidence is an inscription from the late third or the fourth century AD mentioning a synagogue. It is announced in C. Koukouli-Chrysantaki, Τυχαια Ευρηματα-Εντοπισμοι, *AD* 42 (1987) Β΄ 2, Χρονικα (1992), 444, and described by him in Koukouli-Chrysantaki, 'Colonia', pp. 28–35.

[5] Cf. Lane Fox, *Pagans and Christians*, p. 321.

represented social groups in terms of how sharply each is likely to be under-represented. We can then incorporate that ranking into our model by attaching notional figures to it. The broad aim of this exercise is to see in which directions such slanting moves our model: for example, are there likely to be more Greeks in the church than in the town, or fewer?

Considerations of social accessibility would seem likely to reduce most sharply the proportion of élite. We could lower the likely figure in the church from 3 per cent to, say, 1 per cent. The inaccessibility of the élite will have a fairly sharp restricting effect on the accessibility of their domestic slaves. We ought to lower their figure a bit less sharply than the two-thirds we used for the élite: say, by one-half. Farmers are likely to be less represented than craftspeople or traders, both because of there being fewer opportunities to talk with them and because of Paul's apparent ability to form social links with craftspeople and traders. We will drop the proportion of colonist farmers by one-quarter. Conversely, the members of the service groups seem likely to be over-represented in the church. The same is also likely to be true for the poor, especially if the Christians picked up early their later reputation for giving financial help.

The effect of these changes is to leave roughly the following proportions of the various social groups in our model of the church: élite 0.5–1.5 per cent; commuting peasant colonists 15–23 per cent; service groups 35–55 per cent; poor 20–40 per cent; slaves 12–25 per cent. In table 2, I give the figures for the standard scenario (from table 1) and for the scenario with a high number of colonist farmers.

My model for the church at Philippi therefore consists of 43 per cent service community, 25 per cent poor, 16 per cent slaves, 15 per cent colonist farmers, 1 per cent élite landowners. It is difficult to know how these figures might relate to various scholars' visions of the make-up of Pauline churches. Some clearly envisage less diverse communities. The commuting farmers are the main group which is not usually recognised. Scholars such as Meeks associate urban living solely with urban work.[6] This is probably because his primary concern is with very large cities such as Corinth, Ephesus and Antioch. At Philippi, this association breaks down. Meggitt recognises the likely presence of casual agricultural labourers in

---

[6] Meeks, *First Urban Christians*, p. 9.

Table 2. *The composition of the population model of the church of Philippi, under two scenarios*

	Service	Slaves	Colonist farmers	Poor	Elite	Roman	Greek, etc.
Town (standard scenario)	37	20	20	20	3	40	60
Church (with slant for social accessibility)	43	16	15	25	1	36	64
Town (high colonist farmer)	32	20	30	15	3	48	52
Church (with slant for social accessibility)	39	16	23	21	1	42	58

Paul's churches.[7] At Philippi this would undoubtedly be so but there would also be the substantial group of commuting colonist farmers who either rented or owned their land. However, contrary to Friedrich (see below), these do not constitute a fairly wealthy middle-class group. Most would be at or close to subsistence level – although I expect that a limited number would be far enough above it for comfort.

Meggitt would want to remove my 1 per cent élite. I agree that there are no indicators of élite members of the Philippian church in Acts or the letter. Lydia is certainly not one.[8] However, while we can produce arguments to show why we would expect the élite to be under-represented in the churches, that is all we can ultimately do. We cannot exclude the possibility of them altogether. We might disagree over whether they should be 67 per cent under-represented, as I have suggested, or 90 per cent under-represented, but the possibility of the odd one or two members of the decurial class being in the church cannot be ruled out. I would be happy to lower my 1 per cent figure but I would still want some figure for the élite in my model. Of course, in a church of limited size – given its signs

[7] Meggitt, *Paul, Poverty and Survival*, p. 97 n. 108.
[8] Ibid., p. 69.

of organisation (Phil. 1.1) we might say 50–100 members – 1 per cent means one person or less. Given the influence that one convert might have on a family, a notional figure of 1 per cent means that there was probably no member of the élite in the church but that there is a possibility that there were two or three.

At the other end of the spectrum, Kyrtatas might wish to reduce my figure for slaves. However, the arguments which he uses to exclude almost all slaves from the early Church are unconvincing. In particular, he asserts that the New Testament instructions directed to slaves could just as well have been aimed at pagan slaves of Christian households.[9] This does not fit the form of argument used in those passages at all. I do agree with him that many of the Christian slaves that there were would have served Christian masters.[10] The typical Christian slave in my model is the extra pair of hands owned by a family of craft-workers.[11]

In contrast to the standard view, my model estimates the proportion of Roman citizens in the church at only 36 per cent. Even if we push the figure for the number of colonist farmers in mid-first-century Philippi up to its likely maximum, the proportion of Roman citizens in the church remains at only 42 per cent. The common exegetical assumption that the bulk of the hearers are Roman citizens seems unreasonable.

Moving in the other direction, would there be any limit on the likely proportion of Greeks? At its extreme, one could envisage a church without any élite or any colonist peasant farmers. We probably ought then to largely exclude their slaves. This leaves the church consisting of service groups and their slaves, and the poor. If we take those in the proportions I have estimated for the town, we have 57 per cent service groups, 31 per cent poor, 12 per cent slaves. Looking at the general New Testament pattern of church development, I see no reason to exclude Roman members of service groups and the poor. If, as above, we use estimates of Romans forming one-third of the service groups and one-quarter of the poor, this model of the church would have 27 per cent Romans to 73 per cent Greeks. The interesting point is that you can push the figures for slanting the composition of the church very hard in a

[9] Dimitris J. Kyrtatas, *The Social Structure of the Early Christian Communities* (London: Verso, 1987), pp. 45–6.

[10] Ibid., p. 43.

[11] On the ability of people living at subsistence level to own slaves, see Meggitt, *Paul, Poverty and Survival*, pp. 129–32.

number of directions (another interesting direction is to increase the proportion of slaves) and the proportion of Romans stays above one-quarter. The main way to challenge this would be to revise downwards my (rather arbitrary) estimate of Romans forming a third of the service groups. However, the effects of the freeing of slaves on the one hand, and of the impoverishment of peasant colonists through concentration of landholding on the other, make me reluctant to lower the estimate. Including family members, my estimate means 1,800 Romans engaged in service activities (including crafts and trade) in a city of 15,000 – at most about 450 households. After almost a century of the colony, I cannot see the figure being very much lower than that.

In round figures, the limits for my model of the composition of the kind of church likely to occur in a town like Philippi are 25–40 per cent Romans and 60–75 per cent Greeks. The terms refer basically to citizenship. Many Romans would be freedmen or freedwomen, who would not be ethnically Romans. The 'Greeks' would include some slaves who were not of Greek origin. There is, however, one ethnic aspect to the Greeks in the church. There would probably be very few, or no, Thracians. My assumption that the church consists of people from the town largely excludes Thracians, who lived further out in the territory. There is very little evidence of them in the town at all.[12]

Having made much of the importance of using numbers, I now need to turn round and say that the specific figures in my model are not very important: they are only a means to an end. What we are trying to do is to get a sense of who the likely groups in the church were, and what were their likely proportions. I wish to counter the standard view in which most Christians are Romans. I also wish to have a reasonable basis for gaining a 'feel' for what issues would be important for the various early hearers of the letter as they lived in Philippian society and in the Philippian church.

3. Checking the model against data from Philippians and elsewhere in the New Testament

It is characteristic of much of scholarship that Karl Bornhäuser can look at a letter, two out of three of whose named addressees are Greek women, and take as his exegetical foundation the idea that

---

[12] Pilhofer, *Philippi*, p. 89.

the recipients are Roman, male, ex-soldiers. It is important to check our model against NT passages which give us clues as to the composition of the Philippian church.

We cannot build a great deal upon the individuals in the letter but they are worth noting, and do fit with our model: Εὐοδία, Συντύχη, presumably *Clemens*, but probably not Σύζυγος.[13] Then we can add Ἐπαφρόδιτος. I have not managed to make headway on the likely social status of bearers of these names, although Συντύχη sounds like various slave names.

If we widen our scope to Acts 16 we can add Λυδία, a woman who is a 'God-fearer' and a migrant trader from Asia. Scholars have usually argued that she must be quite well off, both because of the level of capital required for trade in purple[14] and because she could accommodate Paul's party. She seems to have been head of her household, both because it is ὁ οἶκος αὐτῆς (16.15) and because they were baptised with her. Justin Meggitt argues that she is more likely to have been a fairly poor producer of dark vegetable dyes. He demonstrates that none of Lydia's characteristics – selling 'purple', autonomy, heading a household, showing hospitality, and travelling – need indicate wealth.[15] I agree that, even together, they do not suggest élite status. However, each factor decreases the probability of her being very poor. Together, they suggest an income above subsistence. How should we envisage her household? Maybe three or four Asian relatives and half-a-dozen slaves, either domestic or engaged in her work. Possibly we should also add to our church the slave-girl, formerly with the πνεῦμα πύθωνα (verse 16). She presumably still belonged to her masters, but they seem to have given her considerable freedom of action, given her ability to trail around after Paul (verses 17–18). We then have the miraculous night in the prison. One issue in assessing this passage must be the relationship between Acts and the foundation-stories remembered by various churches. Details of who were early converts seem particularly likely to be well remembered. It is therefore worth our considering the gaoler and his household. He is some sort of low-

---

[13] Cf. Peter T. O'Brien, *Commentary on Philippians* (NIGTC; Grand Rapids: Eerdmans, 1991) pp. 480f. He leaves the conclusion open, but does note that Σύζυγος has never been found elsewhere as a proper name.

[14] W. M. Ramsay, *St. Paul the Traveller and the Roman Citizen* (London: Hodder & Stoughton, 1925[15]), p. 214.

[15] Meggitt, *Paul, Poverty and Survival*, p. 69 n. 164; pp. 120–1, 129–33, 144–9. Most of the discussion is related to Phoebe (Rom. 16.1).

status Roman official. Peterlin argues, particularly from Pliny (*Ep.* 10.9), that a gaoler would usually be a public slave and that it is not a profession one would continue in if freed.[16] Peterlin's argument for the first point seems quite strong, but not his argument for the second point. Slaves stayed in all kinds of jobs after being freed. The setting in Acts, where the gaoler has his own οἰκία in which there must be at least a few people (because Luke uses the word, πᾶσιν, in describing them) fits more naturally the situation of a freedman. The household could be the immediate family and, say, two or three slaves.

If, out of interest, we add all these up, we get three Roman adults (and, say, three children), about seven free Greeks (four of whom are from Asia) and about nine slaves. Of those whose gender is known, four are women, three are men. Twenty-two is a fair nucleus for a church and we could try to extend the social pattern of this group by arguments about further inroads being likely among friends and relatives from the same groups. However, there are too many variables and uncertain factors in the listing above to make going further in this direction of better than marginal value. The listing does however function somewhat like the inscriptions in the town in that it is another piece of evidence against which to test our model and our model sits quite happily with it.

More searching questions are asked of our model by the references in the letter to Roman institutions and civic issues. If it were not for the counterpoise presented by Euodia, Syntyche and Epaphroditus, there would be a strong *prima facie* case for the audience being Roman citizens, given the references to τὸ πραιτ-ώριον (1.13) and ἡ Καίσαρος οἰκία (4.22), the use of the Latinised Φιλιππήσιοι (4.15), the use of πολιτεύεσθε (1.27) and πολίτευμα (3.20), the use (according to Geoffrion[17]) of the *topos* of the citizens banding together under threat (1.27–30) and, as I will argue (in chapter 5, below), strong allusions to the Emperor.

With regard to the points about specific Roman institutions, their presence in the letter is sufficiently explained by the Roman-ness of the context at Philippi. There is no justification for going

---

[16] Davorin Peterlin, *Paul's Letter to the Philippians in the Light of Disunity in the Church* (NovT Supp. LXXIX; Leiden: E. J. Brill, 1995), pp. 144ff.

[17] Timothy C. Geoffrion, *The Rhetorical Purpose and the Political and Military Character of Philippians: A Call to Stand Firm* (Lewiston: Mellen Biblical Press, 1993), e.g., p. 36.

beyond that to argue that the recipients must also be Roman. τὰ κατ᾿ ἐμὲ μᾶλλον εἰς προκοπὴν τοῦ εὐαγγελίου ἐλήλυθεν, ὥστε τοὺς δεσμούς μου φανεροὺς ἐν Χριστῷ γενέσθαι ἐν ὅλῳ τῷ πραιτωρίῳ (1.12f.) is a statement specifically about the progress of the Gospel in a Roman and, the hearers would expect, a hostile environment. It is particularly natural if written to Christian Greeks in a pagan, Roman-dominated environment.[18] οἱ ἐκ τῆς Καίσαρος οἰκίας (4.22) are not actually a strikingly Roman group of people: they are slaves or *liberti* (freedmen or freedwomen) employed by the Emperor in a wide range of roles, particularly administrative ones.[19] If slaves, the Christians are not Roman at all. If *liberti*, they are ethnically non-Roman but now are Roman citizens. Again, the growth of a Christian community (citizen, non-citizen or, as is presumably the case, mixed) in this context could be a great encouragement to the church in the Roman context of Philippi.

Two issues surround Φιλιππήσιοι (4.15). The first, whether non-citizens would be called 'Philippians' at all, has been considered recently by Papazoglou. She concludes,

> Il semble en effet que l'ethnique *Philippensis* n'était pas réservé aux seuls colons romains et qu'un habitant de Philippes de condition pérégrine pouvait aussi s'appeler Φιλιππεύς.

> It seems in fact that the 'ethnic' title *Philippensis* was not solely limited to Roman colonists and that an inhabitant of Philippi who was a non-citizen could also call himself Φιλιππεύς.[20]

This then raises the second issue of whether a congregation with a majority of non-citizens would be addressed using the Latin-based Φιλιππήσιοι. O'Brien writes, '[T]he vocative plural of Φιλιππήσιος

---

[18] This is true whether the πραιτώριον is a reference to the Guard at Rome (Lightfoot, pp. 99–102) or to a governor's residence (Hawthorne, p. 35). The parallel phrase καὶ τοῖς λοιποις πᾶσιν favours a reference of τὸ πραιτώριον to a group of people, and hence favours the former option (O'Brien, p. 93).

[19] Lightfoot, pp. 171–8; Meeks, *First Urban Christians*, pp. 21, 63. Again, there is discussion about whether the reference could fit Ephesus or whether it must point to Rome. Both are possible, but Caesar's household at Rome would be so much larger that Rome seems a more probable place for an identifiable Christian community to develop within the household.

[20] Papazoglou, *Villes*, p. 412, my tr.

. . . is based on the Latin *Philippenses*, which was appropriate for citizens of a Roman colony.[21] Caird suggests that it was perhaps used, 'out of deference to their civic pride in their colonial status'.[22] I suspect that this is unnecessary. I even think that Collart may be going too far in saying that Paul deliberately chose the word to reflect the Romanness of the colony,

> [E]n employant . . . la forme étrange Φιλιππήσιοι, Paul avait entendu rendre hommage au caractère latin de la colonie.

> [I]n using . . . the unusual form Φιλιππήσιοι, Paul wished to pay homage to the Latin character of the colony.[23]

It seems to me that Paul could have been using the term quite unreflectively because it may simply have been a term in current use. Pilhofer does point out that the term is never used in non-Christian texts.[24] However, the Latin term from which it was transliterated was. The colony had been established for ninety years, and everyone will have been used to coinage that described the city as *Colonia Augusta Iulia Philippensis*,[25] a title also attested on inscriptions. This seems likely to have had a strong effect on the name which Greek-speakers gave to inhabitants of the city. There are quite marked examples at Philippi of Greeks Hellenising Latin words. The two known inscriptions of Greek members of general professions are of a cashier of the ἀργενταριι and a town-crier, a πραίκων. Each term is a transcription of a Latin one.[26] Collart and Ducrey also argue that Βέρνας, the name of the Greek who signed a rock-relief on the hillside, was probably a transcription of the Latin *Verna*.[27] Since *Philippensis* was a Latin term in common use, Φιλιππήσιος could easily have been a common Greek term, even though it does not turn up in the (limited) contemporary sources. If it was a term in common use, then Paul need have had no special

[21] O'Brien, p. 531.

[22] G. B. Caird, *Paul's Letters from Prison (Ephesians, Philippians, Colossians, Philemon)* (New Clarendon Bible; Oxford: Oxford University Press, 1976), p. 153.

[23] Collart, *Philippes*, p. 303, my tr.

[24] Pilhofer, *Philippi*, pp. 116f.

[25] Collart, *Philippes*, pp. 238ff.; *RPC, I*, no. 1653 is a Claudian coin carrying this legend. Note that the second and third words are in the opposite order to that found in inscriptions.

[26] Collart, *Philippes*, p. 271.

[27] Collart and Ducrey, *Philippes*, p. 221.

reason for using it. Having said that, even if the term was chosen unconsciously, its very commonness would still testify to the predominance of Latin, and hence of Roman institutions, in the colony.

We have looked at the issue of the list of individuals reported to be in the church and at the issue of Roman features of the letter.[28] A third issue is that of the Philippians' financial support for Paul. Our suggestion of a church centred on fairly low-status non-colonists runs counter to the common conception of the Philippian church as the wealthy financiers behind Paul's missionary endeavours. Gerhard Friedrich, in particular, argues for a comfortable financial position for the Philippians:

> Im Gegensatz zu andern Orten setzt sich diese Gemeinde warscheinlich nicht aus Proletariat, sondern größtenteils aus Angehörigen des Mittelstandes zusammen, so daß es keine krassen sozialen Unterschiede gibt und der Verdacht auf Bevorzugung und Benachteiligung von Besitzenden und Besitzlosen nicht entstehen kann, wenn Paulus irgendwelche Gaben annimt. Die in Philippi angesiedelten Veteranen sind keine Sklaven, sondern freie Menschen, die meistenteils Grundbesitz als Eigentum haben . . . Eine Gemeinde, die finanziell so gut gestellt ist, kann Paulus materiell unterstützen.

> In contrast to other places, the [Christian] community is probably composed not of the proletariat but mainly of members of the middle class, so there are no gross social differences, and the suspicion of favouring those with property and disadvantaging those without cannot arise if Paul accepts some gifts. The veterans settled in Philippi are not slaves but free people, who mainly own their land . . . A church that is financially so well placed can give Paul material support.[29]

This common conception seems likely to be distorted. First, Paul was not generally externally financed in his mission work. He did have to do his tentmaking work, sometimes even to an extent that

---

[28] Material on citizenship and on the Emperor will be discussed at length, below. I will argue, below, that it is not a strong option to read πολιτεύεσθε (1.27) in the sense of, 'Live as a good citizen of Philippi (or Rome)'.

[29] Friedrich, pp. 92f., my tr.

must have disrupted his other activities, as 1 Thessalonians 2.9 suggests – an instructive example because we know that on this particular mission he received money from Philippi (Phil. 4.16). It seems likely that, rather than being generally financed, Paul worked where possible but was then helped out, in what would seem a financially precarious livelihood, by occasional gifts.[30] If Acts 18.3 (in a section with strong circumstantial detail), 1 Corinthians 4.12 and 2 Corinthians 6.5 are combined with 2 Corinthians 11.8–9 then a similar picture seems to emerge. In fact, the rhetoric of 1 Corinthians 9, in which Paul uses the example of not using his right to support as a preacher, only sounds really forceful if Paul gained most of his income from his own hands rather than from churches to which he previously preached. If this is the case then there need not have been a steady, substantial supply from Philippi. In fact, we know that there had been a considerable gap before the gift brought by Epaphroditus (4.10). Furthermore, the passage that follows – . . . πεινᾶν . . . ὑστερεῖσθαι – would be something of an indictment of the Philippians if they had been regarded as having any general responsibility for Paul's upkeep.

Second, the amounts of money which would make a substantial difference to an itinerant missionary accustomed to hardship need not be great. Certainly they would not be great enough to require a high average level of wealth in a congregation of any reasonable size.

Third, giving can even come out of poverty and we have the direct testimony of 2 Corinthians 8.2–3 that, paradoxically, ἡ κατὰ βάθους πτωχεία αὐτῶν ἐπερίσσευσεν εἰς τὸ πλοῦτος τῆς ἁπλότητος αὐτῶν ὅτι κατὰ δύναμιν, μαρτυρῶ, καὶ παρὰ δύναμιν, gave towards the Collection. Wayne Meeks has argued that the rhetoric of this passage should make one cautious about taking a description of the Macedonian situation from these verses.[31] However, the κατὰ βάθους πτωχεία cannot be more than 'partly' hyperbole[32] and since κατὰ βάθους is so emphatic, we must be left with some evidence of financial hardship in Macedonia. This fits our model far better than it fits a model of a church full of wealthy Roman veterans.

The standard citizen or veteran model of the Philippian church

---

[30] Meggitt, *Paul, Poverty and Survival*, pp. 77–9.
[31] Meeks, *First Urban Christians*, p. 66.
[32] Ibid.

has difficulty both with the social data relevant to Philippi, and with the NT data, especially 2 Corinthians 8 and the Greek names in Philippians. The model for which I am arguing fits the data more naturally.

4. Living in Philippi

Many of the factors which governed life for the group of Christians in Philippi will have been ones common to life in many Graeco-Roman cities. Some factors, however, would be influenced by the particular nature of Philippi. Four factors seem particularly striking: the centrality of agriculture; the relatively modest size of the city; the ethnic and social profile of the population; the emphatic Roman domination of the colony. The last of these is the point I wish to emphasise, but the other three contribute to the way in which the last would be experienced.

The mines were long exhausted. Trade, although significant along the Via Egnatia, would be far from dominant. The city was neither a provincial capital nor the old capital of a country. The economic focus was thus much less on non-agricultural factors than it was in Corinth, Athens, Ephesus or Antioch. Positively, the agricultural hinterland was wide, fertile, accessible and, judging by inscriptions, farmed from local centres right across its extent and therefore farmed quite intensively.[33] Collart concludes that the colony was essentially agricultural.[34] This then has an important socio-political consequence. Agricultural land was the essential economic component of a Roman colony (in contrast to trade, for example, which was not bound up with being a colony *per se*). The centrality of agriculture for the economics of Philippi therefore meant that almost the whole population was, economically, closely involved in the colonial system. A clear contrast would be Corinth, where the major economic element of maritime trade was not directly connected to agricultural land and hence not to Corinth's nature as a colony.

The theme of close involvement with the colonial system is continued by comparing Philippi's population with that of Corinth. Alcock uses Engels' estimate of 80,000 for the urban population (and of 20,000 for the rural population, an example of a low rural–

---

[33] Cf. Alcock, *Graecia Capta*, pp. 60, 80f.
[34] Collart, *Philippes*, p. 275; cf. Papazoglou, *Villes*, pp. 407f.

urban ratio).[35] This is more than five times my estimate for Philippi. In Corinth, large swathes of the population could probably live in anonymity, unseen by the city authorities. In Philippi, there was probably still a certain amount of anonymity, but much less of it. Individual shop-keepers, for example, would be known quite widely in the city and, if they got involved in any trouble, they would be unlikely to be able to sink quickly back into metropolitan anonymity. The same would be true, to a more marked degree, of a broader group, such as the church.

The main 'ethnic' peculiarity of Philippi is the proportion of Romans to 'Greeks' in the population. There are, however, further ethnic complexities within each of those broad categories.

'Romans' meant primarily grandchildren and great-grandchildren of veteran or peasant colonists. These descendants, themselves called 'colonists', would be basically of Italian stock: the peasants came from Italy and the most identifiable group of veterans were Praetorians. To these, three other groups of Roman citizens would need to be added.

The first and, I would imagine, largest would be *liberti*: freed slaves of colonists. We have direct evidence of these through inscriptions concerning the *Seviri Augustales*,[36] an organisation created for *liberti* in connection with the imperial cult.[37] Along with *liberti* there would be their freeborn descendants.

The second group would be Roman citizens who had moved to the area after colonisation. Apart from a few traders, this group will have consisted of newly retiring veteran soldiers. Although, as I have argued above, the numbers of these will not have been very great, their status and wealth were significantly above those of ordinary citizens and quite a fair proportion probably attained decurial status. We have epigraphical evidence of benefaction by veterans at Philippi.[38]

The third group would be native or immigrant Greeks who were granted citizenship at Philippi. General Roman policy and the form of colonisation at Philippi suggest that this group was likely to be very small. There was almost certainly no general grant of

[35] Alcock, *Graecia Capta*, p. 160, citing D. W. Engels, *Roman Corinth: an Alternative Model for the Classical City* (London: University of Chicago Press, 1990), p. 82. Engels' study has been subject to sharp criticism, but his figures are presumably of the right order.

[36] Collart, *Philippes*, pp. 268f.

[37] Garnsey and Saller, *Roman Empire*, p. 121.

[38] Collart, *Philippes*, pp. 293f.

citizenship at colonisation. As Sherwin-White writes, 'Once only, in the exceptional circumstances of the foundation of the veteran settlements at and around Numidian Cirta by the adventurer Sittius and his private army, in and after the time of Caesar, there are indications that a large body of non-Romans acquired Roman status under the mantle of a colony.'[39] Brunt, after surveying a wide range of cities in the Balkans, argues, 'It . . . seems extremely unlikely that . . . [various towns] . . . and Philippi, which possessed the *Ius Italicum*, i.e. counted as Italian towns beyond the confines of Italy, admitted more than a handful of provincials.[40]

A grant to a limited number of the local Greek élite is more plausible. Sherwin-White cites Carthage and Augusta Praetoria as places where this happened.[41] However, it seems more likely that there were few if any families of sufficient prestige, living in the small town of first-century BC Philippi, to have been given citizenship and kept their land and high status. The demand for land for colonists will have been such a strong force against such a move that it seems much more likely that the local élite will have lost their land and status, or moved away. In the period after colonisation, economic weakness and the constitution of the colony will then have tended to lock the Greeks out from magistracies which would have been the most likely route to citizenship.[42] Citizenship was distributed extremely sparsely among Greeks in the East[43] and Philippi seems likely to have been a place where it was particularly sparse.

I therefore disagree with Lazarides who wrote, 'The social situation of the residents of the colony who belonged to other nationalities remains unknown. It is probable that they also belonged to the class of free Roman citizens, to whom had been given the *Ius Italicum*.'[44] Papazoglou seems correct in describing the Greeks as mainly non-citizens.[45] In the middle of the first century AD, I would suggest that almost all would have been in this category.

Lack of citizenship was clearly not such a major issue as, for example, lack of land. Even in experience of legal processes, difference in status between rich and poor seems to have been a

[39] Sherwin-White, *Citizenship*, p. 352.
[40] Brunt, *Italian Manpower*, p. 253.
[41] Sherwin-White, *Citizenship*, p. 352 n. 3.
[42] Garnsey, *Legal Privilege*, p. 266.
[43] Garnsey and Saller, *Roman Empire*, p. 15.
[44] Lazarides, Φίλιπποι, p. 23, my tr.
[45] Papazoglou, *Villes*, p. 412.

more important factor than citizenship.[46] However, citizenship was
never irrelevant: 'Discrimination in favour of citizens as opposed to
aliens was . . . a permanent feature of the Roman judicial system. It
was practised in all spheres of the law where aliens were technically
excluded, as from the *ius civile*, and where they were not, as in
criminal law as administered by the *cognitio* procedure.'[47] In AD
17, when astrologers who were citizens were exiled from Rome,
foreigners were put to death.[48] Citizens whom Pliny found guilty of
being Christians were 'put down for dispatch to the city': aliens
were simply executed.[49] A while later, Marcus, the governor of
Lyons, had Christian non-citizens sent to the beasts, while citizens
were merely decapitated.[50] More generally, aliens were subject to
coercitio – various kinds of punitive action carried out by magistrates as a form of coercion and without judicial procedure *per se* –
while citizens could, in theory at least, appeal against such treatment.[51] At Philippi, non-citizens must have been very restricted in
their opportunities to acquire land. Furthermore, lack of access to
civil law would weaken still further a position of acute economic
and military weakness which would seem likely to erode any landholding which they had.

My catch-all term 'Greeks' covers five groups. The first are the
indigenous tribes with their Thracian names and religious habits,
no doubt linked with much mixing of population across the border.
This Hellenised group also furnishes a number of later Latinised
inscriptions[52] which demonstrate the persistence of an economically
viable, indeed reasonably successful, social group living particularly
at the margins of the territory. Representations of the Thracian
'rider god' are found all over the area, giving a repeated reminder
of the presence and religious influence of this group. Most of the
colony's villages also carried Thracian names. It appears as though
non-Thracian Greeks living in the villages were somewhat absorbed. The second and third groups were the descendants of the
Thasian and Macedonian colonists of the fourth century BC. They
pale somewhat before other groups, who make a more obvious

[46] Garnsey, *Legal Privilege*, p. 270.
[47] Ibid., p. 262. *Cognitio* procedure was a judicial procedure set up under the
Principate which was less formal than the traditional one (ibid., p. 5).
[48] Ibid., p. 261.
[49] Pliny, *Ep.* 10.96. Garnsey, *Legal Privilege*, pp. 74, 268.
[50] Eusebius, *E.H.* 5.1.47. Garnsey, *Legal Privilege*, pp. 130, 261, 270.
[51] Garnsey, *Legal Privilege*, p. 261.
[52] Collart, *Philippes*, pp. 297ff.

cultural mark (in particular a religious one) on the area. The presence of oriental cults such as that of Isis directs attention to the fourth group, migrant workers from various parts of the Hellenistic world – although, of course, these cults were not restricted to such people. The fifth group are slaves, many of whom must have come from the Greek-speaking East.

So, Philippi was agricultural, of modest size and of unusual ethnic (and social) mix. Our fourth peculiar factor is the extent of domination of the colony by Romans and Roman institutions.

In Ephesus, the Roman Empire ruled by means of a primarily Greek élite. This was the general strategy of Rome in the East: to bolster the local élite and form them into a force useful to Rome.[53] In Corinth and Pisidian Antioch, the Romans ruled but a strong Greek influence remained and the Roman culture, in a reasonably short time, largely succumbed.[54] In Philippi, the Romans ruled without the medium of any Greeks, and Latin ruled unchallenged until well into the third century.

Latin was carefully cultivated. The leader of the Latin actors was, uniquely as far as we know, a civic employee.[55] There was a substantial public library which will have been a vehicle for the encouragement of Latin.[56] Civic inscriptions are all in Latin and the coins are 'decorously Roman'.[57] On both, the colonial title is carefully used.[58] The Greeks would have lived in a city where they were surrounded by Latin.

Romans owned almost all the land. Romans had all the political control in the city. Romans largely monopolised wealth and high status. Of course, Greeks in other cities knew that they were under the Roman Empire. However, they were citizens of their cities, under Greek immediate government and with Greeks holding much of the wealth and status and land. The experience of empire was far more acute for the Greeks of Philippi.

One effect of this would be that, in Philippi, the issue of status would be perceived as being very closely tied in with the Roman colonial system. John Elliott defines status as '[t]he relative rank or

---

[53] Bowersock, *Augustus*, is an exposition of this theme. See also S. R. F. Price, *Rituals and Power: The Roman imperial cult in Asia Minor* (Cambridge: Cambridge University Press, 1984), pp. 98ff.
[54] Alcock, *Graecia Capta*, pp. 168f.; Levick, *Colonies*, pp. 134ff.
[55] Collart, *Philippes*, pp. 272f.
[56] *Ibid.*, pp. 338f., 359.
[57] Levick, *Colonies*, p. 161.
[58] *Ibid.*

position of an individual in a particular group with accompanying prescribed behaviour'.[59] Throughout the Greek East, the arrival of Rome reinforced the importance of status and made the hierarchy of status more rigid. The maintenance of status and the proper observation of distinctions of status were imperatives of society. At Philippi, they would be particularly seen as imperatives of the Roman social order in the town.

The Greeks of Philippi were almost all economically dependent on Romans. 'Service groups' means quarrymen who cut marble for Romans, *venatores* who hunted beasts in the arena at shows paid for by Romans, cashiers who handled Romans' money.[60] Shopkeepers sold to Romans in the town and to Romans who came in from the country. Greeks who worked on the land worked for Romans. The land-centred economy of the colony meant that almost everyone, down to the very poorest, was directly or indirectly dependent on Roman money. The social context for poor Greeks, or Greeks who subsisted but struggled, was not simply a context in which power went with wealth, as it would in Ephesus, but of power going with wealth which was held by Romans. This perception for the Greeks is an effect of Philippi's ethnic mix, with its high Greek component, being combined with absolute Roman control of local power. If power is monopolised by one, highly identifiable group who are not a great majority, particularly if they are an immigrant group, then the social situation is bound to be perceived principally in terms of the identity of that group. The social situation at Philippi will have been one identified peculiarly acutely as one dominated by Romans. Many Greeks no doubt welcomed the Roman presence in Philippi: primarily the migrant workers who were probably attracted by the presence of the Romans and for whom the *Pax Romana* provided the whole basis of their economic opportunity. Yet, even though many were not necessarily anti-Roman, their perception must still have been of Roman control of everything about Philippi. Passages in Paul's letter which impinge on Roman institutions are likely to have carried a particular impact to his hearers.

Not all Romans in Philippi were wealthy landowners. The Greeks

[59] John Elliott, *Social Scientific Criticism of the New Testament* (London: SPCK, 1995), p. 134. Cf. Malina, *NT World*, p. 28; Garnsey and Saller, *Roman Empire*, p. 118.

[60] The examples are known occupations of Greeks at Philippi. See Collart, *Philippes*, pp. 305, 266, 270, 271.

would have known this but it was unlikely to have prevented them from viewing the issue of power in ethnically polarised terms. The poorer Romans seem likely to have had a somewhat different perception. Power was, of course, in the hands of Romans, and they would see the relative lack of power of the Greeks (although they would also see that some were better off than themselves). They would probably have had a rather bitter-sweet perception of their own Romanness: they were of the ruling group but far from ruling. They would have felt ways in which their position was better than its Greek equivalent: probably in terms of better treatment by magistrates; possibly in quite a substantial way in terms of support by a patron. They would probably, however, see the main axis of social power as being that of wealth and status, rather than that of ethnicity. Such people in the church might view some of Paul's references in a somewhat different light from the Greeks.

The standard view on the nature of Philippi and the Philippian church has a vital strength. It distinguishes Philippians from Paul's other letters to churches which he founded, by recognising the importance at Philippi of Roman citizenship and Roman institutions. My estimate for the proportions of Romans and Greeks in the town is of 40 per cent Romans to 60 per cent Greeks – or, two Romans to every three Greeks. Even after slanting the figures to estimate the composition of the church, we still have 36 per cent Romans to 64 per cent Greeks – or, one Roman to every two Greeks. No other city in which Paul founded a church is likely to have had this many Romans. In none of the other cities was the experience of everyday life so firmly under the control of local, visible Romans.

But the standard view loses sight of the shape of Philippian society. First, it simply loses the social diversity: landowners, farmers, service-providers, slaves and poor. The town seems to be envisaged as an undifferentiated group of financially secure citizens. Second, it loses the difference between citizen and non-citizen, between colonist and non-colonist, between the somewhat smaller Roman group, whose leaders controlled the colony's resources, and the larger Greek group, who lived in the colony while possessing very little of such control.

We need now to ask whether our departure from the standard view makes a significant difference to the way in which the letter is likely to have sounded to its original hearers. We will turn first to what may have been, for the hearers, the sharpest issue in the letter, the theme of suffering.

3

SUFFERING AND UNITY

The two most important themes in Paul's letter to the Philippians are the themes of suffering and of unity. I will argue that the theme of suffering provides the most notable structural feature of the letter: an extended three-fold parallel between Paul, Christ and the Philippians.[1] This is designed to encourage and guide the Philippians in their situation of suffering. The theme of unity provides, at 1.27–2.11, the most substantial rhetoric in the letter, located at the most significant point. In this passage the themes of suffering and unity are intertwined. I will argue that the likely economic realities of the situation of the Christians in Philippi make such an intertwining almost inevitable.

In this chapter, I first need to defend the idea that at least some of the Philippian Christians were suffering. I then need to consider what that suffering was likely to have involved and to explain why issues of suffering and unity were likely to be linked.

1.   Philippians are suffering

This proposition is supported by a wide range of evidence: the pervasiveness of the theme of suffering in the letter; the specific evidence of 1.27–30; the call to rejoice together in 2.17–18; the presentation of the church relative to its surrounding society in 2.15–16 and 3.20–1; the testimony of 2 Corinthians 8. There is also Philippians 1.7, on which exegetes differ sharply but which probably supports the idea that the Philippians were suffering.

The theme of suffering runs through the whole letter.[2] Paul's

---

[1] Timothy and Epaphroditus may also have a role in such a scheme. See R. A. Culpepper, 'Co-Workers in Suffering. Philippians 2:19–30', *Rev Exp* 77 (1980), pp. 349–58.

[2] Throughout my book, my central evidence will be drawn from Philippians 1.12–2.30, which all scholars agree to be from a single letter. I do, however, follow

suffering enters almost every section: the thanksgiving (ἔν . . . τοῖς δεσμοῖς μου, 1.7); the report (1.12–26, *passim*); the call to steadfastness (τὸν αὐτὸν ἀγῶνα . . . οἷον . . . ἀκούετε ἐν ἐμοί, 1.30); the call to rejoice together (εἰ καὶ σπένδομαι, 2.17); possibly the report on Epaphroditus (λύπην ἐπὶ λύπην, 2.27); the argument about trust in the flesh (τοῦ γνῶναι . . . τὴν κοινωνίαν τῶν παθημάτων αὐτοῦ, συμμορφιζόμενος τῷ θανάτῳ αὐτοῦ, 3.10); the appreciation for the gift (οἶδα καὶ ταπεινοῦσθαι, etc., 4.12–14). Christ's suffering appears in 2.6–8 and 3.10. Epaphroditus' suffering is discussed in 2.26–30. The issue of the Philippians' suffering may occur in 1.7 (ἔν τε τοῖς δεσμοῖς μου . . . συγκοινωνούς μου τῆς χάριτος). It certainly occurs at 1.28–30 and probably at 2.17–18. In view of the link between standing firm and suffering in 1.27–30, it may also be safe to infer an allusion to suffering in the call to stand firm at 4.1. More widely, the way in which Paul links the Philippians' experience of suffering to his in 1.30, and the general rhetoric of the letter, suggest that the Philippians' suffering is in view when Paul writes of his own and that of others (see chapter 4, below).

One recent approach to showing the theme's pervasiveness has been that of Gregory Bloomquist. He adopts a breakdown of the letter in terms of formal rhetoric and then demonstrates the presence of, and considers the function of, the theme of suffering in every part.[3] Bloomquist adds further weight to the case from a *wirkungsgeschichtlich* perspective by noting use of Philippians in patristic and later martyrological texts.[4] Another important study which argues for suffering as a central theme in the letter is Nikolaus Walter's article, 'Die Philipper und das Leiden'. The main thrust of his article is to contrast how alien the idea of suffering for God would be to Gentile Christians with how familiar an idea it was in contemporary Jewish (and, from there, Christian) thought.[5]

the majority of recent scholars in seeing Philippians as one letter. Wayne Meeks' change of view on this issue is symptomatic of the general trend ('The Man from Heaven in Paul's Letter to the Philippians', in B. A. Pearson, ed., *The Future of Early Christianity: Essays in Honor of Helmut Koester* (Minneapolis: Fortress Press, 1991), p. 331 n. 6). Many elements of NT texts that were once seen as indicating redactional seams are now seen as features of rhetorical, epistolary or narrative technique. My own study adds support to arguments that the letter as a whole is thematically and structurally coherent.

[3] L. Gregory Bloomquist, *The Function of Suffering in Philippians* (JSNTS 78; Sheffield: JSOT Press, 1993), esp. chs. 7–10.

[4] Ibid., ch. 1.

[5] Nikolaus Walter, 'Die Philipper und das Leiden. Aus den Anfängen einer

A third scholar to argue for the theme of suffering is Robert Jewett.
It is the first and most substantial of the themes which he sees as
tying the letter together.[6] Ernst Lohmeyer builds a whole commentary around the theme of suffering (albeit handled in a rather
unusual way).[7] In view of the weight that Paul gives to the theme of
suffering and the way in which he ties the Philippians into it, it
seems likely that Paul knows of actual suffering among the
Christians at Philippi.

We can build four arguments from 1.27–30. The centre-point is
the τὸ ὑπὲρ Χριστοῦ ... πάσχειν (verse 29). This is given an
interpretative context by the link to Paul's situation (verse 30), by
the ideas of struggle and opposition in the verses, and by the
function of verse 29 as reason.

ὑμῖν ἐχαρίσθη τὸ ὑπέρ Χριστοῦ ... πάσχειν. The natural way
to take this is that Paul knows of suffering among the Philippians,
that he reminds them that this is for Christ, and that he is likely to
be using this reminder to argue that there is some particular value
in the Philippians' sufferings, a value of which they were insufficiently aware. The closest parallel to this verse is unambiguously in
a context of external attacks upon the church:

> ... ὑπὲρ τῆς ὑπομονῆς ὑμῶν καὶ πίστεως ἐν πᾶσιν τοῖς
> διωγμοῖς ὑμῶν καὶ ταῖς θλίψεσιν αἷς ἀνέχεσθε, ἔνδειγμα
> τῆς δικαίας κρίσεως τοῦ θεοῦ, εἰς τὸ καταξιωθῆναι ὑμᾶς
> τῆς βασιλείας τοῦ θεοῦ, ὑπὲρ ἧς καὶ πάσχετε (2 Thess.
> 1.4–5; cf. 1 Thess. 2.14)

Verse 29 seems clear in itself but the link, in verse 30, to Paul's
situation makes it still clearer: ... τὸ ὑπὲρ αὐτοῦ πάσχειν, τὸν
αὐτὸν ἀγῶνα ἔχοντες οἷον εἴδετε ἐν ἐμοὶ καὶ νῦν ἀκούετε ἐν ἐμοί.
Gnilka, Houlden and O'Brien have each argued that this need not,
or cannot, refer to suffering of the same kind as Paul is undergoing[8]

heidenchristlichen Gemeinde', in R. Schnackenburg et al., eds., *Die Kirche des
Anfangs: Für Heinz Schümann* (Freiburg: Herder, 1978), pp. 417–34.
    [6] Robert Jewett, 'The Epistolary Thanksgiving and the Integrity of Philippians',
NovT 12 (1970), p. 51.
    [7] Ernst Lohmeyer, *Der Brief an die Philipper* (Göttingen: Vandenhoeck &
Ruprecht, 1928). Lohmeyer, p. 4, sees disunity at Philippi as stemming from pride
that some have in the 'perfection' of martyrdom. Later scholars have not been
persuaded by this.
    [8] Joachim Gnilka, *Der Philipperbrief* (Herders Theologischer Kommentar, X:3;
Freiburg: Herder, 1968), pp. 101f.; J. L. Houlden, *Paul's Letters from Prison* (PNTC;
Harmondsworth: Penguin, 1970), pp. 65f.; O'Brien, p. 162.

– the Philippians are not all in a Roman prison[9] – but, instead, means that theirs comes under the same theological rubric as his, ὑπὲρ Χριστοῦ.[10] However, even if (as seems unlikely) the parallel is only at this more general and theological level, for Paul to draw the Philippians into a sphere of suffering which can be categorised with his, probably means that he sees them as undergoing harsh treatment for the sake of the Gospel, as he did.[11]

The link to Paul seems explicitly to cite experiences which Paul had had in Philippi (οἷον εἴδετε) and the account of his present experiences (verses 12–26) which they had just heard (νῦν ἀκούετε). The latter seems particularly likely to mean that the Philippians are actually suffering. An alternative suggestion, that the reference was to the Christian opposition to Paul in verses 15–17, would seem unlikely to be heard by the Philippians as being the ἀγών, in parallel with πάσχειν, referred to in verse 30. There are sufferings in verses 12–26 which are more obvious than the opposition. It is also unlikely that Paul faced an ἀγών against Christian opponents in Philippi which the Philippians could have 'seen'.

The second context which helps our exegesis of verse 29 is the struggle and opposition in verses 27–30 as a whole. Timothy Geoffrion has argued that the whole range of imagery in use there reflects the *topos* of the call for the citizens of a Greek city to band together in order to deal with an external crisis facing the community.[12] Without attempting to adjudicate on the specifics of Geoffrion's idea, it does seem safe to see 1.27–30 as directed to persuading a community to band together to ward off some sort of external threat. The struggle is seen particularly in the στήκετε, συναθλοῦντες, the need to be μὴ πτυρόμενοι, and the ἀγών. In 1.28, Paul talks of opponents, ἀντικείμενοι, in the face of whom the Philippians are likely to πτύρεσθαι, panic.[13] These opponents will face ἀπώλεια, a term which suggests that they are external to the Philippian church. This is probably true whichever sense is given to the term, whether of defeat in a contest, as Loh and Nida argue,[14] or of destruction. The latter option seems much the

[9] A. Plummer, *A Commentary on St. Paul's Epistle to the Philippians* (London: Robert Scott, 1919), p. 36; Houlden, pp. 65f.

[10] Gnilka, pp. 101f.

[11] In any case, these writers do accept that the Philippians have suffered.

[12] Geoffrion, *Rhetorical Purpose*, pp. 35f.

[13] See ibid., pp. 66ff., for a discussion of the term.

[14] I.-J. Loh and E. A. Nida, *A Translator's Handbook on Paul's Letter to the*

stronger, especially given 3.18–19 which speaks of τοὺς ἐχθροὺς τοῦ σταυροῦ τοῦ Χριστοῦ, ὧν τὸ τέλος ἀπώλεια.

The third context is the function of verse 29 within the rhetoric of verses 27–30. It seems to function as a reason for something preceding it. The ideas in the verse are well suited to acting as a reason and, of course, there is the ὅτι. One way in which the argument might work is if one allows a link of interest between God and Christ. For the Philippians to suffer ὑπὲρ Χριστοῦ would then, in Greek thought, be a strong reason for God to benefit them in return, in this case by providing their σωτηρία.[15] If verse 29 does function as a reason, then the πάσχειν will probably describe something that the Philippians have experienced, rather than, say, a future danger. Paul appeals to their experience as the basis for an argument.

An attempt to avoid taking verse 29 as implying that the Philippians have suffered can be made by seeing the opponents of verse 28 as false teachers rather than attackers. Moises Silva takes this approach: 'Whether the Philippian church was experiencing opposition from the pagan environment . . . is difficult to prove. Because Paul appears to be greatly concerned about Judaizers (see comments on 3.2), it is reasonable to assume that the same group is primarily in view here as well.'[16] As I have argued, verses 29–30 seem to be about actual suffering – and I cannot imagine the Philippians putting tensions caused by the presence of false teachers into this category – and seem to indicate attack from outsiders. More specifically, if these teachers have made any substantial inroads into the community,[17] it would seem very unlikely that Paul would introduce them simply as οἱ ἀντικείμενοι (verse 28) – with ὑμῶν surely understood (given the earlier μὴ πτυρόμενοι). The term is not previously explained and thus would seem very unlikely to be understood by the Philippians as referring to these teachers. Furthermore, πτύρεσθαι seems an odd word to use with regard to teachers. The danger would be much more of being persuaded than

---

Philippians (London: United Bible Societies, 1977), p. 42. They argue from the context relating to war and contests. See also the *Jerusalem Bible* translation of the verse.

[15] See C.-H. Kim, *Form and Structure of the Familiar Greek Letter of Recommendation* (SBL Diss. Series 4, 1972), p. 120.

[16] M. Silva, *Philippians* (Wycliffe Exegetical Commentaries; Chicago: Moody, 1988), p. 92; cf. p. 9. On J.-F. Collange's approach, see below.

[17] As Collange seems to suggest (see below).

of being panicked. I will return to the suggestion about false teachers as opponents below.

The specific evidence of suffering in 1.27–30, and the link there between Paul's suffering and that of the Philippians, suggests that, of the various possibilities for the reason behind the insistent theme of suffering in the letter, the correct one is the most straightforward, namely, that the Philippians were actually suffering. The insistence of the theme suggests that Paul saw there being some problem in the church in connection with it.

Less clear than 1.27–30, but still useful, is the evidence of 2.17–18. In verses 17–18 we have Paul's imagery about being a drink-offering on or with the Philippians' sacrifice and then the call to rejoice, themselves and with him. The sacrifice language immediately follows a 'flash-forward' to the Day of Christ, from which viewpoint Paul looks back on his life's work. The visit to that high viewpoint raises the temperature of the next verse. The 'sacrifice and service' therefore seem likely to represent something very heavyweight, such as suffering with a possibility of death. Paul's being 'poured out' seems to refer to his death. Against Collange, it is not significant whether σπένδομαι was used of the pouring of blood. The libation was poured out once, with the sacrifice, and thus is most naturally read as referring to Paul's death.[18] In that case, for the Philippians' 'sacrifice and service' to refer to their financial gifts would seem absurdly trivial. There is clearly a range of viable possibilities, such as the Philippians' Christian life as a whole,[19] but, again, a reference to the Philippians' suffering would seem particularly easily heard. This is followed by Paul's χαίρω καὶ συγχαίρω πᾶσιν ὑμῖν and his call, τὸ δὲ αὐτὸ καὶ ὑμεῖς χαίρετε καὶ συγχαίρετέ μοι. Paul's rejoicing is unexpected: εἰ καὶ σπένδομαι χαίρω. Paul rejoices, even if he is to die, and he calls the Philippians to rejoice with him, even if that is to happen to him: συγχαίρετέ μοι. If this is correct, then Paul's συγχαίρω πᾶσιν ὑμῖν presumably refers to the Philippians' sacrifice and service and, like σπένδομαι, that is presumably also something which would be expected to preclude rejoicing. It therefore seems likely to refer to present, or imminently threatened, suffering. Paul's call, χαίρετε, seems then to be a call for the Philippians to rejoice (in a way in which they are

[18] J.-F. Collange, *The Epistle of Saint Paul to the Philippians*, tr. A. W. Heathcote (London: Epworth, 1979), p. 113. See O'Brien, pp. 301–6.

[19] F. W. Beare, *A Commentary on the Epistle to the Philippians* (New York: Harper, 1959), p. 94, suggests various options.

not doing now) in this suffering. For Paul to feel a need to call for this probably means that there has been suffering at Philippi and that the Philippians have (understandably) not been rejoicing in it – a problem which presumably expressed itself in some tangible way evident to Paul. This kind of reading of verses 17–18 makes the verses fit well as a conclusion to the unit from 1.27 to 2.18.[20]

Two passages in the letter suggest an externally beleaguered church at Philippi. Philippians 3.20–1, in which Paul and the community σωτῆρα ἀπεκδεχόμεθα, coming from their πολίτευμα in the heavens, seems to paint the picture of a city under siege or at least in great trouble. The possible implication of this for the Philippians' suffering is reinforced by the description of their present state as τὸ σῶμα τῆς ταπεινώσεως. The presence of threatening forces could be further reinforced by the reference to Christ's subjection of all things. Philippians 2.15–16 suggests a similar situation, this time by its sharp depiction of contrast between the Philippian community and the rest of society. The Philippian Christians are almost 'angelised' (albeit on condition that they do not grumble) and society demonised: ἄμεμπτοι, ἀκέραιοι, τέκνα θεοῦ, ἄμωμα, φαίνεσθε ὡς φωστῆρες ἐν κόσμῳ, λόγον ζωῆς ἐπέχοντες, in contrast to γενεᾶς σκολιᾶς καὶ διεστραμμένης. The natural home of this kind of literary form is a situation where a community feels itself a threatened minority. That can be the result of paranoia, but it is often the result of actual suffering.

We can also gather support from the reference in 2 Corinthians 8.1–2 to . . . ταῖς ἐκκλησίαις τῆς Μακεδονίας . . . ἐν πολλῇ δοκιμῇ θλίψεως, which probably includes Philippi, especially since the topic is the giving of money. We discussed 2 Corinthians 8 with regard to money, above. In a similar way to the comment Paul makes on their poverty, the Macedonian suffering is stated by Paul to be extremely deep, so, even if we were to tone the idea down to allow for rhetoric, there is still evidence of suffering.

Philippians 1.7, συγκοινωνούς μου τῆς χάριτος πάντας ὑμᾶς ὄντας, has a certain ambiguity. Some scholars relate it to the Philippians' suffering[21] while others – the majority – relate it to their financial support of Paul.[22] I have argued elsewhere that the

---

[20] For 1.27–2.18 as a unit, see, e.g., O'Brien, pp. 143, 297; Hawthorne, p. xlix.
[21] Most notably, Lohmeyer, p. 26. Also Lightfoot, p. 85.
[22] E.g., Beare, p. 53; O'Brien, p. 70.

balance of probabilities favours a reference to suffering.[23] The most cogent argument for this is that it makes verses 3–7 into a very Pauline chain of reasoning, which also follows the pattern in verses 27–30. In verses 3–7, the reasoning is 'you have suffered, therefore you share with me in grace (verse 7), therefore I am confident of your salvation (verses 3–6)'. If the ὅτι in verse 29 is connected with the σωτηρία in verse 28, the reasoning is more-or-less the same. Both pieces of reasoning fit with Paul's general outlook (e.g. Rom. 8.17). In contrast, Paul seems unlikely to argue from financial support to assurance of salvation – or even to perseverance in the ability to offer financial support (to take an alternative interpretation of verse 6). Philippians 1.7 seems, therefore, to offer evidence in support of Philippian Christians having suffered.

In a sense, the argument of this section as a whole has proved nothing that is contentious, since the great majority of commentators think that the Philippians were suffering. However, my aim has been to build an exegetical platform. The presence of suffering in Philippi seems sufficiently probable for it to act as a basis of interpretation. This is something that commentators, with the notable exception of Ernst Lohmeyer, have not tended to do in any great depth.

2. Suggestions of Jewish Christian or Jewish opponents in 1.27–30

Before proceeding further, I need to give further attention to the main scenario which is suggested as an alternative to the idea that the Philippians were, or had been, actually suffering. I will also argue against the related suggestions that attacks that the Christians faced came from a Jewish source.

The suggestion that the ἀντικείμενοι of verse 28 are Jewish Christian false teachers has been championed by Jean-François Collange. He notes the striking parallels between 1.27–2.18 and chapter 3 and argues that the situation in chapter 1 is an earlier stage of the same crisis as in chapter 3 (which he thinks was a separate letter).[24]

---

[23] Peter Oakes, 'Jason and Penelope Hear Philippians 1.1–11', in Christopher Rowland and Crispin H. T. Fletcher-Louis, eds., *Understanding, Studying and Reading. New Testament Essays in Honour of John Ashton* (Sheffield: Sheffield Academic Press, 1998), pp. 161–4.

[24] Collange, p. 71.

> Allied to the false apostles who are disparaged in *2 Corinthians*, these itinerant Jewish Christians supported their preaching by an appeal to a series of superior qualities due to their Jewish origin or to more or less exotic spiritual phenomena. They thereby introduced a kind of rivalry within the community which was unfaithful not only to the fraternal spirit which should reign there but also to the humility of the Cross which was its origin.[25]

Collange sees the point at issue in Philippians as being the nature of Christianity – whether it is a religion which follows the Cross and the way of suffering.[26] This has the advantage of linking the issues of unity and suffering in 1.27–30, issues which, as Collange rightly argues, are intertwined in these and the succeeding verses.[27] He is, however, linking the issues in an unusual way. The opponents do not cause the suffering. Instead, the question under dispute is whether Christianity includes suffering. By arguing for their position on this question, the Jewish Christian adversaries cause disunity.

I have argued, above, that the topic of suffering appears in verses 27–30 because Philippians have actually been suffering. This seems a more probable reason for its inclusion here than does the idea that a heretical group has appeared, who differ in their understanding of the nature of the Gospel. The primary issue in 1.27–30 seems not to be the definition of the nature of the Gospel but a call to live in accordance with the Gospel. Of course, the issue of the nature of the Gospel is indeed vital in Philippians. However, what Paul does is first to call for action on the basis of the Gospel, whose nature he seems to assume that he and his hearers agree upon (1.27). He then uses definition of the Gospel – for example, by using 2.6–11 – as a rhetorical strategy to shape the hearers' action and to strengthen them in that action. His argument seems best to fit a situation of actual suffering in which action is needed, rather than a situation of a clash of ideas about whether the Gospel involves suffering.

Collange's idea shares the difficulties of other approaches involving false teachers and no actual suffering in 1.27–30. In particular, Paul's unexplained introduction of false teachers as οἱ ἀντικείμενοι

---

[25] Ibid., p. 72.
[26] Ibid., p. 14.
[27] Ibid., p. 71.

seems implausible. In an attempt, I imagine, to introduce the topic of these teachers' doctrine at a more programmatic point in the text, Collange then overloads the τοῦ Χριστοῦ in 1.27a. He writes that it 'in the present context and in view of 1.29f. and 2.5–11 can mean only one thing, that the Gospel exhibits a "glory" attributable not to itself but to Christ, and by that very fact becomes effective, through struggles and sufferings, in the steady achievement of real progress, especially in brotherly community life.'[28] When the Philippians hear verse 27, the τοῦ Χριστοῦ is unlikely to alert them to these things.

Collange is also forced to a very unusual translation of verses 28b–29. He begins a new sentence at ἥτις:

> What is for them a sign of perdition is in fact your salvation, and it comes from God, (29) namely, that you have been graciously allowed (to live) for Christ, which not only means believing in him but also suffering for him.[29]

He explains that the ἥτις (feminine by attraction to ἔνδειξις), 'an indefinite relative pronoun often used to introduce sentences of a general kind (cf. Matt. 5.39, 41 etc.), is explained by the phrase opening with "*hoti*" (verse 29): "what is . . . namely, that it is necessary to suffer".'[30] Collange may have strong extracanonical linguistic evidence, which he does not cite, for his reading. However, a brief survey of the use of ὅστις in the NT suggests that his translation is untenable.

Of 158 instances, 141 seem to refer backwards to a previous referent. Of those which refer forwards, i.e., introduce a previously unstated person or thing, 11 are in a pair, ὅστις . . . αὐτος (etc.), while the other six leave the second pronoun unstated. All these 17 use ὅστις in a rather indefinite sense. They introduce what are effectively 'if . . . then' sentences, 'If someone does X, then . . .', for example,

ὅστις δὲ ὑψώσει ἑαυτὸν ταπεινωθήσεται. (Matt. 23.12)

Collange's suggestion refers forwards, so it is considerably less probable than one which refers backwards. His ἥτις . . . ὅτι construction, even allowing for the attraction of ἥτις into the feminine, seems not to be a kind of construction known in the NT.

[28] Ibid., pp. 73f.
[29] Ibid., p. 72.
[30] Ibid., p. 75.

Finally, the essential grammatical idea of the NT sentences beginning with ὅστις seems to be to set up an indefinite group (of persons, things or actions) and then to say what happens in the case of that group. This kind of construction therefore seems completely inapplicable to a sentence in which the referent is a definite one – something like, 'the nature of Christian existence'.

In contrast with the suggested Jewish Christian groups who are false teachers, those who suggest Jews as opponents think that they might have brought more concrete trouble. Houlden suggests Jews in Philippi as 'much the most likely source' of the 'long drawn-out antagonism' that he sees 1.27–30 as attesting.[31] He does not, however, advance any particular argument for this. The Jews come in because he sees the strength of the polemic in 3.2ff. as indicating that they were quite prominent in Philippi. On this basis he disregards the evidence of Acts 16. He sums up Acts 16 by noting that 'it does not sound as if the Jews in Philippi were very prominent'. He goes on to say, 'However, the evidence of *Philippians* tips the balance the other way.'[32]

The near-absence of archaeological evidence of Jews at Philippi,[33] although naturally open to question when used to argue *e silentio*, does suggest that Houlden has made a historical misjudgement here. He seems to misapply the standard scholarly tool of preferring Paul's letters to the accounts in Acts. What he has done is to give the primary source so much priority over the secondary one that he prefers a conclusion from extremely unclear evidence in Philippians over rather clear evidence in Acts – and in a passage which commands more support than most for its historical usefulness. Even if the targets of Paul's polemic in 3.2ff. are Jews, it is extremely unsafe to infer anything about the prominence of the Jewish population in Philippi. Houlden's view of the opponents of 1.27–30 depends on his conclusion that Jews were a prominent group in Philippi. His view seems unfounded.

Gerald Hawthorne develops a suggestion of Jews in more detail than Houlden. He suggests that 'the most likely source of the trouble threatening the Philippians was Jews, possibly from Thessalonica'.[34] Although the primary form of danger was persuasion, which Paul seeks to counter in chapter 3, Hawthorne also sees a

[31] Houlden, pp. 34, 65.
[32] Ibid., p. 34.
[33] See pp. 58f., above.
[34] Hawthorne, p. xlvi.

danger of attack. One of the two possibilities he sees for suffering among the Philippians is 'because of persecution that might come upon them for rejecting the message of fanatical Jewish missionaries'.[35]

The primary problem with Hawthorne's reconstruction of the opponents in Philippians is that it sounds historically quite implausible. He speaks of, 'Jews, who had their own missionaries proclaiming a message of righteousness and perfection that was attainable *now* simply by submitting to circumcision and complying with certain laws.'[36] Martin Goodman has argued that there were no groups of Jewish missionaries in this period.[37] Whatever one's assessment of Goodman's overall case, the historical evidence would seem highly unfavourable for such strange groups as Hawthorne seems to suggest. I cannot imagine any strand of first-century Judaism producing Hawthorne's missionaries. I think one has to be extremely suspicious of supposed Jewish groups who are reconstructed essentially from mirror-reading of a NT text.

If the trouble caused by Hawthorne's Jews in 1.27–30 is only in the form of persuasion, turning some Philippians from Christianity, then various of the arguments above, against the idea that the ἀντικείμενοι are simply missionaries of some sort, would apply. If the trouble consists of persecution instigated by these 'fanatical Jewish missionaries' then Hawthorne is not only going beyond what seems historically plausible but also beyond the picture in Acts. There, Jews frequently respond aggressively to Paul 'coming on to their patch' and acting in ways that affect their community. The most that then happens is that some follow Paul to his next destination and try to cause trouble for him there (Acts 14.19). This is a natural move for members of the Jewish community to make. If they saw Paul as a troublemaker in their own town, they are unlikely to be happy to see him start his work in the next town. This rather natural picture in Acts is different from Hawthorne's picture of events in Philippi. He sees a missionary group of Jews from Thessalonica coming to Philippi to convert the established, Gentile church and then instigating persecution of them when they refuse their message. This seems quite implausible.

It is also noteworthy that even Thessalonian Christians suffered

[35] Ibid., p. xlvii. The other possible source is the Roman authorities.
[36] Ibid., p. xlvii.
[37] Martin Goodman, *Mission and Conversion: Proselytizing in the Religious History of the Roman Empire* (Oxford: Clarendon Press, 1994).

at the hands of their συμφυλέται (1 Thess. 2.14), who were probably Gentiles, rather than those of the Thessalonian Jews who had, according to Acts, stirred up trouble for Paul himself, and his supporters, while he was there (17.5ff.).

Suggestions of Jewish Christian or Jewish opponents in 1.27–30 seem unlikely to be correct. The verses, therefore, probably refer to opposition from other people in Philippi.

3. 'To suffer for Christ' (1.28): what does it mean?

Scholars have generally tried to treat a church as an undifferentiated group, defined only by their Christianity. Our modelling of the Philippians suggests that a better starting-point may be the various groups within the church. These give a much greater social specificity to the question, what would 'suffering for Christ' be likely to mean? We can consider each group in this way. We can also ask whether some groups are more likely to suffer than others.

We ought to begin with the most numerous group in our model of the church, craft-workers. If we consider a family of Greek craft-workers, all of whom are Christians, what would 'suffering for Christ' be likely to involve for them? Let us imagine that our family are bakers and consist of a married couple called Simias and Ianthe, three children, an elderly grandmother and a slave-girl. They make and sell bread from a one-room bakery and shop. They live in the bakery and in a low mezzanine room above it. When trade is good, they just make ends meet. They sell half their bread as a regular order to three élite families. The rest is sold from their shop to a mixture of customers from the town and the countryside. Simias has for many years been a member of a burial club. A number of the members are also bakers and these contacts provide our baker with access to extra oven-space which he needs whenever he receives an order which is larger than usual.

What could 'suffering for Christ' mean for this family? The most obvious possibility is that problems might arise over the burial club. Simias might stop paying his subscription or the club might hold a celebratory meal, at the grave of a former member, which Simias was expected to attend but did not. The result of such unfriendly behaviour by Simias was likely to be damage to his relationships with some other members of the club. Some could be regular customers who might change where they bought bread. More seriously, the other bakers might deny him access to oven-space when he needed it. Since our family of bakers were living at subsistence level already, any such economic suffering would be very serious. Although an organisation such as a burial club did not perform major social functions, disruption of relationships with other members could cause substantial suffering.[38]

Problems could also arise at the shop. Ianthe has removed the shrine to the god that was popular among Greek bakers.[39] This had been quite visible from the shop counter and, although most customers did not notice its absence, some did and started to spread word that Simias and Ianthe were dishonouring the gods. This was particularly unpopular among the other bakers. Extra oven-space became impossible to find and our bakers had to change their supplier of flour. They ended up paying 10 per cent more than they had previously. This, again, was a severe problem.

Things became worse as word went round that the family were members of a strange, subversive, Jewish organisation. Some people challenged Simias and Ianthe over this and they responded by seeking to persuade them to join the organisation and join in the dishonouring of the gods. The daughter of one of the other bakers was actually persuaded. Her father came round in a rage, along with three friends. They beat up Simias and started breaking up the shop. Neighbours, worried that a fire might start, ran to the magistrates. Simias and the other baker were taken off to answer for the disturbance. The magistrates had seen one or two of these troublesome Christians before. Simias received a further beating and a night in prison. Simias was unable to work for a week. This was a particular problem because the usual neighbourly extra pairs of hands for such an emergency were unavailable. However, Ianthe and the rest of the family coped with the work. In fact, the work-load proved unexpectedly light because, two days after Simias' night in prison, one of the three élite families who were their main customers stopped their order. Simias and Ianthe lived in terror of the other two doing the same.

---

[38] Garnsey and Saller, *Roman Empire*, pp. 156f.; Lane Fox, *Pagans and Christians*, p. 85; Meggitt, *Paul, Poverty and Survival*, pp. 171f.

[39] D. G. Orr, 'Roman Domestic Religion: The Evidence of the Household Shrines', *ANRW II.16.2*, ed. W. Haase (Berlin: de Gruyter, 1978), pp. 1580f., lists deities popular with various trades at Pompeii.

The sufferings of Simias and Ianthe and their family
sprang from a variety of primary causes: principally abandon-
ment of pagan worship,[40] also suspicion of secretive associa-
tions,[41] suspicion of Jewish activities,[42] and attempts at evangelism.
When they met violence, this disturbance acted as a secondary
cause of further trouble, namely, being taken before the magistrates. Association in the magistrates' mind with other troublesome
Christians contributed to Simias being punished. That punishment
itself cause notoriety which led to loss of custom.

The crucial form of suffering for the bakers was economic.
Broken relationships, broken reputations and broken heads would
all be serious forms of suffering in themselves. However, for a
family on a subsistence income, the most serious aspect of each of
these would be the long-term economic effect that it produced.

Greek service groups, such as craft-workers, together with their
slaves, formed 35 per cent of our model of the church. Commuting
colonist farmers, their families and slaves, formed a further 19 per
cent. What might suffering mean for such families?

Suffering must be less likely for this group than for service
groups. This is because the farmers would have less interaction with
other people in the town. Part of the family would be out at the
fields all day. Other family members would be service-users in
town, rather than service-providers. They would therefore be far
less vulnerable.

The least vulnerable of all would be colonist farming families
who still owned their land and who were not in debt. For them, a
night in prison or a beating might not have great economic
consequences, especially as the family income might be a little
above subsistence level. At this date, it seems unlikely that Christians would have faced punishments, such as confiscation of land,
which would have affected families with capital assets. For such a
family, the main secondary concern would be loss of honour.[43]

---

[40] See Lane Fox, *Pagans and Christians*, pp. 38, 95, 98; G. E. M. de Ste Croix,
'Why were the early Christians Persecuted?' *Past and Present*, 26 (1963), p. 24;
Goodman, *Mission*, p. 105.

[41] See Robert L. Wilken, *The Christians as the Romans saw them* (New Haven:
Yale University Press, 1984), ch. 2; Bormann, *Philippi*, pp. 223f.

[42] See Louis H. Feldman, *Jew and Gentile in the Ancient World: Attitudes and
Interactions from Alexander to Justinian* (Princeton: Princeton University Press,
1993), chs. 3–4; Acts 16.20.

[43] On the importance of the issues of honour and shame, see Malina, *NT World*,
chs. 2, 3.

However, by the middle of the first century AD, most colonist farmers in Philippi would probably either have lost ownership of their land and be renting, or be somewhere on the very slippery slope of debt which tended to lead to loss of ownership.[44] These farmers were economically vulnerable. Their landlords would probably be uninterested in the religious activities of their tenants. However, trouble with the magistrates might be a different matter. Notoriety could quite conceivably lead to either cancellation of a tenancy or foreclosure on a debt. Either would usually mean the ruin of the farming family. Again, suffering can be coped with if it stays at the immediate level of occasional violence or punishment by the authorities. The suffering becomes acute when economic consequences follow.

The vulnerability of tenant colonist farmers lay in their dependence on élite landowners. A similar dependence would be characteristic of many Roman families in the service groups. These constitute 18 per cent of our model. Whether the families had come 'down' economically from being colonist farmers, or whether they had come 'up' from slavery, through manumission, their service work was particularly likely to be linked to the élite and some might also receive benefaction from them. Freed slaves generally became clients of their former owners and often continued to perform the same services for them as before.[45] The freedman or freedwoman would then be economically dependent on their relationship with their patron. Far more than would be the case for a landlord–tenant relationship, a patron–client relationship could easily be disrupted if the client either engaged in activities of which the patron disapproved or gained a reputation as a troublemaker.

A poor family (25 per cent of our model) will have still been alive only because they partially functioned like part of the service groups. They would therefore have faced similar problems, sharpened by the desperate nature of their situation. Another possible source of income would be casual building or agricultural work. The ability to obtain this could be affected by any notoriety. If the family were unusually fortunate and were receiving some direct financial assistance, that would be totally dependent on the main-

[44] Oakman, 'Countryside', pp. 157f.
[45] Alison Burford, *Craftsmen in Greek and Roman Society* (Ithaca: Cornell University Press, 1972), p. 38; M. I. Finlay, 'Freedmen', *Oxford Classical Dictionary*, ed. N. G. L. Hammond and H. H. Scullard (Oxford: Clarendon Press, 1970²), p. 448.

tenance of good relations with the donor. The poor were particularly liable to harsh treatment by magistrates. Again, however, the
long-term economic consequences of trouble would be the most
serious aspect of suffering.

I do not want to spend time discussing what suffering might face
members of the decurial class. If there were any in the church, the
number would be small. They would also probably be in mixed
relationships, the consequences of which will be discussed below.
The meaning of suffering for an élite family which was completely
Christian would be an interesting issue but does not seem likely to
be relevant to a study of Philippians.

All first-generation Christians would be involved in mixed relationships to some extent. A fair proportion would be involved in a
close mixed relationship: Christian wife to pagan husband (or vice
versa); Christian slave to pagan owner (or vice versa); Christian son
or daughter to pagan parents (or vice versa).

Lilian Portefaix discusses various aspects of the situation of a
Christian woman married to a non-Christian.[46] There were various
evident possibilities for tension centred on domestic or public
religion. One imagines that matters might become particularly
critical if the husband came to feel that he was shamed by his wife's
refusal to behave in the appropriate way.[47] If the tensions became
great, then, in a first-century urban context in particular, divorce
would seem quite a strong probability – 1 Corinthians 7.15 may
well reflect such a situation. As Portefaix points out, this could be
economically disastrous for a woman and, as she also points out,
the Christian faith exacerbated this by banning prostitution, the
main means of support in the most desperate cases.[48]

There are some problems with Portefaix's reconstruction of the
social location of these women. Portefaix's focus on women, which
gives her book its dynamism, unfortunately also leaves her without
an overall model of the make-up of the church in which to place her
women. The resulting confusion is most evident on the issue of
citizenship. Her explicit discussion of the audience of the letter
emphasises Greeks: 'From the fact that the proper names in the
letter are mainly Greek it may further be deduced that the first
Philippian Christians were principally of Greek origin.'[49] The

---

[46] Portefaix, *Sisters*, pp. 43ff., 53ff., 146f., 167, 186, 193ff., 200.
[47] See note 43.
[48] Portefaix, *Sisters*, pp. 181f.
[49] Ibid., p. 137. The fact that most names in the letter are Greek is indeed

description of family life on which she builds her reconstruction of women in marriage-difficulties is, however, characteristically Roman, involving the absolute rule of the *paterfamilias*[50] and a domestic religion which is discussed in terms of *lares*, *penates*, *genius*, etc.[51] She writes that citizenship 'might have been inconceivable'[52] for most of the hearers but she worries about the hearers' participation in civic cult processions.[53] If they were not citizens, this would not have been an issue for them. Portefaix's work would have gained a great deal in clarity and precision if she had delineated a number of types of women hearers with various possible combinations of circumstances (for example, Greek freedwoman who is a former adherent of Dionysus and has a Christian husband).

However, Portefaix's general argument about Christian women married to pagans seems correct. D. G. Orr notes the wide range of domestic shrines and street shrines found in Pompeii.[54] We do not have a Greek Pompeii to study, but there is scholarly consensus that, in Greek culture too, acts which acknowledged the gods' position would enter every sphere of life. Robin Lane Fox writes that 'we can appreciate the gods' role on every level of social life and their pervasive presence . . . in early Christians' existence.'[55] He also comments that the lack of privacy in daily living in that period meant that it was impossible to conceal one's personal religion.[56] Roman or Greek women converts who were married to pagans almost certainly faced tensions and some probably had their relationship disrupted. Losing a valued relationship would itself be an acute form of suffering. Losing status that went with that relationship would also be felt strongly. However, again, the most substantial long-term form of suffering would be economic.

Christian sons and daughters of pagan parents would probably

important and is badly neglected by the commentators. '[I]t may . . . be deduced' is, however, one of a number of logical leaps which Portefaix needs to defend in more depth.

[50] Ibid., pp. 192, 178(!). The effective power of the *paterfamilias* seems, in any case, to have declined substantially by the time of the Empire. See Garnsey and Saller, *Roman Empire*, pp. 126ff.
[51] Portefaix, *Sisters*, pp. 44f., but cf. n. 71.
[52] Ibid., pp. 138f.
[53] Ibid., p. 49.
[54] Orr, 'Roman Domestic Religion', pp. 1557–71, 1572.
[55] Lane Fox, *Pagans and Christians*, p. 82. See p. 83, on Greek family cults.
[56] Ibid., p. 62.

be regarded as rebelling against family traditions.[57] Various consequences might flow from this. These could range from beating to repudiation. The adult child of a craft-worker might well work for their family. Repudiation by the family would then bring unemployment and probable destitution.

Christian slaves with pagan owners were likely to have great difficulty in attending Christian gatherings. However, any such converts that there were must have had some degree of freedom of action in order for them to have been converted in the first place. They could, for example, be public slaves who acted as low-level administrators. If an owner discovered that a slave was engaged in a disreputable activity, various punishments might follow. These could range from restriction of movement to beating or, ultimately, to the selling of the slave. Such a sale could well leave the slave in a less favourable situation, especially if it was known that the sale had come about because the slave had become a troublemaker. Should we describe the suffering of Christian slaves as having a strong economic component? I think that most slaves would say, yes. As well as their living conditions being in themselves a kind of economic issue, slaves would be very keen to save up money (their *peculium*[58]) in the hope of buying manumission. The kinds of slaves who had enough freedom of movement to come into contact with Christians were particularly likely to be engaged in this. The means of acquiring money was either through tips from the owner or through other earnings in the course of business – earnings allowed purely through the favour of the owner. If the favour of the owner was lost, the hope of saving for manumission was lost. Gratuitous manumission would also become unlikely. A Christian slave with a pagan owner ran a very great economic risk in living a Christian life.

If the Christian in a mixed relationship was the one on whom others were dependent, he or she clearly ran less risk than when the positions were reversed. Christianity was probably not sufficiently recognised as a crime for denunciations by family members to be a substantial possibility or threat. Relationships could be disrupted. 1 Corinthians 7.12 implies the possibility that a pagan wife might leave a Christian husband. This could in itself bring suffering but, unless the dowry was very large, it would not immediately result in economic suffering. It could, however, be part of a pattern of

---

[57] Ibid., p. 83.
[58] M. I. Finley, 'Peculium', *Oxford Classical Dictionary*, ed. N. G. L. Hammond and H. H. Scullard (Oxford: Clarendon Press, 1970^2), p. 793.

breakdown of relationships which did have serious economic consequences.

We have now considered each of the groups in our model of the church. For almost every group, the most serious long-term suffering seems likely to have been economic. This was true even though the initial forms of suffering that each group was likely to face varied a great deal: withdrawal of facilities by fellow craftspeople; withdrawal of custom; violence; summary justice from magistrates; cancellation of tenancy; foreclosure of debt; breaking of patron–client relationships; withdrawal of financial assistance; divorce; repudiation by family; withdrawal of opportunities to earn *peculium*; being sold. The only groups for whom any long-term suffering seems less likely to have been economic were colonist farmers who owned their land and were not in debt, and economically dominant partners in relationships with non-Christians. In fact, even these groups, if they were suffering, would be likely to suffer economically.

We know that Philippian Christians were suffering. If, in the Philippian context, the most serious long-term component of suffering would be economic, then Paul's intertwining of material on suffering and unity in the letter has particular force.

Before looking at this issue, we need to consider a possible objection to the view that I have been putting forward.

4.   Descriptions of Christian sufferings in early texts

My suggestion that the most important form of suffering at Philippi was probably economic has to face the objection that this does not appear to fit the descriptions of Christian suffering in texts from the first three centuries of the Church's life. We therefore need to give some attention to these texts.

At least twenty of the twenty-seven books of the New Testament mention the persecution of a Christian or of Christians as a broader group. (The exceptions are 1 Timothy, Titus, 2 Peter (but 2.9), 1 John (but 3.13), 2 John, 3 John, Jude.) Since we are considering Philippi we should exclude persecution which is particularly described as being by Jews. A number of texts refer to possible or actual death (Matt. 10.21 [and parallels]; 24.9; John 21.18–19; Philippians 1.20–3; 3.10; Revelation 2.13; 6.9, 11; 11.7–10; 13.10, 15; 18.24; 20.4). There is a prediction of torture at Matthew 24.9 and of imprisonment at Luke 21.12 and Revelation

2.10. Evidence of actual imprisonment comes in Hebrews 10.34 and repeatedly in Paul's letters and the Acts of the Apostles. The author of Revelation was exiled to an island (Rev. 1.9). Paul describes himself and the other apostles as being beaten (1 Corinthians 4.11; 2 Corinthians 11.23–5 (various forms of beating)) and himself as having been stoned (2 Corinthians 11.25; Acts 14.19). Hebrews 10.34 refers to the 'plundering of possessions'. Mob violence is reported in Acts 14.19; 17.5–9.

Many of these forms of suffering involved the Roman legal process. Such process enters the story explicitly at Matthew 10.18 (and parallels); Acts 16.19–24; 17.5–9; chapter 21 onwards; 2 Timothy 4.16; James 2.6. Another kind of legal process is indicated at 1 Corinthians 7.12–16, which discusses the possibility of divorce instigated by a non-Christian spouse, clearly on account of the Christian's faith.

The post-Biblical accounts of Christian suffering predominantly have death as the form of suffering. In AD 112, Pliny asks Trajan about putting Christians to death and is sufficiently confident to carry this out for non-citizens before writing to Trajan. Trajan clearly does then support Pliny's policy (Pliny, *Ep.* X, 96, 97). Most sources record death in the most extreme judicial forms. In 155, Polycarp is burnt (*Martyrium Polycarpi*, xv-xvi). In 177, the martyrs of Lyons are sent to the beasts in the amphitheatre.[59] Nero goes beyond even the legal extremes (Tacitus, *Ann.* XV, 44).

There are some records of suffering other than death. In 52, Jewish Christians were probably expelled from Rome after riots (Suetonius, *Claudius*, XXV, 4).[60] Before matters at Lyons reached the stage of condemnation to the arena, Christians were 'excluded from public buildings, baths and markets' and 'even the mere appearance of any one of us was forbidden' (Eusebius *H.E.* V, i).[61] Tertullian complained that Christians faced trial without proper representation or even personal defence (*Apol.* ii). Somewhat later (253–60), the first rescript of Valerian forbade assembly and the use of Christian cemeteries. The second rescript decreed that Christian members of the élite should have their property confiscated. If they

---

[59] See W. H. C. Frend, *Martyrdom and Persecution in the Early Church* (Oxford: Blackwell, 1965), p. 7.

[60] How widely this affected the Jewish community as a whole is a matter of debate (Feldman, *Jew and Gentile*, p. 97; see Acts 18.2).

[61] *Epistle of the Gallican churches*, in Henry Bettenson, ed., *Documents of the Christian Church* (Oxford: Oxford University Press, 1963²), p. 12.

remained Christian they then faced death if male, or exile if female. Members of Caesar's household would lose their property and become agricultural slaves.[62]

Does all this Biblical and post-Biblical evidence suggest that economic suffering was not the predominant form of suffering among the earliest Christians? In order to answer this, we need to ask what sort of overall picture these texts paint. The NT letters and Acts highlight the troubles of the apostles. Sometimes this contrasts with the experience of the churches (1 and 2 Cor.). Sometimes the churches suffer too (1 Thess.). The Gospels predict Christian life heavily marked by persecution, both judicial (Matt. 10.18) and non-judicial (Matt. 5.11). The post-Biblical texts give the impression of churches living without trouble for most of the time but with sporadic outbreaks of persecution which brings deaths.

We also need to consider the intended functions of the texts. The relevant passages in the Gospels seem designed to encourage steadfastness under persecution, as do texts from Revelation. Post-Biblical Christian texts seem generally to see the martyrs as exemplary. Post-Biblical non-Christian texts either discuss issues relevant to the task of a provincial governor (Pliny) or record events of historic importance (Suetonius and Tacitus).

These combinations of types of picture and types of function make it almost inevitable that there is a focus on the most dramatic forms of suffering, especially death. The sources – and the present-day scholars – give little or no attention to more mundane forms of suffering in Christian communities. For example, they generally ignore the suffering of other members of churches in which some were martyred. Only a limited proportion of early Christians can have been killed but the kind of context in which such killing could take place would surely have generated economic difficulties for a far larger number of Christians.

Some texts do indicate forms of economic suffering. 'Plundering of possessions' (Heb. 10.34) could refer to a mob or a magistrate. The economic consequences of divorce (1 Corinthians 7.12–16) have been discussed above. Revelation foretells prevention of trade (Rev. 13.17). Expulsion from Rome – either alone or with other members of the Jewish community (Suetonius, *Claudius*, xxv, 4) would have sharp economic effects. Exclusion from market-places

---

[62] Bettenson, *Documents*, pp. 13f.

(at Lyons; Eusebius *H.E.* V, i) and confiscation of property, both from members of the élite and from imperial slaves (Valerian, Second rescript) were directly economic sanctions.

The preserved accounts talk particularly about deaths. Unspectacular, economic, suffering must have taken place among, for example, the children of the martyrs. But this is not as 'newsworthy' or so useful as an example to others.

In fact, this gives us a surprisingly strong argument from silence in Philippians (and other places where Paul talks about Christian suffering). Since Paul mentions no deaths or other very dramatic forms of suffering at Philippi, we can safely assume that the suffering is of an unspectacular kind. Such suffering is likely to have had a strong economic component. We can strengthen our argument further with the evidence of 2 Corinthians 8.2. Paul writes of the churches in Macedonia that

> ἐν πολλῇ δοκιμῇ θλίψεως ἡ περισσεία τῆς χαρᾶς αὐτῶν καὶ ἡ κατὰ βάθους πτωχεία αὐτῶν ἐπερίσσευσεν εἰς τὸ πλοῦτος τῆς ἁπλότητος αὐτῶν·

The great suffering and the deep poverty seem linked. Whether the text refers to Philippi or Thessalonica or both, our case for economic suffering is strengthened by this.

In Philippians 1.29–30, Paul compares the Philippians' sufferings to his, both during his visit there and at the time of writing. As various scholars have argued, the sufferings cannot be exactly the same as his.[63] However, the sufferings attributed to Paul in Acts 16 are of kinds which some of the Philippian Christians could be facing: mob-violence, appearance before magistrates, judicial beating, a night in prison. Even assuming that Paul is referring in 1.29 to these rather than to economic suffering, it still seems likely that the move from these verses to the call to unity in 2.1–4 would be driven by the economic effects of the suffering. In the first-century Philippian context, the most prevalent factors that would link issues of suffering and unity would be economic.

5. The issue of unity in a suffering church

I have argued that at least some of the Philippian Christians had been suffering. The presence of substantial suffering will always

---

[63] Gnilka, pp. 101f.; Houlden, pp. 65f.; O'Brien, p. 162.

have an effect on the issue of unity in a church. This is particularly important for the study of Philippians because, as we will consider in chapter 6, Paul closely intertwines the issues of suffering and unity in the letter.

At the very least, suffering in a church increases the importance of unity. Geoffrion has effectively argued for this in presenting evidence for the widespread expression of the need for unity among Greek citizens or troops in the face of enemies.[64] Members of a church facing attacks would no doubt see themselves in an analogous situation which carried analogous imperatives. The actual situation of the church members would also carry practical imperatives. These imperatives would be primarily economic. A distinction between first-generation Christianity and that in subsequent generations is that the complex of economic and other relationships within which the Christian will have lived the earlier part of his or her life will generally have been with people who were not (and did not become) Christians. I have argued that it would have been the breakdown of these relationships which constituted the most significant form of suffering. In that situation, what the Christians would need to do in order to survive is to enter into a new set of economic and other relationships among themselves (although, for the Christian community to be viable, some at least would need to maintain some relationships with non-Christians – and I imagine that almost all would have done so to an extent). In a situation of suffering, it was bound to be necessary, in particular, for the better-off in the church to enter into new or deeper economic relationships with others in the church.

If, as seems to have been the case at Philippi, suffering was fairly substantial, then such economic rearrangement would probably have needed to be fairly substantial too. For the wealthier parties in these new arrangements, the changes would seem likely to have involved at least three major dangers. First, the fresh demands on their purse could deplete their wealth. This is clearly a sufficient problem in itself but, within Graeco-Roman society, it ran against social imperatives which would be regarded as having moral force. If a craftsman, say, had inherited both a flourishing business and some land outside the city, and if he then sold the land in order to provide for poor fellow-Christians, the craftsman would not be maintaining his family's status and his act was liable to be judged

[64] Geoffrion, *Rhetorical Purpose*, pp. 36, 65.

as dishonourable.[65] Such considerations would also particularly apply to any élite landowners, whose status was directly measured by their landholding.[66]

A second danger follows from a second strategy that a wealthier Christian might adopt to enable him or her to enter fresh economic relationships, namely, that of breaking some existing relationships. The seriousness and dangers of doing this could be very great. The family of a wealthy Christian woman has bought bread from a particular family of bakers for three generations. The wealthy family provide a tenth of the bakers' business – the bakers stand in what is, more or less, a client relationship to them. The Christian wishes to stop the trade, without any honourable reason: she simply wants to switch her custom to Simias and his family, who have been unable to get people to buy their bread since he had his encounter with the magistrates. Such a move would seem sure to impugn the family honour of the Christian woman.[67] It would also lead to enmity from the non-Christian family of bakers[68] and they would voice their grievances to other wealthy customers (many of whom, by the nature of the patterns of such relationships, were liable to have relationships with the Christian's family). This would spread the opprobrium among people who could do the Christian harm. In any case, such a breaking of economic relationships would be likely to bring the Gospel into disrepute. This highlights an asymmetry which must have been particularly difficult for converts. Their relationships with equals or superiors in status seem likely to have been endangered, whereas they are likely to have been expected to maintain relationships with those of lower status.

The third danger comes from the immense weight that Roman society placed on law and order. To be a disorderly element was to merit strong condemnation. This contrasts with various present-day societies where disorderly groups such as Greenpeace receive a fair degree of toleration if the beliefs of the group are regarded as having merit. In Roman society, if someone was regarded as a troublemaker then there was a moral imperative for others not to associate with him.

Suffering will generally heighten the economic need for unity. It

---

[65] Malina, *NT World*, pp. 76f.; cf. MacMullen, *Social Relations*, pp. 105f.

[66] MacMullen, *Social Relations*, p. 90.

[67] Malina, *NT World*, p. 86.

[68] Cf. P. Marshall, *Enmity in Corinth: Social Conventions in Paul's relationship with the Corinthians* (Tübingen: J. C. B. Mohr, 1987), pp. 19f., ch. 2.

also clearly heightens the need for unity in many other ways, especially general relational ones. Suffering also produces forces which threaten unity. It becomes dangerous to remain or become united with people who are suffering. As I have argued above, there are specific dangers of this in the Graeco-Roman context. These are particularly marked when rearrangements of economic relationships are needed.

At Philippi, we would therefore expect there to be forces, arising from suffering, that tended to disrupt the unity of the church. The suffering at Philippi would also make unity a more vital issue than normal.

All this, I would argue, provides us with a coherent context for understanding the specific ways in which Paul responds to the intertwined issues of suffering and unity at Philippi.

4

PAUL AND THE PHILIPPIANS

Paul's response to the Philippians' suffering provides the most important thematic element in the construction of the letter, a pervasive three-fold parallel drawn between Christ's suffering, Paul's suffering and the Philippians' suffering.[1] Also, Paul's response to suffering, together with the related issue of unity, provides the topic for 1.27–2.11, the passage which is in the most important rhetorical position in the letter and which carries the letter's most weighty rhetoric. In this chapter, we will focus mainly on Paul as a model for the suffering Philippians. That will take us across the whole of the letter. In chapter 6, we will look at Christ as a model. That will mean particularly looking at 1.27–2.11. Chapter 5 will prepare for chapter 6 by looking at a comparison that Paul seems to draw between Christ and the Roman Emperor.

1.   Paul as a model for the suffering Philippians

The basic thematic structure of Philippians is a series of exemplary parallels which focus particularly on the issue of suffering. Paul writes about himself in two major blocks: 1.12–26 and 3.4–16. The function of these blocks can be contrasted with the function of most passages where Paul writes about himself in other letters. In the other letters such passages usually have the function of defending Paul or explaining what he is doing (e.g., Gal. 1–2; 2 Cor. 10–12; Rom. 15). Philippians is different. Here, Paul primarily writes about himself in order to give an example of the way he wants the Philippians to live.

Of course, if Paul presents himself as a model, he would always see Christ standing behind this as a prior model. In 2.6–8, Christ is

---

[1] On the pervasiveness of the theme of suffering, see the discussion on pp. 77–9, above.

the pattern for the Philippians' behaviour. In 3.10–11, his is the pattern for Paul's suffering. Stephen Fowl has argued that 2.6–11 also provides the basic pattern for Paul's whole presentation of his life in 3.4–11.[2] In fact, the link may be more complex than that. Philippians 3.4–11 is partly given shape by Paul's rhetoric designed to combat the 'Judaisers' (see below). More fundamentally, we need to ask whether 3.4–11 is essentially shaped by 2.6–11 or whether both 3.4–11 and 2.6–11 are essentially shaped by the needs of the Philippian situation. However, Paul would undoubtedly see any similarity between his pattern of life and that of Christ as representing him following Christ as a model. Where Paul provides an example to his churches, it will always be, 'Be imitators of me as I am of Christ' (1 Cor. 11.1).

These two examples and their outworking among the Philippians occupy the bulk of the letter. We may be able to add 2.19–30 to this structure. Epaphroditus and Timothy seem also to act as examples for Philippian behaviour.

The best way to explain the parallel structure is to give a brief reading of the letter.

Greetings. I rejoice that you have always shared in grace with me in my sufferings. I long to see you and pray that your love for each other may continue to grow (1.1–11). I want you to know that my sufferings have turned out for the benefit of the Gospel. My attitude to my sufferings and possible death is one of concern for the Gospel and confidence in Christ (1.12–26).

Stand firm together as you face opposition. Your sufferings are for Christ and are like mine. So be united, looking to each other's interests. Imitate Christ who willingly gave up status and was obedient right through the worst possible suffering. Because of this, God raised him to the position of supreme authority. So, keep going down the path which is bringing about your salvation. Do not quarrel. Even though I and you are suffering, I still rejoice. Rejoice with me (1.27–2.18).

I hope to send you Timothy, who is concerned for you and has stood the test. I am sending back Epaphroditus, who has been seriously ill. Honour people like him, because he risked his life for Christ (2.19–30).

---

[2] Stephen E. Fowl, *The Story of Christ in the Ethics of Paul: An Analysis of the Function of the Hymnic Material in the Pauline Corpus* (JSNTSup. 36; Sheffield: JSOT Press, 1990), pp. 99–101.

Watch out for the circumcision group. For the sake of gaining Christ, I have given up all such fleshly means of confidence. Being justified by faith in Christ, I want to become like him in his sufferings, death and resurrection. I am not yet perfect but I press on. You need to think this way too (3.1–16). Imitate me and those who follow our pattern. There are many who live as enemies of the Cross, whose sights are set on earth. Yours should be set on heaven, from where your transformation will come. So, my beloved brothers and sisters, my joy and my crown, stand firm (3.17–4.1).

Euodia and Syntyche, settle your quarrel. All of you – rejoice, pray, lead good lives, keep to my teaching and imitate me (4.2–9). I was delighted by your gift – but, remember, God is all I need when I suffer. However, your gift was good and I rejoice in our friendship. God will supply all your needs. Glory to him. Greetings (4.10–23).

To suggest that what Paul writes about himself in Philippians is consistently aimed at presenting himself as a model for the Philippians in their situation of suffering means questioning the conclusions of a number of recent studies of the letter in which Paul's own suffering is seen as a central issue in its own right. According to these studies, there is disquiet among the Philippians which focuses on the nature of Paul's sufferings. I will discuss this idea, below. First, however, we should look at the evidence that Paul's consistent aim is to present himself as a model. We need to consider textual links that the letter makes between Paul and the Philippians. We then need to consider how Paul would expect the content of the sections about himself to have been heard.

Philippians is remarkable for the numbers of links that are made between Paul's way of life and that of his hearers. The most pointed call to take Paul's behaviour as a model is in 3.17:

Συμμιμηταί μου γίνεσθε, ἀδελφοί, καὶ σκοπεῖτε τοὺς οὕτω περιπατοῦντας καθὼς ἔχετε τύπον ἡμᾶς.

The focus is on way of life: περιπατεῖν. The aspects of his life to which he has just drawn attention are surrender of privileges (3.7–9), willingness to suffer (verse 10), and determination to press on to the goal (verses 12–14). The behaviour of Paul and those like him is then contrasted with that of some who are 'enemies of the Cross of Christ', who behave in some manner associated with the stomach and shame, and who fix their thoughts, and consequent

actions, on 'earthly things' (verses 18–19).[3] The literary context for
the link in 3.17 between the behaviour of Paul and that of the
Philippians carries strong messages about loss, suffering, perseverance, and about not focusing on earthly things.

In Philippians 4.9, the whole of the letter's exhortation ends with
a further call to imitate Paul:

> ἅ καὶ ἐμάθετε καὶ παρελάβετε καὶ ἠκούσατε καὶ εἴδετε ἐν
> ἐμοί, ταῦτα πράσσετε.

The content of what they are supposed to have seen in Paul's life is
not made clear. However, the text matches 1.30,

> τὸν αὐτὸν ἀγῶνα ἔχοντες ὃιον εἴδετε ἐν ἐμοὶ καὶ νῦν
> ἀκούετε ἐν ἐμοί.

Here, what the Philippians saw is Paul's 'struggle'. Given 1.29, this
'struggle' must be sufferings that Paul underwent at Philippi. We
know that Paul did run into trouble there. As well as the account in
Acts 16, Paul tells the Thessalonians that he and his companions
arrived at Thessalonica

> προπαθόντες καὶ ὑβρισθέντες . . . ἐν Φιλίπποις. (1 Thess.
> 2.2)

If we ask what Paul had in mind when he called on the Philippians
in 4.9 to take him as a model, the most likely area for imitation is
Paul's behaviour under suffering.

Three other texts link Paul's experience of suffering and that of
his hearers. They are 2.17–18,

> ἀλλὰ εἰ καὶ σπένδομαι ἐπὶ τῇ θυσίᾳ καὶ λειτουργίᾳ τῆς
> πίστεως ὑμῶν, χαίρω καὶ συγχαίρω πᾶσιν ὑμῖν· τὸ δὲ αὐτὸ
> καὶ ὑμεῖς χαίρετε καὶ συγχαίρετέ μοι,

1.30,

> τὸν αὐτὸν ἀγῶνα ἔχοντες οἷον εἴδετε ἐν ἐμοὶ καὶ νῦν
> ἀκούετε ἐν ἐμοί,

and, less certainly than the others, 1.7,

---

[3] If κοιλία (v. 19) means the stomach as the seat of hunger (Majority Text of
Luke 15.16), and αἰσχύνη is a euphemism for idols (LXX Hos. 9.10; Jer. 3.24; 3
Kings 18.19, 25), then the 'enemies of the Cross' could be those who return to (or
stay with) idolatrous worship to escape economic suffering.

καθώς ἐστιν δίκαιον ἐμοὶ τοῦτο φρονεῖν ὑπὲρ πάντων ὑμῶν, διὰ τὸ ἔχειν με ἐν τῇ καρδίᾳ ὑμᾶς, ἔν τε τοῖς δεσμοῖς μου καὶ ἐν τῇ ἀπολογίᾳ καὶ βεβαιώσει τοῦ εὐαγγελίου συγκοινωνούς μου τῆς χάριτος πάντας ὑμᾶς ὄντας.

Each of these has been discussed in chapter 3, above.[4]

Philippians 1.30 is particularly important for a consideration of Paul's role as a model because, here, he explicitly cites the suffering which he had just described in 1.12–16: ὑμῖν ἐχαρίσθη . . . τὸ ὑπὲρ αὐτοῦ πάσχειν, τὸν αὐτὸν ἀγῶνα ἔχοντες οἷον εἴδετε ἐν ἐμοὶ καὶ νῦν ἀκούετε ἐν ἐμοί. Whatever other implications this linking of their sufferings and his might have from the point of view of their relationship with Paul, the primary implication in the immediate literary context is probably that the Philippians are to read into their own situation the kind of comments that Paul has made about his. This in turn suggests that Paul wrote those comments with this transfer in mind.

We should also note that Paul picks up two of the points that he makes in 1.12–26 and says the same thing about the Philippians. Paul rejoices during his sufferings, then calls them to rejoice during theirs:

. . . εν τούτῳ χαίρω· ἀλλὰ καὶ χαρήσομαι . . . (1.18)

. . . χαίρω καὶ συγχαίρω πᾶσιν ὑμῖν· τὸ δὲ αὐτὸ καὶ ὑμεῖς χαίρετε καὶ συγχαίρετέ μοι. (2.17f.)

Despite his sufferings, Paul rejoices in the spread of the Gospel and in his confidence of σωτηρία. And he does not call the Philippians to rejoice only at 2.17f.: the topic is a recurring motif. Given the pervasiveness of suffering as a theme in the letter, the joy seems primarily to be joy while suffering.

Σωτηρία itself forms the second point of contact. Paul argues that his and their suffering will lead to salvation:

οἶδα γὰρ ὅτι τοῦτό μοι ἀποβήσεται εἰς σωτηρίαν . . . (1.19)

. . . ἥτις ἐστὶν . . . ἔνδειξις . . . ὑμῶν δὲ σωτηρίας. (1.28)

Paul's σωτηρία in 1.19 is linked to the help of the Spirit and the prayers of the Philippians. It will come whether Paul lives or dies

---

[4] Pages 82f., 79f., 83f.

(1.20–2). It is expressed somehow in Paul's not being ashamed but glorifying Christ (1.20). Taking contemporary Greek usage (Epictetus, *Diss.* 4.1.163–7, on Socrates), the present context, and Paul's usage elsewhere (e.g. Rom. 5.9), σωτηρία could mean something like preservation of character as a faithful follower of Christ, together with the consequent hope of life after death. If we should also give weight to the direct echo of Job 13.16, then the consequent hope ought also to include vindication.[5]

Paul develops in a number of ways the idea of the Philippians' suffering leading to salvation. First, he argues that their lack of terror in the face of their opponents is evidence of the Philippians' salvation (1.28). Either the salvation in particular[6] or their situation in general[7] – depending on the referent of the difficult τοῦτο – is from God. In either case, this gift from God will lead to their ending up in a situation of salvation. This gift, in turn, either springs from, or consists of, suffering for Christ. The Philippians' suffering leads to salvation. Second, Paul tells, in 2.5–11, the story of Christ who lowered himself, was obedient under suffering right through to death and who, because of his actions, was then exalted. Philippians 2.5 calls the hearers into some sort of following Christ in his actions. The hearers seem bound then to hear in verses 9–11 a promise that this following will lead to some sort of salvation (although there is also another, more important, strand of verses 9–11: see chapter 5, below). Third, the imperative with which Paul in 2.12 picks up the lesson of 2.5–11 is 'bring about (κατεργάζεσθε) your own salvation!'

Following Stephen Fowl, I think that we may be able to read τὴν ἑαυτῶν σωτηρίαν κατεργάζεσθε as a summing up of Paul's call to them from 1.27 onwards,[8] 'Bring about your own salvation' – by following the way of suffering together for Christ that Paul is calling them to. This way of suffering is, for the Philippians, their route to salvation (whether eschatological or in terms of the safety and health of their church). This reading is somewhere between the

---

[5] See Richard B. Hays, *Echoes of Scripture in the Letters of Paul*, (New Haven, Yale University Press, 1989), pp. 21–4; Peter Oakes, 'Quelle devrait être l'influence des échos intertextuels sur la traduction? Le cas de l'épître aux Philippiens (2:15–16)', in D. Marguerat and A. Curtis, eds., *Intertextualités* (Geneva: Labor et Fides, 2000).

[6] Loh and Nida, p. 42.

[7] O'Brien, p. 157.

[8] Fowl, *Story of Christ*, p. 96.

conventional, 'doctrinal' reading and J. H. Michael's 'social' reading.[9] Michael makes σωτηρία the immediate object of Paul's exhortation: he calls the Philippians to work at 'the well-being of their community'.[10] However, comparison with 1.19 (τοῦτό . . . ἀποβήσεται εἰς σωτηρίαν), 1.28 (ἔνδειξις . . . ὑμῶν . . . σωτηρίας) and, I think, the overall flow of the argument in 1.27–2.18, suggest that σωτηρία is likely to be a benefit gained as a result of aiming at some other immediate object, such as faithfulness to Christ. I would not stand radically against O'Brien's or, particularly, Silva's 'doctrinal' readings since each emphasises that the working out of salvation is by doing the things which Paul is calling for in the context.[11] However, a distinction ought to be drawn since I think that Paul is not introducing any new thought at all with the clause, τὴν ἑαυτῶν σωτηρίαν κατεργάζεσθε, but is simply saying, 'Follow the path which I have just shown you (which, as you have seen, leads to salvation).' O'Brien and Silva are introducing a new, doctrinal, motive: 'Put into practice (or fully develop) your Christian salvation' (salvation being defined for the Philippians from general teaching by Paul). My reading also enables κατεργάζεσθε to have a more common meaning ('bring about') than does the 'doctrinal' view ('work out').

A third link in 1.12–26 between Paul and the Philippians is the term εὐαγγέλιον. Paul's report about his circumstances is not the kind of account you would expect in a normal letter of friendship. He leaves out most things that concerned friends might want to know. Instead, he focuses on προκοπὴν τοῦ εὐαγγελίου (1.12). He then turns to the Philippians and urges them, ἀξίως τοῦ εὐαγγελίου . . . πολιτεύεσθε, and he characterises them as συναθλοῦντες τῇ πίστει τοῦ εὐαγγελίου (1.27). When he says they are τὸν αὐτὸν ἀγῶνα ἔχοντες as he is, it is not only that they, like he, are suffering. They, like he, are suffering for the Gospel.

William Kurz also sees a link in 1.21–6 between Paul's behaviour and the behaviour to which he is calling the Philippians in the area of self-sacrifice for the sake of others. Paul's desire is for the release of death and going to be with Christ. However, he comes to a willingness to accept the postponement of this for the sake of the

---

[9] J. H. Michael, *The Epistle to the Philippians* (MNTC; London: Hodder & Stoughton, 1928), pp. 98, 101f.; Hawthorne, pp. 98f.

[10] Michael, p. 102.

[11] Silva, pp. 134–40; O'Brien, pp. 278–80.

Philippians.[12] The Philippians are then called to show concern for each other.

In 1.12–26 we have Paul, the Gospel, suffering, salvation, joy, and concern for others. Philippians 1.27–2.18 clearly has many differences from 1.12–26 but here, for the Philippians too, we have the Gospel, suffering, salvation, joy, and concern for others. The report about Paul seems to be presenting a model in preparation for the exhortation to the Philippians which follows immediately after the report.

The final autobiographical passage in the letter is 4.11–13. Here too, the description seems too elaborate to be simply a statement of financial independence. The best way of explaining both the specific content of the verses and Paul's desire to insert it, despite the awkwardness of doing so, into a passage expressing appreciation for the Philippians' gift seems to be to see it as a final touch in Paul's presentation of his experience as a model of Christ's ability to sustain the Christian under suffering.

As well as Paul offering himself as a model, Timothy and Epaphroditus seem, as Culpepper argues, to be presented as models too.[13] This is seen in the unexpected turns that their biographical sections take. In Timothy's case, Paul appears to become gratuitously insulting towards those around him. He does this in order to contrast Timothy who τὰ περὶ ὑμῶν μεριμνήσει with the others who τὰ ἑαυτῶν ζητοῦσιν, οὐ τὰ Ἰησοῦ Χριστοῦ (2.21). This is strikingly comparable with the call to the Philippians not to be τὰ ἑαυτῶν . . . σκοποῦντες, ἀλλὰ καὶ τὰ ἑτέρων (2.4). If Timothy is being presented as a model, this makes some sense of Paul's bringing in the otherwise rather irrelevant people around himself. In the case of Epaphroditus, much of the praise of him could have an exemplary edge to it. However, Paul does need to support Epaphroditus since his return could easily be seen as shameful, both for him and even for the Philippian church. The church could suffer shame if they thought that they were seen to have given a defective gift in sending to Paul a helper whose health did not hold up.[14] Paul needs to ease Epaphroditus' return. However, he then

---

[12] William S. Kurz, 'Kenotic Imitation of Paul and of Christ in Philippians 2 & 3', in F. F. Segovia, ed., *Discipleship in the New Testament* (Philadelphia: Fortress Press, 1985), p. 118.

[13] Culpepper, 'Co-Workers in Suffering'.

[14] See the discussions in Seneca, *De Ben.* 2.21.5–6; 5.6.2–7, on the difficulties of sending a gift back. Paul could have felt himself in such a position and in danger of insulting the Philippians by sending back Epaphroditus.

generalises by calling for the Philippians to honour all who risk their lives for the sake of the work of Christ (2.29–30). Kurz points out that Epaphroditus follows Christ in going μέχρι θανάτου (2.30; 2.8)[15] and Christ is a model for the Philippians. In any case, for a suffering church, praise of people who risk their lives is bound to be heard as exemplary.

2. Hearing the model

If we accept that Paul is presenting himself and others as models, then we need to ask how these passages are likely to have sounded to the Philippians.

Two general points need to be made. The first is that some of these passages also performed other functions besides presenting models. As Loveday Alexander has rightly argued, Philippians 1.12 marks a transition to a section of 'reassurance about the sender'.[16] As part of Paul's relationship with the Philippians, they will want news of how he is getting on. They will also be interested in news about his mission. Paul's immediate focus on the Gospel would not necessarily signal to the Philippians that he was trying to make an exemplary point. Although the Philippians might be surprised that, in the present circumstances, Paul has news of evangelistic fruit, they would not be surprised that Paul gives them that news first. They would just think that that was the way Paul was. Similarly, chapter 3 probably has another function in addition to exemplification. It is just about possible that the 'dogs' (3.2) and the 'enemies of the cross of Christ' (3.18) are simply there as negative examples.[17] However, the intensity of the rhetoric does make it seem that, whoever these groups (or this group) are, they actually pose some practical threat to Philippian Christians. Probably the danger is that Christians will join with members of one of these groups in some way and abandon Pauline Christianity. The autobiographical section in chapter 3, then, probably has some role in defining and legitimating boundaries. Christians are the true inheritors of Jewish privileges (3.3). Paul has abandoned his impeccable Jewish privileges for the sake of gaining Christ and righteousness in him (3.4–9). This approach to life rules out, say, any 'Judaising'

---

[15] Kurz, 'Kenotic Imitation', p. 113.

[16] Loveday Alexander, 'Hellenistic Letter-Forms and the Structure of Philippians', *JSNT* 37 (1989), pp. 91–5.

[17] See Geoffrion, *Rhetorical Purpose*, p. 151.

approach to Christianity. Such an approach is rendered illegitimate. If it is out of court for Paul, the archetypal Jew, it must be out of court for his Gentile Philippian followers. Paul's argument, of course, in its own way operates by means of example. He uses his own case rather than arguing simply from Christian existence in general. However, this boundary-defining use of example is a different function from that in my general argument that Paul is offering, throughout the letter, an example of the proper attitude to suffering. The two functions only really coincide if, as some scholars have argued, either the central problem with the opponents in chapter 3 is precisely their opposition to suffering[18] or the temptation to 'Judaise' is linked to seeking legal protection from persecution.[19] I am not persuaded by the case for either of these suggestions and, anyway, I am loath to attach my general argument to a particular kind of solution to the very vexed question of the identity of the opponents in chapter 3.[20]

My second general point about how these 'exemplary' passages would be heard is that they were likely to be heard in a two-edged way. An example of your leader joyfully suffering and renouncing privileges could be both encouraging and disturbing. These two effects could, to an extent, be split among different members of the church. I have argued that the most significant long-term effects of suffering in a first-century church would be likely to be economic. This would bring a need for rather difficult economic rearrangements for members of the Christian community. Paul's example would encourage those who had, at some cost, made such rearrangements already. For any who had not done so, or who felt a need to do more, Paul's example could be disturbing and challenging. This observation would extend more broadly to those who had suffered heavily or very little since becoming Christians. Paul the sufferer could encourage or disturb. For many, he could do both. I have tentatively explored elsewhere the issues around rather different Philippian hearers hearing Paul in Philippians 1.1–11.[21]

---

[18] Fowl, *Story of Christ*, p. 98.

[19] M. Tellbe, 'The Sociological Factors Behind Phil 3:1–11 and the Conflict at Philippi', *JSNT* 51 (1994), pp. 97–121.

[20] The complexities of the issues are set out by Robert Jewett, 'Conflicting movements in the early church as reflected in Philippians', *NovT* 12 (1970), pp. 362–90, and Chris Mearns, 'The Identity of Paul's Opponents at Philippi', *NTS* 33 (1987), pp. 194–204.

[21] Oakes, 'Jason and Penelope'.

Having raised these two general issues, we can now turn to the specifics of the passages. The first striking note in 1.12–26 is the μᾶλλον in verse 12. The progress of the Gospel is unexpected. Bloomquist argues that this indicates the central issue of the letter: reassuring the Philippians who have become concerned that Paul's imprisonment threatens the future of the Gospel.[22] I will argue, below, that Bloomquist is not right. Bloomquist is, however, right in drawing attention to the weightiness of the verse. This seems to be best explained if Paul views the progress of the Gospel despite his suffering as being a pattern promising the same in the Philippian situation, contrary to expectation. Two features strengthen this conclusion. One is that Paul characterises the Philippian situation as being, like his, a struggle on behalf of the Gospel. As noted above, they are, and are called to be, συναθλοῦντες τῇ πίστει τοῦ εὐαγγελίου (1.27) while Paul says, εἰς ἀπολογίαν τοῦ εὐαγγελίου κεῖμαι (1.16). The second feature is that, as many commentators observe, Paul then explains the progress of the Gospel in a way which emphasises the Roman nature of the context, ἐν ὅλῳ τῷ πραιτωρίῳ. This seems likely to offer encouragement to the Philippians in their strongly Roman context. In verses 12–13, a suffering Philippian Christian would probably go beyond simply hearing good news about the Gospel in Paul's situation and would take encouragement that the same could be replicated in their situation. This would be especially so since the progress centred on the process of people simply becoming aware that one was suffering for Christ.

Philippians 1.14–18 is a very strange passage. It is clear why he introduces the topic of 'speaking the word', as a means of progress for the Gospel, but it is far from clear why he gives the elaborate, and almost poetic, development of this topic in terms of contrasting groups of preachers. The most likely explanation, again, is that he has the Philippians in mind. But what would he be aiming at? Gordon Fee suggests that Paul is concerned about internal unrest at Philippi and that this concern has been heightened by Paul's recent experience of strife in Rome. Under such circumstances, Paul models a focus on the Gospel.[23] As Markus Bockmuehl writes, 'By his own tolerance here, Paul may also wish to set an example to his readers at Philippi of how to handle personal

---

[22] Bloomquist, *Suffering*, pp. 147–9.
[23] Gordon D. Fee, *Paul's Letter to the Philippians* (NICNT; Grand Rapids: Eerdmans, 1995), pp. 123–4.

animosity within their own church.'[24] How this might relate to suffering depends on how, and to what extent, the issues of suffering and unity are related in the Philippian church. In my scenario, divisions would be most likely along economic lines. In such a case, different approaches to Christian mission might even develop, leading to a situation to which the picture of rival preachers in verses 15–17 was sharply relevant. This, however, is speculative. What we can say is that Paul's response to those around him gives a pattern which would promote unity and might defuse, say, the quarrel between Euodia and Syntyche, who were both workers for the Gospel (4.2–3).

Another possibility for 1.15–17 is that the crucial issue is the last one named, that is, stirring up trouble for those suffering. At Philippi, either people suffering or people not suffering could become worried that any evangelistic activity by the church might accidentally exacerbate suffering in the church. The point of Paul's story could be that he does not care if evangelism even deliberately exacerbates suffering. He would not want suffering to stop evangelism.

Philippians 1.19–22 would work more straightforwardly as a model. Anyone suffering for their faith would tend to move fairly rapidly from hearing the verses as news about Paul's attitude towards suffering and possible death to hearing them as a possible pattern for their own attitude. The pattern would function as exhortation and promise. It effectively calls the sufferer to make the glorification of Christ their aim, an aim which overrides any other considerations such as living or dying. The promise is two-fold. First, the resources are available from God and one's fellow-Christians to maintain one's Christian faith whatever the circumstances. Second, death means joyful union with Christ.

Verses 23–6 do not function as a straightforward pattern. Although, as Karl Barth argues, the whole of Paul's report in 1.12–26 is strongly apostolic,[25] the actions and attitudes of verses 12–22 are potentially applicable to any Christian. The logic of verses 23–6, however, depends specifically on Paul's apostolic responsibilities. He thinks that his mission to the churches gives him some insight into how God will use him in the future.

---

[24] Markus Bockmuehl, *The Epistle to the Philippians* (London: A. & C. Black, 1997), p. 78.

[25] K. Barth, *The Epistle to the Philippians*, tr. J. W. Leitch (Richmond: John Knox, 1962 (ET of 1947 edn)), *in loc.*

Kurz's suggestion that the passage models consideration for others[26] offers a possible way forward for my argument. Another possibility is that Paul could be using his own case to exemplify the idea that God (rather than, say, the Roman authorities) decides the outcome of any situation. Any outcome is determined on the basis of God's priorities. These are two possibilities for patterns. It is possible, however, that this passage simply fulfils other functions. It expresses Paul's feeling of responsibility towards the Philippians and his expectation of being with them again and encouraging their further development. This probably gives enough audience-related points for them to hear the passage without seeking further messages from it.

Before leaving 1.12–26, it is worth putting it into a further context to strengthen the idea that Paul's attitude under suffering would be seen as an admirable one and hence worthy of emulation. An indication of first-century thinking about proper behaviour under suffering can be gleaned from Epictetus, who writes particularly fully on the topic. He would have been generally delighted by Paul's attitude. Paul shows no worry about his own suffering but he is very concerned about it, in the sense of regarding how he behaves under suffering as being a vital matter. This combination is what Epictetus would regard as the essence of right thinking in this situation.[27] Paul is right to regard living as being for God (1.21)[28] although he ought really to regard death as indifferent rather than as gain.[29] Epictetus would particularly admire the way that Paul not only does not worry about his suffering but even does not worry about others seeking to take advantage of his suffering and to make things worse for him. Epictetus would also admire the purely utilitarian argument which Paul uses on the issue of whether he would live or not. Epictetus would say that Paul has grasped (in the limited field of the Philippian church) the precise issue which determines whether one stays alive, namely, whether one is still useful to the Universe (i.e., to God).[30] He would even heartily agree with Paul's specific aim for the Philippians, namely that they would boast in God on account of Paul (verse 26).[31] Epictetus would, of

---

[26] Kurz, 'Kenotic Imitation', p. 118, see above.

[27] Epictetus, *Diss.* 3.8.1f.; 4.6.34f.

[28] *Diss.* 1.14.15; 1.20.15.

[29] *Diss.* 1.27.7; 2.1.4; 3.8.1f.

[30] *Diss.* 3.13.14f.; 3.24.93f. P. Oakes, 'Epictetus (and the New Testament)', *Vox Evangelica* 23 (1993), pp. 46f., 49.

[31] *Diss.* 1.16.15; 4.8.30ff. Oakes, ' Epictetus', pp. 51f.

course, see Paul's metaphysics as hopelessly deluded. In particular
he would see Paul's conviction, that the utilitarian argument of
verses 24–6 meant that he would definitely live, as being Paul
imagining that he could second-guess God. For Epictetus, none of
us know when the Universe will cease to need us and, hence, when
God is going to 'sound the retreat', i.e., cause you to die or lead
you to commit suicide.[32] However, Epictetus and, I think, most
first-century hearers would regard Paul's attitude to his suffering as
extremely commendable.

The other main autobiographical passage is 3.3–14. As Kurz,
Fowl and others have noted, Paul's path broadly mirrors that of
Christ.[33] Paul begins in a privileged position, he renounces his
privileges, then faces suffering, then finally gains higher privileges
than he began with. There are points at which the comparison is
limited. Jesus abandons his privileges for the sake of others. Paul
abandons his because he sees something better that he himself can
gain, namely, knowing Christ. In fact, concern for others has no
direct part in any of Paul's autobiography here. This means that, as
a model for the Philippians, it functions somewhat differently from
Christ's model in 2.6–11. Christ models willingness to lose status
and suffer for the sake of others (see chapters 5 and 6, below). Paul
models willingness to lose and suffer in order to gain a higher prize.
However, Christ does end up gaining a higher prize too, so the
difference is diminished a little. More importantly, each model calls
the Philippians to the same actions: willingness to lose privileges
(which, in the context of Philippi, probably centres on status) and
to suffer. Christ's model calls, 'Be willing to lose privileges for the
sake of others.' It also promises reward. Paul's model calls, 'Be
willing to lose privileges in order to gain Christ.' It too promises
further reward.

Christ gives a model for Christian service and reward. Paul's
model is of the whole Christian life, from conversion to death and

[32] *Diss.* 3.26.27f.
[33] Kurz, 'Kenotic Imitation', p. 105; Fowl, *Story of Christ*, pp. 99–101. Brian
Dodd, 'The Story of Christ and the Imitation of Paul in Philippians 2–3', in Ralph
P. Martin and Brian J. Dodd, eds., *Where Christology Began: Essays on Philippians 2*
(Louisville: Westminster John Knox, 1998), pp. 154–61, argues that Paul's behaviour relates to that of Christ on a soteriological rather than an exemplary basis. I
agree with his criticism of some supposed echoes in 3.2–11 of terminology in 2.6–11.
As will be seen below (pp. 126f.), I see the similarity of pattern between 3.2–11 and
2.6–11 as most immediately stemming from the needs of the Philippian situation,
rather than from Christ's example or from soteriological considerations.

resurrection. It is necessarily Paul's own life that is depicted. However, if Paul was simply presenting a model to guide the Philippians who were facing the kind of social situation for which I have been arguing, then he need not have focused solely on his religious privileges. He would have been better expounding whatever social privileges he had. He could have said that he had advanced to a high standing in Judaism and could look forward to a comfortable life as a respected teacher with a home, a family and an honoured position in the community but had, instead, renounced all these social privileges for the sake of Christ.

In Paul's model there is something about religious privilege or, more specifically, Jewish religious privilege (verses 4–8). This is followed by something about righteousness and faith and knowing Christ (verses 8–9). If we view the first section as being about specifically Jewish religious privilege then this second, rather doctrinal, element can be absorbed into the same topic, as happens in Galatians. If the first section is about religious privilege in general – Jewish for Paul, pagan (possibly including Imperial cult) for most Philippians – then the 'doctrinal' section probably needs to be making a separate point (especially because of the reference to the Law in verse 9). The third section (verses 10–11) is about suffering and then resurrection. The final section (verses 12–14) is about knowing that one is not perfect but pressing towards the goal.

We cannot completely rule out the possibility that the first section is about privileges in general. Paul gives some possible indicators of generality. He is talking about πεποίθησιν . . . ἐν σαρκί (verse 4) which, although particularly suitable for anti-Judaising polemic (cf. Gal. 6.12), could somehow pick up on Paul's wider use of σάρξ. He also characterises his privileges as ἅτινα ἦν μοι κέρδη (verse 7) and ends up saying that he lost τὰ πάντα (verse 8). However, I think that the totality of verses 2–9 means that the primary aim of Paul's model in verses 4–9 must be to prevent the Philippians following a Judaising path. In verses 2–9 we have, first, 'rhetoric of reversal' suitable for 'Judaisers' (verse 2),[34] then a claim to Christian appropriation of Jewish symbols (verse 3), then a list of Jewish privileges (verses 4–6), and finally a doctrinal statement which is particularly appropriate to persuading the hearers not to adopt Torah (verses 7–9). In addition to the situation of economic suffering that I have argued is present

---

[34] Cf., for example, Fee, p. 295.

at Philippi, Paul also perceives a danger (which could be fairly immediate or rather remote) of Philippians following the teachers of some 'Judaisers', i.e., people somewhat akin to those urging circumcision in Galatia.[35]

However, a warning about Judaisers is not the only thing that was likely to be heard in the passage. Paul carries on and talks about suffering, death and resurrection. Although, for Paul, persecution can be linked with resistance to circumcision groups (Gal. 6.12), this seems unlikely here. In verse 10, Paul is giving a general characterisation of his Christian life. He has left concerns about Judaisers behind. One could argue that Paul has got carried away by the sweep of his story and is not trying to make a point at all, but three things weigh against this. First, Paul, having written this, will shortly call for imitation. Second, in verse 10 we are back with the issue of suffering, which has been central to most of the models for imitation earlier in the letter. Third, the Philippians are suffering so they will be listening for any material on this topic that they could apply to their own lives.

As Paul did in 1.12–26 and Christ did in 2.6–11, in 3.10–11 Paul again models the message that the way of suffering for Christ leads to salvation. He has said this to the Philippians explicitly in 1.27–30. He spends much of the rest of the letter reinforcing this explicit message by means of models who suffer and find, or hope to find, salvation through it.

We can probably sharpen the point of 3.10–11 still further. Paul's model of being conformed to Christ's sufferings and death reinforces 2.5 in its call to be conformed to the pattern of Christ's sufferings (and reward) in 2.6–11 (see chapter 6, below).

O'Brien challenges the place of 3.10 in this pattern by denying both that the παθήματα (in κοινωνίαν παθημάτων αὐτοῦ) are those experienced by Christ and that συμμορφιζόμενος (in συμμορφιζόμενος τῷ θανάτῳ αὐτοῦ) is to do with Paul actually dying. Instead, he gives each of the clauses a technical rather than a straightforward meaning. τὰ παθήματα Χριστοῦ are 'the birth pangs of the Messiah', i.e. the sufferings of God's people prior to the Messiah's return,[36] rather than what Christ suffered. συμορφιζόμενος τῷ θανάτῳ αὐτοῦ is an example of Paul's general language about dying

---

[35] Mearns, 'Opponents', p. 202; Jewett, 'Conflicting movements', pp. 302–7; Fowl, *Story of Christ*, pp. 98f.
[36] O'Brien, pp. 405f.

and rising with Christ (at baptism),[37] rather than a reference to actually dying. Thus, in neither clause does Paul's experience parallel that of Christ.

The texts which O'Brien cites to support his case are not convincing. Romans 8.18 does not mention Christ and 2 Corinthians 1.5–7 is ambiguous. In contrast, two non-Pauline texts (1 Pet. 4.13; Heb. 2.10) unambiguously show that the phrase, παθήματα Χριστοῦ, was used by early Christians to speak of Christ's actual sufferings. The parallel between Philippians 3.10–11 and 1 Peter 4.13 is particularly striking. In a chapter which begins, Χριστοῦ οὖν παθόντος σαρκὶ . . ., the author goes on to write,

> ἀλλὰ καθὸ κοινωνεῖτε τοῖς τοῦ Χριστοῦ παθήμασιν χαίρετε, ἵνα καὶ ἐν τῇ ἀποκαλύψει τῆς δόξης αὐτοῦ χαρῆτε ἀγαλλιώμενοι.

If, in verses 10–11, Paul is heard as a model for any Christian life, irrespective of whether Jewish or Gentile, then the audience seem likely to hear that to an extent in verses 4–9 too. The main message may be about avoidance of Judaisers. A secondary message, of renunciation of privileges for the sake of Christ, is likely to be heard too, especially on second and subsequent hearings of the letter. This is because of 2.1–11. In chapter 2, what the Philippians are called to involves at least the willingness to lose privileges. Christ then models loss of privilege and obedient suffering. Paul does this too in chapter 3. From Paul's model, the Philippians would feel called to be willing to lose privileges for the sake of gaining Christ. In the Philippian context this would mean willingness to lose privileges for the sake of Christ's work in Philippi. In my scenario, at Philippi, this would mean willingness to risk losing money and status for the sake of others. Even though Paul, in chapter 3, models loss for the sake of gaining Christ, rather than loss for the sake of others, the practical consequences of following this model in Philippi are likely to be loss for the sake of others. What Paul models powerfully here is his key point that faithful following of Christ is, despite loss and suffering, the way of salvation.

I doubt whether we need to read opponents into 3.12–16. Paul seems basically to be modelling day-by-day perseverance to the very end. This is very appropriate to a situation of suffering. The

[37] Ibid, pp. 400, 410.

references to Paul's not yet being perfect could reinforce his model by means of an argument from greater to lesser. The beginning of verse 12, 'Not that I have received (all this) or already been made perfect', implies that the hearers may be thinking that Paul, given the story he has just told, or given the high spiritual status that they might ascribe to him generally, has already arrived at perfection and need do no more. Paul says, No, I need to keep chasing towards the goal. The hearers are likely to respond by thinking that if even Paul needs to do that, then they certainly do.

This could fit a problem with a heresy of perfectionism[38] but I think it is more likely to be addressing a problem of Christian inertia. Certainly today few Christians imagine themselves to be perfect but a great many have an inertia which means that they do not see a need for any fresh spiritual effort. In Philippi, some Christians could be away from the sharp edge of evangelism or mutual support partly through an inertia in which they saw themselves as spiritually 'OK' (after all, they were Christians) so not needing further great effort, especially if this was likely to draw them into suffering. This kind of scenario seems more plausible than the introduction of perfectionist heretics on the slim basis of verses 12–16.

My conclusion avoids the problems associated with reading the τέλειοι in verse 15 as representing a group sharply at variance with Paul. These τέλειοι are addressed by Paul. They are thus unlikely to be among the 'opponents' in chapter 3 since they are generally not addressed. Furthermore, Paul classes himself with these τέλειοι: φρονῶμεν. O'Brien's arguments for taking τέλειοι as 'mature' and ὅσοι as potentially, but not necessarily, inclusive of anyone at Philippi (cf. Rom. 6.3, etc.) seem persuasive.[39] Paul is making a play on words. He includes himself among the τέλειοι but a consequence of this is that he should not think, τετελείωμαι. This only makes sense if the two words mean different things so τέλειος in verse 15 probably refers to maturity. This could be an ironic re-use of an opponents' term but there is no need for that to be the case. Paul could just enjoy the play on words. The most difficult clause for my view is εἴ τι ἑτέρως φρονεῖτε. On my reading of verses 12–14, Philippians are unlikely to think that what Paul says is unreasonable. It is their actions that may not be in line

[38] H. Koester, 'The Purpose of the Polemic of a Pauline Fragment (Philippians III)', *NTS* 8 (1961–2), pp. 317–32; Jewett, 'Conflicting movements', pp. 372–6.
[39] O'Brien, pp. 433–7.

with it. The best way of easing my problem is probably to suggest that verse 15 may refer back to the whole of chapter 3 so far, or even to Paul's argument in the letter as a whole. In either case there would be plenty of scope for people to 'think differently'.

3. Scholarly approaches to the autobiographical passages

My approach to the autobiographical passages can be summed up in two propositions. First, the most pervasive feature of the autobiographical passages is that Paul presents himself as a model for the Philippians. Second, Paul's main aim in offering himself as a model is to respond to the situation of suffering among the Philippians. I would summarise the main message that the model carries to the Philippians as being that continuing in the way of faithful suffering for Christ is the route to their salvation – salvation which encompasses both the preservation and growth of the church at Philippi and also their life after death. A consequence of my approach is that I am arguing for a fair amount of unity between the models in 1.12–26; 3.4–14; 4.11–13 and even those of Timothy and Epaphroditus in 2.19–30. These models also share a basic unity with Christ as a model in 2.6–11.

All scholars on Philippians offer some support for these propositions but many would disagree sharply with me at certain points. Gregory Bloomquist agrees with me at many points but essentially represents the most important alternative perspective to mine. He, like a number of other recent scholars such as Davorin Peterlin, sees Paul's situation itself as the most important issue in the letter. I am arguing that it is the Philippians' situation that is most important, and that Paul mainly writes about his own situation in order to present a model for them in their situation.

Bloomquist describes Philippians as 'a rhetorical address, the focus of which is entirely on Paul'.[40] He sees 1.12–14 as stating the key issue of the letter. This passage 'reveals Philippians to be primarily intended as an authoritative letter of comfort in which Paul reassures the Philippian believers of the gospel's advance in the light of Paul's imprisonment.'[41] Bloomquist's view is related to that of a number of other scholars who see the fact of Paul's imprisonment as being a theological problem for the Philippians.

---

[40] Bloomquist, *Suffering*, p. 138.
[41] Ibid., p. 149.

Peterlin, for example, sees the Philippian community as divided over whether Paul's imprisonment must mean that he has compromised 'his Christian vocation', a worry stemming from a triumphalist form of Christianity.[42] Robert Jewett sees Paul himself as facing 'divine-man' missionaries who think that imprisonment and suffering are incompatible with the kind of successful picture that a servant of God ought to present.[43]

Bloomquist sets up a court scene. The Philippians are the jury. Paul is trying to convince them that his suffering actually advances the Gospel. They are also co-defendants, since they too have suffered.[44] They are also witnesses, since their progress in the Gospel has come as a result of Paul's sufferings at Philippi.[45] The bulk of the rest of Paul's case is a series of parallels between Paul, Christ and others. Paul shows that he embodies the Christ-type and that others embody the Christ-type insofar as they embody the Paul-type. By definition, the Christ-type is consonant with progress of the Gospel. Therefore Paul's case is proved and the Philippians can rest assured that his sufferings do not put the future of the Gospel in danger.[46]

The question is, who is operating the parallels in the right direction, Bloomquist or myself? Bloomquist's radical Paulocentricity is surely incorrect. He writes, 'In 1.27–2.18 Paul's desire is to underscore his choice of suffering in this world for the sake of the community, rather than glorification. So he invokes the Christ-hymn of 2.6–11 to show how Christ is personified in himself.'[47] This is an implausible reading of the function of 1.27–2.18. In 1.27–2.18, Paul is aiming to persuade the Philippians to action rather than to reinforce an image of himself. Bloomquist also uses structural arguments from rhetorical and epistolary theory to maintain that 1.12–14 states the main concern of the letter, 1.18b–26 gives its main argument, and 4.8–20 recapitulates its main ideas.[48] The other sections give examples which reinforce these 'key sections'. Since the 'key sections' are all to do with Paul, this inevitably leads Bloomquist to conclude that the central issue is to do with Paul. Bloomquist's reading of 1.27–2.18 shows the

---

[42] Peterlin, *Disunity*, p. 51.
[43] Jewett, 'Conflicting movements', pp. 362–71.
[44] Bloomquist, *Suffering*, p. 159.
[45] Ibid., p. 146.
[46] Ibid., p. 168.
[47] Ibid., p. 135.
[48] Ibid., pp. 123f., 126, 136–8, 148–50, 152–7, 187–90.

dangers of leaning heavily on arguments based on supposedly
normative structural schemes. Many scholars have commented on
the inadvisability of doing this.[49] Bloomquist's choice of 1.12–14 as
the rhetorical heart of the letter also ignores the relative persuasive
weight that Paul puts into various passages. Paul's persuasive effort
is far more intense in 1.27–2.4 than in 1.12–14. Once Bloomquist's
structural scheme is set aside, his possible secondary purpose for
the letter, of reassurance to suffering Philippians,[50] can benefit
from much of his data.

Scholars such as Peterlin, who see the Philippians as having a
theological problem with Paul's suffering, tend to read the letter
too much in terms of ideas rather than experiences and actions. We
have seen this approach (in chapter 3, above) in the discussion of
Collange's reading of 1.27–30. Suffering is turned from a Philippian experience to a Philippian theological concern. The letter does
not read like this. Especially in 1.27–2.18, the Philippians are seen
to be facing concrete pressures which require concrete action.
Clearly they do need to have a correct theology of suffering. Paul is
concerned to show them that faithful suffering leads to salvation.
But the point of that is to help them in the suffering that they face,
rather than to defend the legitimacy of Paul's imprisonment.

Peterlin also represents a second type of challenge to my view of
the letter. This second approach sees disunity at Philippi as the
central issue. The letter is usually seen as focusing on the dispute
between Euodia and Syntyche (4.2–3).

In Peterlin's case, the disunity stems from differing views about
Paul. Bruce Winter sees the central issue as competition for office
and honour within the Christian community.[51] Nils Dahl thinks
that Euodia and Syntyche have some personal rivalry related to
their work for the Gospel: for example, rivalry over who had
suffered or given most.[52] The strengths of this second approach are
that it relates to a known issue (Euodia and Syntyche's dispute),

[49] Markus Bockmuehl, *The Epistle to the Philippians* (London: A. & C. Black,
1997), pp. 23f., 38f.; Jeffrey T. Reed, *A Discourse Analysis of Philippians* (JSNTSS
136; Sheffield: Sheffield Academic Press, 1997), pp. 448–50, 453f., arguing that
letters did not follow patterns of rhetorical structure.

[50] Bloomquist, *Suffering*, p. 150.

[51] B. W. Winter, *Seek the Welfare of the City: Christians as Benefactors and
Citizens* (First-century Christians in the Graeco-Roman World; Carlisle: Paternoster,
1994), p. 99.

[52] Nils A. Dahl, 'Euodia and Syntyche and Paul's Letter to the Philippians', in
L. M. White and O. L. Yarbrough, eds., *The Social World of the First Christians:
Essays in Honor of Wayne A. Meeks* (Philadelphia: Fortress Press, 1995), pp. 7, 14.

that language in the most intense exhortatory passage (2.1–5) is picked up in 4.2–3, and that an *inclusio* between 1.27 and 4.1–3 could be seen as framing the exhortatory heart of the letter.

I think that the structural point is probably incorrect. *Inclusio* occurs where elements from the beginning of a section of text are picked up again at the ending of it. Philippians 4.1, not 4.3, seems to be an ending. In 4.1 Paul uses terms from earlier in the letter to form an emotionally charged rhetorical flourish to mark the conclusion of his exhortation for the Philippians to 'stand firm', στήκετε. The *inclusio* lies in the recapitulation of the main initial instruction from 1.27.[53] Philippians 4.2–3 is then written in a much lower key than 4.1. Rhetorical flourish has given way to calm persuasion. The repetition of συναθλέω in 4.3 (from 1.27) does not mark 4.3 as the ending of a section running from 1.27. To do this, συναθλέω would at least need to have the same function, i.e., Euodia and Syntyche would have to be being called to συναθλεῖν – which would mean giving up their quarrel. Instead, the most we have is an echo of the term from 1.27: Euodia and Syntyche have indeed been those who have worked for the faith as Paul wanted in 1.27, now they should mend their quarrel. τὸ αὐτὸ φρονεῖν in 4.2 strongly echoes 2.2. The echo suggests to Euodia and Syntyche that this is how they should apply the call of 2.1–4. It does not mean that 1.27–4.3 was a section directed primarily at Euodia and Syntyche. More generally, 1.27–4.3 does not even make sense as a section on unity in the Philippian church. In contrast, it is quite viable to describe 1.27–4.1 as a section on standing firm under pressure. Unity can be one major element of standing firm but it does not account for enough material to make it the central issue in the letter. If we make Paul's response to Philippian suffering the main issue of the letter we account for more material. One reason for this is that suffering in a church will tend to raise the issue of unity but disunity in a church does not tend to raise the issue of suffering. Admittedly, someone writing to a disunited church could, as a rhetorical strategy, play up any real or supposed suffering. This could encourage unity. However, in Philippians there is far too much weight on one's approach to suffering itself (e.g., 3.10–11) for the introduction of the topic to be merely a rhetorical move designed to deal with a problem of disunity.

A third alternative approach to mine is to see the letter as

---

[53] Geoffrion, *Rhetorical Purpose*, pp. 206–9.

primarily relational rather than responsive: what Paul writes flows from his relationship with the Philippians rather than from the requirements of the particular current situation at Philippi. Loveday Alexander and, to an extent, Markus Bockmuehl would represent such an approach.[54] The response to this lies mainly in some of the exegesis above. The passion of Paul's rhetoric at certain points such as 2.1–4 suggests that we are taking too far our proper caution about mirror-reading if we deny that Paul is likely to know of some problem at Philippi to do with unity. The same is true of suffering, especially since we have Paul's explicit comment in 1.29 to support our mirror-reading. Furthermore, one piece of information that Paul's note on Euodia and Syntyche gives us is that Paul must have heard news about the situation at Philippi quite recently.

This 'relational' approach to the letter involves suggesting that Paul's advice to the Philippians stems from Paul's general experience, or from his own immediate situation, or from his general long-term knowledge of the Philippians. Each of these clearly does have some input. The 'Judaisers' of chapter 3, whom Paul describes in very indefinite terms, could quite plausibly arise from Paul's general concerns for his churches, rather than from information about a specific group. His situation at Rome also affects what Paul writes but, given the weight of material of various kinds in the letter, it seems more likely that Paul chooses Roman material which addresses the Philippian situation than that he is trying to shape the Philippians' actions in such a way as to help them avoid specifically the Roman situation. Having said all this, the relational approach does account for a number of elements in the letter. It is clearly part of what the letter is about. However, the number of elements for which the approach does not account exceeds those for which it does.

A new twist is given to the relational approach by Sean Winter's DPhil thesis, 'Worthy of the Gospel of Christ'. He sees the primary purpose of the letter as being to increase the commitment of the Philippians to their relationship with Paul. Winter's exegetical basis for this is to see the letter's opening and closing as the keys to understanding the letter's 'rhetorical situation'. He criticises earlier approaches, including my own, for failing to give enough weight to the opening and closing. Winter's criticism is reasonable. My

---

[54] Alexander, 'Hellenistic Letter-Forms', pp. 93–5; Bockmuehl, p. 33.

argument would be stronger with an analysis of these passages that incorporated them into my overall thesis. I think that this could be done. Conversely, however, I think that, in the case of Philippians, the body of the letter is much more important than the letter-frame for understanding both its actual and its 'rhetorical' situation.

My approach has links with the work of a number of scholars. I noted Bockmuehl's unwillingness to see the letter as primarily being responsive to a situation. On the other hand, Bockmuehl's commentary is probably the one that most systematically draws attention to passages in which Paul acts as a model for the Philippians.[55] The work of Kurz has been used several times, above. He sees Paul's 'kenotic imitation' of Christ, and the subsequent call for imitation by the Philippians, as the central feature of the letter.[56] He does not, however, explore the issue of what situation at Philippi brings about the need for such imitation.

Stephen Fowl's work takes a similar line. He sees 3.1ff. as polemic against those (who are Judaisers) with a view different from Paul's of the right response to the Philippians' situation. In particular, they do not accept that walking worthily of the Gospel might entail suffering.[57] Fowl's particular point is that Paul presents a view which conforms to Christ's precedent in 2.6–11.[58] That passage forms the basis upon which Paul argues.[59] As I have discussed above, I am reluctant to relate the issue of suffering to the particular views of certain teachers. I think the material on suffering is fully accounted for by actual suffering at Philippi. Fowl also has a logical problem in demonstrating his thesis. Paul tackles a particular situation at Philippi. Fowl's thesis is that Paul uses a suitable story of Christ to address that situation and then models his own and the Philippians' behaviour on that story. The problem for Fowl is that the situation at Philippi is logically prior. The particular story of Christ was chosen because its features fit the situation. Those same features appear in Paul's story and in the exhortation to the Philippians. It is very difficult to prove (as Fowl needs to) that, instead of the needs of the Philippian situation shaping Paul's telling of both Christ's story and his own, the shape of Paul's story and his exhortation to the Philippians came via the

---

[55] Bockmuehl, e.g., pp. 73, 74, 78, 81, 87, 90, 93, 95.
[56] Kurz, 'Kenotic Imitation', pp. 115, 122.
[57] Fowl, *Story of Christ*, p. 98.
[58] Ibid., pp. 99f.
[59] Ibid., p. 101.

story of Christ. However, Fowl's argument that 3.3–11 is addressing the same concerns as 1.27–2.18, about suffering and salvation, seems convincing.

Wayne Meeks' valuable short article on 'The Man from Heaven' in Philippians, takes his previous work on John and re-applies it. As in John, the portrayal of Christ is for community-building but, in Philippi, the community's situation, and hence the portrayal, is different. All the figures in the letter exemplify a form of practical reasoning modelled most directly in 2.6–11. Meeks picks up on issues such as friendship, joy, concern for others, equanimity about other preachers, confidence and self-sufficiency.[60] However, as was the case for Kurz, he does not have space to explore the nature of the community-building needed at Philippi in any detail.

On 1.12–26, Duane Watson reaches a conclusion similar to mine but deduces it in terms of formal rhetorical categories:

> Verses 12–26, besides serving to elicit personal pathos through a show of concern outweighing personal desire, provides an example of love determining action towards others and of a life lived for the gospel. It provides a basis for the call to imitation in 3.17, 4.9. In light of the whole epistle, this example of Paul's life functions like the figure of thought known as exemplification which clarifies and vivifies the message, providing the Philippians with a tangible model of living a life worthy of the gospel in spite of opposition, the central concern of Phil. (1.27–30).[61]

While I agree with much of this, I am not convinced that Paul is setting out to elicit *pathos* and one probably ought to say that the function of Paul's life actually has a further dimension beyond straightforward exemplification. Paul is, for the Philippians, a figure of respect and authority, so his life constitutes something of an authoritative example, rather than simply an illustration 'which clarifies and vivifies'. L. W. Hurtado makes this point, in the related case of Christ, with his idea of 'Lordly example'.[62]

Finally, it is worth reflecting on Philippians as a text that has

[60] Meeks, 'Man from Heaven', pp. 329–36.
[61] Duane F. Watson, 'A Rhetorical Analysis of Philippians and its Implications for the Unity Question', *NovT* 30 (1988), pp. 64f.
[62] L. W. Hurtado, 'Jesus as Lordly Example in Philippians 2:5–11', in P. Richardson and J. C. Hurd, eds., *From Jesus to Paul: Studies in Honour of Francis Wright Beare* (Waterloo, Ontario: Wilfred Laurier University Press, 1984).

historically been heard in the Church.[63] Bloomquist documents, up to the Reformation, the important role that Philippians had in thinking on martyrdom.[64] One later example is the use of Philippians 1.29 on the Martyrs' Memorial in Oxford, dedicated to Cranmer, Latimer and Ridley. As well as the theme of suffering coming through clearly to many generations of hearers of the text, the idea of Paul as a model must have been almost universally heard. The main mode of hearing of the text has been through preaching. My experience is that preachers always see characters in the text as (positive or negative) examples. In the case of Philippians, the very earliest exposition of the text – maybe even on the day the letter was received – will have been directed to a Christian community in which some were suffering. Whatever else a preacher said about a passage such as 1.12–26, they were bound to apply it to the situation of suffering members of the congregation. Such people would probably have already been hearing it in that manner, anyway. The act of expounding the passage would have reinforced this way of hearing it. Paul himself is bound to have been aware that this was likely to happen. If he wished to prevent it, he would have needed to write something specifically to do so. He certainly would not have concluded his exhortation to the Philippians by saying, '. . . whatever you have learned and received and heard and seen in me, put these things into practice'.

[63] Bockmuehl, pp. 42–5.
[64] Bloomquist, *Suffering*, ch. 1.

5

CHRIST AND THE EMPEROR

Before focusing on how Christ functions in Philippians 2 as a model for the Philippians, we need to prepare part of the argument by considering the imagery of 2.9–11. A central element of this, I would argue, is a comparison between Christ and the Roman Emperor.

1. Previous studies

At the beginning of the twentieth century there was a period of interest in the relationship between the Emperor-cult and the Christ-cult. Work was produced by Lietzmann, Wendland, H. A. A. Kennedy, Lohmeyer and, particularly, Deissmann in his *Licht Vom Osten.* Study basically focused on titles: in particular, κύριος, σωτήρ, θεός and υἱὸς θεοῦ.[1] The general conclusion was that NT titles developed independently but would have seemed offensive to the Imperial cult and were the focus of conflict later. Deissmann comments that 'there arises a polemical parallelism between the cult of the emperor and the cult of Christ, which makes itself felt where' Septuagint or Gospel terminology 'happen to coincide' with Imperial cult concepts 'which sounded the same or similar'.[2] Philippians 2.11 was quite often cited, but only really for the title, κύριος.[3]

Lohmeyer, in his *Christuskult und Kaiserkult* (1919), noticeably failed to mention 2.11, presumably because he already held a strong conviction of the Near-Eastern origin of the passage: his study,

---

[1] See Deissmann's exhaustive list: Adolf Deissmann, *Light from the Ancient East: The New Testament Illustrated by Recently Discovered Texts of the Graeco-Roman World*, tr. L. R. M. Strachan (London: Hodder & Stoughton, 1927 edn), pp. 338–78.

[2] Ibid., p. 342; cf. H. A. A. Kennedy, 'Apostolic Preaching and Emperor Worship', *The Expositor* (April, 1909), p. 299.

[3] Kennedy, 'Emperor Worship', pp. 292f.; Deissmann, *Light*, p. 355.

Kyrios Jesus, came out in 1928 (the same year as his commentary) and included a note to the effect that it is a mistake to derive the acclamation as Lord from Emperor-proclamations.[4] In this, I think that he was technically correct (see below), but I think that he chose the wrong issue by discussing 'derivation', and that Emperor-proclamations, as such, are, in the first century, the wrong place to look for the term. Lohmeyer does, however, see the Emperor in 3.20–1:

> Der römischen Bürgerschaft auf Erden, deren Haupt der kaiserliche Soter ist, steht die Bürgerschaft der Christus-gläubigen im Himmel gegenüber, die ihren Soter Jesus Christus zu dauernden Verweilen in ihrer Mitte erst er-wartet. So läßt sich nur schwer der Schluß abwiesen, daß hier zum erstenmal Jesus, der Kyrios der Christuskultes, und der römische Cäser, der Kyrios des Kaiserkultes, in bewußten Gegensatz einander gegenübergestellt werden.

> The Roman citizenship on Earth, whose head is the imperial saviour, stands over against the Christian be-lievers' citizenship in Heaven. They are only waiting for the lasting presence of their saviour Jesus among them. It is thus difficult to reject the conclusion that here, for the first time, Jesus, the Lord of the Christ-cult, and the Roman Emperor, the Lord of the Imperial cult, are set in conscious contrast to one another.[5]

While agreeing with this in general, I have a major reservation about both Lohmeyer's book and the other works cited above. Why need Lohmeyer's final sentence have the term 'cult' in it? The Emperor was not σωτήρ or κύριος simply in the Emperor-cult: he was these things in the life of the whole Empire (see the examples below). If Christ relativises the Emperor in every way, then this clearly does undermine the Emperor-cult, but it also has far wider ramifications for society and politics – and hence for NT study.

In 1938, in his brief work, *Jesus Imperator Mundi*, Karl Born-häuser argued that the background to Philippians 2.6 lay in Caligula's claims to divinity. Bornhäuser then drew the rest of

---

[4] Ernst Lohmeyer, *Kyrios Jesus: Eine Untersuchung zu Phil 2, 5–11* (Sitzungsber-ichte der Heidelberger Akad. der Wiss. 18:4; Heidelberg: Winters, 1928), p. 60 n. 1.
[5] Ernst Lohmeyer, *Christuskult und Kaiserkult* (Tübingen: J. C. B. Mohr, 1919), p. 28, my tr.

verses 6–8 from the figure of the Isaianic Servant. On verse 10, he made the general observation that more knees bowed to Jesus than to any Caesar. His overall suggestion for Philippians was that Paul was showing to veterans, who once served Caesar, what serving Christ was like. Apart from the contrast with Caligula, Bornhäuser saw the main comparison with the Emperor as again lying in titles: Χριστός, κύριος and σωτήρ.

Comparison with Caligula would indeed have been a live issue in Paul's day, especially for a Jewish writer. Bornhäuser's suggestion is also methodologically important. Having dismissed Ewald's Aristotelian reading of μορφὴ θεοῦ (2.6) as incomprehensible to Philippian veteran soldiers, Bornhäuser's alternative approach is to look in the soldiers' experience for a figure who might fit the term.[6] Hence Caligula. I disagree, of course, with Bornhäuser in his view of the make-up of the church. I am also sceptical about the size of the mental jump that he expects the hearers to make at verse 6. They are already jumping from their situation to the story of Christ. This is well signalled. They are unlikely to make, at the same time, a further, unsignalled, jump to comparison of Christ with another figure, such as the Emperor.

This is a very sweeping argument for me to use. One could use it against any view which requires the hearers to move at verse 6 to hearing both the story of Christ and some second story, such as that of Adam or the Isaianic Servant, which was shaping the story of Christ. I do think that such an argument would have some force. However, the figures of Adam or the Servant could already have shaped the Philippians' understanding of Christ, prior to hearing verse 6. It is therefore no great problem to imagine them being perceived there. It is quite a different matter for a figure such as Caligula, who was not a normal part of the early Church's Christology. For the hearers to perceive such a character as implicit in verse 6 would seem to need far clearer signalling than verse 6 (or verses 7–8) presents.

Moving to more recent scholarship: in a 1979 article on the letter to the Romans, Luise Schottroff compares slavery under Sin with the world-wide slavery under the Roman Empire. Dealing with Romans 13.1–7 as an attempt to work out a limited loyalty to Rome, she draws in Philippians 2.9f. as evidence: if Jesus is Lord, loyalty to Rome is limited – they can expect taxes but not the

---

[6] Bornhäuser, *Jesus imperator mundi*, p. 17.

acknowledgement of Caesar as κύριος.[7] Wolfgang Schenk cites this in his commentary, but only as an implication of the passage rather than as the background which shapes it. He sees the background in mythical terms (as written by the Philippians themselves).[8] Eberhard Faust's 1993 book, *Pax Christi et Pax Caesaris*, argues that Ephesians 2 asserts that Christ alone can bring inter-ethnic peace – unlike the Flavian emperors whose attempts were essentially anti-Jewish. Aspects of Faust's argument are also important for Philippians. I will return to his book, below. For Lukas Bormann, the contents of Paul's Gospel in Philippians 2.5–11 'relativieren die religiöse und politische Macht des Prinzeps' (relativise the religious and political power of the Emperor).[9] This is especially because the passage 'betont ... das gegenwärtige Recht der kosmischen Herrschaft Christi ...' (emphasises ... the present claim of the cosmic lordship of Christ).[10] Bormann's essential Imperial comparison, however, seems to be between Paul and the Emperor. Having shown the importance of a special imperial patronage for the town's conception of itself,[11] Bormann's main argument in his book is that Paul has become the key patron of the Philippian Christians. This change of patronage becomes one of the factors that sets the Philippian authorities against the church.[12] Bormann's case could have been quite strong if he had argued that Christ was the new patron. The language in the letter compares Christ, not Paul, with the Emperor. Bormann also has difficulties with his general project of making Paul the Philippians' patron. The model of patronage which he has to construct to allow money to flow in the unexpected direction seems very problematic.[13]

Three scholars have recently made a particular point of noting a comparison between Christ and the Emperor in Philippians 2.6–11: Dieter Georgi, David Seeley and Gordon Fee. Georgi's suggestion is a weighty one because, although his section on 2.6–11 is very brief (three pages), it is part of a sustained treatment of Paul's

[7] Luise Schottroff, 'Die Schreckenherrschaft der Sünde und die Befreiung durch Christus nach dem Römerbrief des Paulus', *Evangelische Theologie* 39:6 (1979), p. 508.
[8] Wolfgang Schenk, *Die Philipperbriefe des Paulus* (Stuttgart: Kohlhammer, 1984), p. 210.
[9] Bormann, *Philippi*, pp. 222f., my tr.
[10] Ibid., p. 219, my tr.
[11] Ibid., p. 197.
[12] Ibid., pp. 218–24.
[13] Ibid., pp. 207–17.

interaction with concepts of rule and authority.[14] For Georgi, the issue in the exhortation of 2.1–4 is the realm of Christ's jurisdiction and the dynamics of his rulership. These are established by verses 6–11. Christ's acts in verses 6–8 have made him the 'first among equals'. For Paul and the Philippians, 'the description of Jesus' exaltation and entrance into heaven must have suggested the events surrounding the decrease [*sic*: the word must be 'decease'] of a *princeps* and his heavenly assumption and apotheosis by resolution of the Roman senate, ratified in heaven.'[15] The dynamics of Jesus' rule are seen in the fact that 'renunciation of ascendancy is the secret of ascendancy'. Jesus' rule 'puts an end to the hegemonic claims of all alienating and murderous power and violence together with their law'.[16]

There is ambiguity in Georgi's understanding of 2.9–11. Explicitly, he sees it as comparable to the apotheosis of the deceased Emperor. Implicitly, however, he sees it as the point of accession to power. It is Christ's death 'that makes Jesus the first among equals and equal to the biblical God'.[17] The 'hymn' establishes Christ's rulership. I think that Georgi needs to choose between apotheosis and enthronement. The latter fits the conclusions that Georgi wants ultimately to draw from the passage. I think the former is incorrect. The apotheosis of the Emperor follows his reign. The events of verse 9 inaugurate the reign of Jesus.

David Seeley sees three backgrounds to Philippians 2.6–11. The three are unified by the theme of rule. Christ exceeds the Emperor's rule, is given some of YHWH's rule (in contrast to Isaiah 45), and, as a righteous sufferer, refuses to bow to tyrannical rule but obeys God's rule.[18] The effect of the hymn is that 'one wing of a fledgling community offers its own religio-political warrant in competition with other communities already on the scene'.[19]

The combination of Seeley's three backgrounds is fairly complex. In verse 6, the author of the hymn uses the word μορφή, meaning

---

[14] Dieter Georgi, *Theocracy in Paul's Praxis and Theology*, tr. D. E. Green (Minneapolis: Fortress Press, 1991 (Ger. 1987)).

[15] Ibid., p. 73.

[16] Ibid., pp. 76–7.

[17] Ibid., p. 74.

[18] David Seeley, 'The Background of the Philippians Hymn (2:6–11)', *Journal of Higher Criticism* 1, (Fall 1994), pp. 49–72; internet edition at http://daniel.drew.edu/~doughty/jhcbody.html#reviews, pp. 11–12. Page numbers are from internet copy of article.

[19] Ibid., p. 3.

'appearance', because Caligula had sought to make himself look like various gods. The same factor explains the mention of regarding equality with God greedily. 'A new community proclaiming the divinity of its lord would do well to distinguish him from the self-aggrandizing madman still fresh in many memories.'[20] The author then describes Christ's self-emptying and servanthood (verse 7) in order to portray him as an ideal ruler.[21] More broadly, verses 6–7 present a pattern of pre-existence and incarnation drawn from worship associated with rulers.[22] In a 'startling and brilliant move', the author of 2.6–11 then juxtaposes this imperial figure with that of the righteous sufferer of Maccabean literature, a figure at the opposite pole of the power structure.[23] The stories of the suffering righteous then provide the pattern of death and rescue after death seen in verses 8–9. This gives God's blessing on Jesus' power and hence on the Christian community.[24] Verses 9–11 are 'based on Isaiah 45, but . . . resonate with ruler worship as well'. For Jesus to have the highest name places him above Caesar. For Jesus to be worth bowing to contrasts him to Caligula who, inappropriately, wanted this honour in worship of him. Jesus' lordship covers the spheres of lordship of both Augustus and Jupiter. Jesus, not the Emperor, is the Lord. The praise of Jesus will exceed the praise offered to the Emperor at public festivals.[25] At the same time, verses 9–11 represent 'an audacious redirection' of the stringently monotheistic Isaiah 45.23. 'Isa. 45.6, 18 proclaim that there is no *kurios* besides God. The hymn says there is, and even adds that it was God himself who conferred that name.' 'This means that the God of Israel is losing a critical signifier of authority to the leader of the Christian churches.'[26]

Seeley analyses Philippians 2.6–11 outside its context in Philippians – as many other scholars do. He uses the Philippians occasionally as audience but does not use verses 1–5. The crucial exegetical effect of this is that it allows Seeley to produce a reading without verses 6–8 having any ethical exemplary function. The reading is strictly Christological. For a church that uses this text, the function of the text is that it defines the status of the church by

[20] Ibid., p. 8.
[21] Ibid., pp. 8–9. Seeley cites some of the same texts that I use below.
[22] Ibid., p. 1.
[23] Ibid., p. 11.
[24] Ibid., pp. 4–6.
[25] Ibid., pp. 9–11.
[26] Ibid., p. 3.

locating the status of its ultimate leader. His reading runs into difficulties because it does not give proper value to the shape of verses 6–8. This can be seen in the different reasons given for the inclusion of μορφή in each of its occurrences. In verse 6 it contrasts with Caligula's dressing up. In verse 7 it is part of a depiction of Christ as an ideal ruler. The two can, of course, be linked but it is much easier to see μορφὴ θεοῦ and μορφὴ δούλου as a pair of terms marking the two ends of a movement. Furthermore, Seeley does not say what it meant for Christ to be ἐν μορφῇ θεοῦ and, given Seeley's insistence that μορφή is about perception by the senses, it is hard to see what he could think that it meant. Again, Seeley's reading does not account for the function of Christ's choice to become human. This is far from an obvious point to put in if someone was designing a passage to present Christ as an ideal ruler.

Seeley switches to the Maccabean Suffering Righteous at verses 8–9a because 'there simply does not seem to be anywhere else' where the sequence of 'obedient death/exaltation' takes place.[27] In assessing this assertion, let us begin with the term 'obedient'. Seeley does not demonstrate any use of the term ὑπήκοος for the Maccabean martyrs. His parallel is only in concept, not terminology. There are several alternative backgrounds with at least this degree of precision. There is the Isaianic Servant who, *pace* Seeley, is clearly an obedient figure, right through to and including his death. There is also Christian experience of Jesus' death and its aftermath. Christians testified to experience and visions of Christ as risen and as exalted.[28] The combination of that with a description of Jesus' death as obedient could arise in various ways. It could arise simply as a reaction against the supposition of wrong-doing produced by the mode of Jesus' death. It could arise via Adam-Christology (Rom. 5.19). It could arise because ὑπήκοος was an important term from early Christian paraenesis, i.e., it could originally be a summary of how *Christians* were to behave (e.g. Rom. 1.5). That term could then be applied to Christ as a model for Christians.[29] More specifically, Wayne Meeks has suggested

[27] Ibid., p. 5.
[28] See, for example, Larry W. Hurtado, *One God, One Lord: early Christian devotion and ancient Jewish Monotheism* (London: SCM, 1998²), pp. 117–22.
[29] Hurtado, 'Lordly Example', pp. 121–23. Seeley's note 14, in which he castigates O'Brien (who is citing Hurtado) fails to grasp Hurtado's line of argument at all.

that ὑπήκοος in Philippians is a term indicating the perseverance under suffering that Paul is calling the community to (2.8, cf. 2.12).[30] Both Adam-Christology and Christian paraenesis provide possible backgrounds for the specific term ὑπήκοος.

Moving to Seeley's stronger point, the Maccabean martyrs do provide a logic for the 'therefore' of verse 9. As Seeley argues, they expected resurrection *because of* their faithful death.[31] Again, once the imprecision of the Maccabean martyrs' link with ὑπήκοος is realised, the Isaianic Servant could fit the 'therefore' (Isa. 53.12). Similarly, the Davidic tradition (Ps. 16.8–11), applied to Jesus in Acts 2.31–2, could provide the logic if Jesus' 'holiness' was seen as especially expressed in his death. More substantively, we need to ask whether the issue in Philippians 2.9 is really about the granting of eternal life expected by the Maccabean martyrs. Elsewhere in Seeley's article, he thinks that verse 9 is actually about Israel's God divesting himself of authority in favour of the Christians' leader – and Seeley also thinks verse 9 is about imperial apotheosis. These are a long way from the Maccabean expectation. I do not see how Seeley can remove the 'therefore' from his verse 9 of Isaiah 45 and emperors, and attach it to Maccabean martyrs. Surely the 'therefore' in verse 9a gives the reason for God's specific action in verse 9b. In fact, I think that neither Isaiah 45 nor imperial apotheosis provide a workable logic for the 'therefore'. I will argue, below, that the 'therefore' falls into place if we see verses 9–11 as being about imperial authority rather than imperial apotheosis. The 'therefore' can then be the logic of the reason for raising someone to a position of authority. Much of Seeley's evidence can then come back in, but with different conclusions.

Gordon Fee arrives at a comparison between Christ and the Emperor in Philippians 2.6–11 from the diametrically opposite direction to Seeley. Fee's approach has much in common with my own. For Fee, the passage is composed by Paul for the Philippian situation, in which the church faces problems over unity and external opposition.[32] The nature of the Philippian situation therefore guides Fee's reading of 2.6–11. In verses 9–11, Christ is seen to be above the Emperor. Even he will bow to Christ.[33]

---

[30] Meeks, 'Man from Heaven', p. 335.

[31] Seeley, 'Background', p. 4.

[32] Fee thinks that this is the way to interpret it, whether it includes pre-Pauline material or not: see pp. 43–6 and his exegesis of the passage itself.

[33] Ibid., p. 31.

Fee's reading of 2.6–11 is linked to the Philippian situation in a more specific way than my own is. Following Mikael Tellbe, he sees the Philippians' suffering as stemming from their refusal to join as 'citizens of Rome in Philippi' in the celebrations of the imperial cult, which was very prominent at Philippi.[34] The passage 'places Christ in bold contrast to "lord Nero", whose "lordship" they have refused to acknowledge' in the imperial cult.[35] I think it is very unlikely that the Philippians' problems stemmed primarily from the imperial cult. It would be one cult among many that they might be seen to abandon. Since, *pace* Fee, most Christians were probably not Roman citizens, the imperial cult is unlikely to have been the most pressing of the issues that they faced. Also, I will argue, below, that the problems addressed in 2.1–4 are social, not cultic. It is therefore likely that Paul is using the representation of Christ in 2.9–11 to address social issues rather than cultic ones.

Finally, I must mention my own doctoral supervisor, Tom Wright. For Wright, Paul's Gospel is the proclamation of who Christ is. This involves proclamation of Christ's Lordship. This is a direct challenge to other 'Lords', especially to Caesar. Philippians 2.11 is a prime example of declaration of such Lordship.[36] I am pleased that my own work on 2.6–11 has encouraged my supervisor further in this direction!

In general, commentators on Philippians may or may not note comparisons between the ascription of the titles κύριος and σωτήρ to Christ and to the Emperor. If they do, however, it does not make an impact on the commentary. In some ways, this is the most annoying feature of the current situation. Peter O'Brien is typical. A particularly pregnant thought is tucked away at the end of a long footnote:

> Here at Phil. 3.20 both terms [sc. κύριος and σωτήρ] are used, and although σωτήρ is not a title its appropriateness is apparent in the context of a letter to Philippi, where the Emperor was regarded as 'saviour'. The Lord Jesus Christ is the only one who can effect the eschatological deliverance, and it is to him that Christians expectantly look.[37]

[34] Ibid., citing Mikael B. Tellbe, 'Christ and Caesar: The Letter to the Philippians in the Setting of the Roman Imperial Cult' (unpubl. ThM thesis, Vancouver, 1993).

[35] Fee, p. 197.

[36] N. T. Wright, 'Putting Paul Together Again: Towards a Synthesis of Pauline Theology (1 & 2 Thessalonians, Philippians & Philemon)', in J. M. Bassler, ed., *Pauline Theology, Vol. I* (Minneapolis: Fortress Press, 1991), p. 206.

[37] O'Brien, p. 462 n. 120; cf. Hawthorne, p. 172.

In the following, I will argue that the comparison between Christ and the Emperor can be seen on a considerably broader front than just the titles κύριος, σωτήρ, etc. Before moving to 2.9–11, we will consider the clearer case of 3.20–1.

2.   Philippians 3.20–1

Three factors suggest a comparison between Christ and the Emperor here: first, the context, which is concerned with ethics and politics; second, the title σωτήρ and the general issue of saving; third, the link between ability to save and power. Two other points can be paralleled in ruler-ideology but seem unlikely to be heard here, namely, the ruler saving by transforming his subjects into his likeness and the ruler as having glory.

a.   Ethical and political context

The Philippian Christians belong to another state.[38] Not only that, but this is the only state to which they belong: ἡμῶν . . . τὸ πολίτευμα . . . (verse 20). The passage is immediately political. This is reinforced because membership of this state defines the Christians' ethics (cf. verse 19). For Roman citizens, their citizenship was supposed to define their ethics, both in terms of what was permissible (Acts 16.21) and in terms of where one's real allegiance lay (Cicero, *de Legibus*, 2.2.5).[39] As Lohmeyer argued, the political nature of verse 20 is a decisive argument in favour of taking the reference to the σωτήρ, who is κύριος 'Ιησοῦς, as a comparison with the Emperor.[40]

b.   σωτήρ and saving

On its own, the title σωτήρ would be far from unequivocal in pointing towards the Emperor. Philippians with some knowledge of

---

[38] For a discussion of the meaning of πολίτευμα here, see Andrew T. Lincoln, *Paradise Now and Not Yet: Studies in the role of the heavenly dimension in Paul's thought with special reference to his eschatology* (SNTSMS 43; Cambridge: Cambridge University Press, 1981), pp. 97–101. He sees the word as carrying the nuance of 'the state as a constitutive force regulating its citizens' (p. 99).

[39] See Sherwin-White, *Citizenship*, p. 154. The relationship between local allegiance and allegiance to Rome is actually quite a complex topic under the Principate: cf. ibid. p. 295, etc.

[40] Lohmeyer, *Christuskult und Kaiserkult*, pp. 27f.

the OT might hear it solely in relation to Biblical references to heroic saviours or to God as saviour. The Philippians could also hear it in relation to other gods as saviours or to figures such as philosophers.[41] In 3.20, however, it seems unequivocal. This is because of the political context and the specific role of this σωτήρ. In 3.20, the σωτήρ is an eagerly awaited figure who comes, from the state to which his people belong (ἐξ οὗ καὶ . . .), to another state where they are living, in order to rescue them. This must be an analogy with a military leader of a state. In the first-century Graeco-Roman context, the only such leader likely to be thought of was the Emperor. In Philippi, this would be yet more likely. There would even be memories of this having happened, a couple of decades earlier, when the Emperor, represented by his legions, presumably arrived to drive out invading Thracians.[42]

Testimony to the use of the title, σωτήρ, for an emperor is widespread. Their precursor, Julius Caesar, is celebrated in an inscription from Ephesus, dated to 48 BC:

> τὸν ἀπὸ Ἄρεως καὶ Ἀφροδε[ί]της θεὸν ἐπιφανῆ καὶ κοινὸν τοῦ ἀνθρωπίνου βίου σωτῆρα.
>
> the god made manifest, offspring of Ares and Aphrodite and common saviour of human life.[43]

Augustus is praised in both a calendar inscription from Priene (*c*. 9 BC) and a response by the Roman governor:

> providence . . . created . . . the most perfect good for our lives . . . filling him [Augustus] with virtue for the benefit of mankind, sending us and those after us a saviour who put an end to war and established all things . . . and whereas the birthday of the god marked for the world the beginning of good tidings through his coming (τῶν δὶ αὐτὸν εὐανγελί[ων]) . . .[44]

---

[41] For the various options see W. Foerster, σωτήρ, *TDNT VII*, ed. G. Friedrich (Grand Rapids: Eerdmans, 1971); O'Brien, p. 463; Hawthorne, p. 172; Collange, p. 140.

[42] See p. 29, above.

[43] Ditt. *Syll.*³ no. 760, tr. in Deissmann, *Light*, p. 344.

[44] Ditt. *OGIS*, no. 458. Quoted from Price, *Rituals and Power*, p. 54 using tr. from N. Lewis and M. Reinhold, eds., *Roman Civilization II* (New York: Harper & Row, 1955), p. 64. See also J. Rufus Fears, 'Rome: The Ideology of Imperial Power', *Thought*, 55 (March 1980), pp. 104f. and Deissmann, *Light*, p. 366.

... he has given a different aspect to the whole world, which blithely would have embraced its own destruction if Caesar had not been born for the common benefit of all. Therefore people would be right to consider this to have been the beginning of the breath of life for them . . .[45]

Vincent Scramuzza has used the frequency of inscriptions ascribing the term, σωτήρ, to Claudius, an emperor particularly relevant for our letter, to argue that Claudius was an emperor of outstanding benevolence.[46] Two of his examples are from Eresus on Lesbos and from Aezani, respectively:

> . . . σωτήρ τᾶς οἰκουμένας . . . (saviour of the world)[47]

> . . . θεὸς σωτὴρ καὶ εὐεργέτης (god who is saviour and benefactor).[48]

The two terms in the second of these inscriptions may be fairly synonymous. Σωτήρ in Imperial inscriptions can have the weaker sense of 'benefactor'. 'Benefactor', of course, is such a broad term that it could include any good activity of the Emperor and could thus cover all the instances of σωτήρ. However, where the context is of rescue from present or threatened crisis, the translation, 'saviour', seems more appropriate. In 3.20, Christ does save: his followers are eagerly awaiting rescue – ἀπεκδεχόμεθα. One corollary of this is that, as well as Imperial use of the title σωτήρ, more general material about the Emperor in a saving role should be considered in looking for the background of 3.20. This takes us to the link between the Emperor as saviour and the Emperor's power.

c. Saving and power

In 3.21, Jesus' saving action, specified as the transformation of our bodies, is said to be κατὰ τὴν ἐνέργειαν τοῦ δύνασθαι αὐτὸν καὶ ὑποτάξαι αὐτῷ τὰ πάντα. This strengthens the likelihood of comparison with the Emperor, whose ability to save his people is precisely in accordance with the power which enables him also to

[45] Price, *Rituals and Power*, p. 55 using tr. from A. C. Johnson et al., *Ancient Roman Statues: a translation* (Austin: University of Texas Press, 1961), p. 119.
[46] Vincent M. Scramuzza, 'Claudius Soter Euergetes', *Harv. Stud. in Class. Philology* 51 (1940), pp. 261–6.
[47] *IGRR*, IV, 12. Quoted in ibid., p. 264, my tr.
[48] *IGRR*, IV, 584. Quoted in ibid., p. 265, my tr.

subject all things to himself. As Eberhard Faust has argued (see section 3.d, below), the link between saving and power was a central element in Roman Imperial ideology. Faust's interest is in its centrality in legitimating the Empire to conquered peoples. It was, however, also central in legitimating, to the Roman people, the idea of having an emperor. It also legitimated the candidature, and then the rule, of any particular emperor. The roots of this logic lie in the Republican period with the legitimation of limited power assigned to a person for a specific task – generally a saving task.

We can see this if we consider Cicero's speech in 66 BC, arguing for Pompey to be given authority needed to conduct the war against Mithridates (*Pro lege Manilia* or *de Imperio Cn. Pompei*), and then Velleius Paterculus' presentation of the accession to power of his former commander, Tiberius.

Cicero outlines at length (6–26) how serious a crisis Mithridates' actions represent. He then argues that Pompey is the man clearly marked out to deal with the crisis. He describes Pompey's experience, gained in saving Rome from the pirates, which also demonstrates that *Est haec divina atque incredibilis virtus imperatoris*, 'Such is his superhuman and unbelievable genius as a commander' (36, tr. Hodge). He then describes his great virtue: his integrity, self-control and trustworthiness, unlike some generals who even left the money given for the conduct of war on deposit at Rome (37f.), and his condescension – 'he whose greatness surpasses that of princes appears in accessibility the equal of the lowest' (41). He describes his prestige, proved by the sudden fall in the price of wheat when he was appointed for the naval war (44). He describes how *universus populus Romanus* called for his appointment last time (44), and he describes his *fortuna* (47). He argues, '. . . will any man hesitate to transfer the conduct of this great war to the man who seems to have been sent into the world by Providence to bring to a conclusion all the wars of our time?' (42)

The pattern seen in the granting of authority for a single task such as fighting a war is maintained for the general task of protecting and benefiting an Empire. Velleius Paterculus makes it clear that, in particular, the protection of the Empire constituted an urgent, continual task. He does this most effectively by describing a series of threats to Italy, especially ones occurring late in Augustus' reign when his powers were failing or had at least been eclipsed by the new star who had risen and who alone could save Rome. The sharpest of these was the Pannonian War (AD 6–9) when '. . . even the courage of Caesar Augustus . . . was shaken with fear' (2.110.6, tr. F. W. Shipley). Levies were raised. All pulled together. But '[a]ll these our preparations would have been in vain had we not had the man to take command. And so, as a final measure of protection, the state demanded from Augustus that Tiberius should conduct the war' (2.111.2). Tiberius is presented in these passages as the saviour and defender, 'the champion and the guardian', 'the constant protector (*perpetuus patronus*) of the Roman Empire' (2.104.2; 2.120.1). The necessity of this saving task is made clear again in 'the crisis which was awaited with the greatest foreboding' (2.123.1), Augustus' death:

> Of the misgivings of mankind at this time, the trepidation of the senate, the confusion of the people, the fears of the city, of the narrow margin between safety and ruin on which we then found ourselves, I have no time to tell . . . Suffice it for me to voice the common utterance: 'The world whose ruin we had feared we found not even disturbed, and such was the majesty of one man that there was no need of arms either to defend the good or restrain the bad.' (2.124.1)

Although Tiberius initially refused power, in the end the people persuaded him that there was a task that only he could fulfil: 'At last he was prevailed upon . . . since he saw that whatever he did not undertake to protect was likely to perish' (2.124.2).

The 'saviour' motif is inherent in the language of urgency and crisis with which Velleius Paterculus surrounds the situation of the Principate. The pervasiveness of the worry, and its removal by Tiberius' acquisition of the power which enabled him to put his goodness and skill into action, is summed up in the reaction of all on his earlier accession to co-regency:

> On that day there sprang up once more in parents the assurance of safety for their children, in husbands for the sanctity of marriage, in owners for the safety of their property, and in all men the assurance of safety, order, peace and tranquility. (2.103.5)

We could consider at length the various terms which suggest the 'saviour' idea, used in describing aspects of Imperial rule. Many of these have been explored by Jean Béranger in his book, *Recherches sur l'aspect idéologique du Principat*. The Emperor is the protector of the people and the State.[49] Moreover, his whole reign is characterised by *cura*, care, concern, taking on the burden of worry for the people.[50] Béranger concludes:

> La *cura rei publicae* n'est point une institution. C'est un état d'esprit. Elle reflète une attitude caractéristique de la Cité. Elle impliquait la reconnaissance d'une monarchie idéale. Les citoyens se confient à un homme puissant, capable, représentant terrestre des forces surnaturelles, pressenties, éprouvés. Aux dépens de sa quiétude personnelle, ce chef accepte de veiller au bonheur d'autrui. La base du pouvoir devient essentiellement morale.

> The *cura rei publicae* is not an institution. It is a state of mind. It reflects a characteristic attitude of the City. It implied the recognition of an ideal monarchy. The citizens place themselves in the hands of a powerful, able man, the earthly representative of supernatural forces that people sensed and experienced. At the expense of his own peace and quiet, this leader accepts the task of looking after the happiness of others. The basis of power becomes essentially moral.[51]

Ovid writes of '. . . *terrarum dominum quem sua cura facit*' – 'you, whose concern makes you master of the world'.[52]

Cura is a particularly good term to illustrate the real width of the backing for the idea that the most characteristic task of the Emperor was as saviour. Rule of the Empire seems to have been seen not as the rule of a majestic king, in a peaceful realm which faced no threats, with merely the positive roles of dispensing benefits and administering justice to his subjects. Rather, it was seen as the handing over of the worries of an inherently crisis-ridden state to one man who had been marked out as the one who could cope with them, who could solve the problems and save the people from the manifold disasters which would otherwise have overtaken them.[53]

Béranger powerfully sums up both how this often worked in

[49] Jean Béranger, *Recherches sur l'aspect idéologique du Principat* (Basel: Reinhardt, 1953), pp. 254–78.

[50] Ibid., pp. 186–217.

[51] Ibid., p. 217, my tr.

[52] Ovid, *Pont.* 2.8.25, my tr. based on that of Béranger, p. 202.

[53] See the many texts cited by Béranger, esp. on pp. 194–7.

practice, as a victorious general was elevated to higher office, and how the resulting authority was inextricably linked with the saving task.

> Le triomphateur, soit le général vainqueur, acclamé spontanément sur le champ de bataille par ses soldats voyant dans la Victoire une manifestation divine. Il apparaît doué d'un pouvoir surnaturel, sauveur du peuple romain. Pour des raisons sentimentales, mystiques, morales, on lui demande d'être le chef de l'Etat. On lui confie alors *l'imperium*, grâce à quoi il possède les moyens légaux de répondre à l'appel et de parfaire sa tâche.

> The triumphant victor, that is, the conquering general, spontaneously acclaimed on the field of battle by his soldiers, who see in Victory a divine manifestation. He seems to be endowed with supernatural power, the saviour of the Roman people. For reasons that are emotional, mystical and moral, people ask him to be head of state. They then confer on him the *imperium*, thanks to which he possesses the legal means to respond to the call and to complete his task.[54]

Dio Cassius writes that, if you find a man with a natural bent for leadership, well-practised, with fortune,

> You must all, with one accord, whenever such an one is found, both support him and make the fullest use of him, even if he does not wish it. Such compulsion proves most noble both in him who exerts it and in him who suffers it: to the former because he may be saved by it, and to the latter because he may thus save the citizens (σώσειεν . . . τοὺς πολίτας), in whose behalf the excellent and patriotic man would most readily give up both body and life.[55]

So far, we have largely considered only Roman literary sources, but there is wider evidence. First, there are public inscriptions, such as the Priene inscription, given above. Second, there are various coin issues. Fig. 11 is a particularly good example, from the period when Octavian was trying to cement his rule in Asia, which had been under Antony's control.

[54] Béranger, *Recherches*, p. 52, my tr.
[55] Dio Cassius, 36.27.6, tr. E. Cary.

Figure 11   Silver Cistophorus, Ephesus(?) 28 BC
Obverse: Octavian. Reverse: Pax standing on a
sword, holding a caduceus (symbolising world
communication), *cista mystica* (symbolising Asia)
behind, laurel wreath (*B.M.C.*, Augustus, 691)[56]

Third, there are non-Roman literary works which effectively
legitimate the rule of emperors on account of their role as Saviour.
A particularly clear example is Philo, *De Legatione ad Gaium*,
144–9, quoted below (p. 161). Fourth, the idea was not wholly a
creation of the Romans. Greek ruler-philosophy pushed in the
same direction as the Roman ideas and, to quite a great extent,
inspired them.[57]

In the first century AD, the one whom most people would see as
saving in accordance with his power to subject all things to himself
was the Emperor.

d.   Pseudo-Pythagorean concepts

Erwin Goodenough, who wrote a seminal article on pseudo-
Pythagorean ruler-philosophy which he argued to be 'the philosophy of state which thrust itself irresistably upon the Roman
imperator',[58] would be able to parallel everything in 3.20–1 with

[56] C. H. V. Sutherland, *The Emperor and the Coinage: Julio-Claudian Studies*
(London: Spink & Son, 1976), Pl. I no. 16, cf. C. H. V. Sutherland, *Coinage in
Roman Imperial Policy, 31BC–AD68* (London: Methuen, 1951 (1971 repr.)), p. 31.
[57] Béranger, *Recherches*, pp. 149f.
[58] Erwin R. Goodenough, 'The Political Philosophy of Hellenistic Kingship', *Yale
Classical Studies* 1 (1928), p. 100.

material relevant to the Emperor. The text that I have not covered is, ὃς μετασχηματίσει τὸ σῶμα τῆς ταπεινώσεως ἡμῶν σύμμορφον τῷ σώματι τῆς δόξης αὐτοῦ (verse 21). Goodenough discusses a range of texts in which the king transforms his people into his likeness. Moreover, this is, religiously and philosophically, the way in which they are saved. Diotogenes writes about virtues required of a King and then says,

> So will he succeed in putting into order those who look upon him, amazed at his majesty, at his self-control, and his fitness for distinction. For to look upon the good king ought to affect the souls of those who see him no less than a flute or harmony.[59]

Ecphantus writes that the need for obedience is 'the basest trace of our earthiness', and goes on to say,

> . . . whatever things can by their own nature use the Beautiful, have no occasion for obedience, as they have no fear of necessity. The king alone is capable of putting this good into human nature so that, by imitation of him, their Better, they will follow in the way they should go.[60]

Goodenough asserts that this harmony, where obedience is not needed, is the aim of Pauline Christianity.[61]

If 3.21 did carry a comparison with the ideas that Goodenough describes, it would need to do so by rather indirect means. The transformation in 3.21 is of the body, not the mind, and is at the Eschaton (and presumably instantaneous) rather than a process during the subjects' lifetime. The issue of the extent to which Goodenough's primarily Hellenistic ideas would be well known in the first century AD is discussed below. Certainly, ideas such as transformation to be like a ruler would be ones which seem likely to be among the less well known in the general population. For these reasons, I would not see transformation to be like a ruler to be an important likely background to 3.20–1. However, it does look a possibility as a distant *religionsgeschichtlich* influence. It is also a more interesting issue when one considers 2.5–11.

On Christ's δόξα in 3.21, Goodenough could produce parallels to

---

[59] Stob. IV, 62, ll. 9ff., tr. ibid., p. 72.
[60] Goodenough, 'Philosophy of Kingship', p. 89.
[61] Ibid., p. 91.

Royal philosophy.[62] More direct parallels to the Emperor could also be drawn. However, the term seems too general to offer support for any such comparison.

3. Philippians 2.9–11

A wide range of factors have convinced me that the Philippians would have heard a comparison being drawn, in Philippians 2.9–11, between Christ and the Emperor. I have arranged them under eight headings.

a. Links with 3.20–1

The verbal and conceptual links between 2.9–11 and 3.20–1 are so strong that, if the comparison with the Emperor would be heard in chapter 3, then it would probably also be heard in chapter 2. This would certainly be the case in second, and subsequent, hearings.

The link is most powerful in the last clause of 3.21. Having heard 2.9–11, the Philippians would be bound to hear τὴν ἐνέργειαν τοῦ δύνασθαι αὐτὸν . . . ὑποτάξαι αὐτῷ τὰ πάντα as being what was conferred on Christ in 2.9–11. The links from 2.5–11 and 3.20–1 are astonishingly full:[63] κύριον Ἰησοῦν Χριστόν (in only these two places in the body of the letter); the direct conceptual links of universal submission and, possibly, of citizenship (with 1.27); the 'accidental' use of cognates of words in 2.5–11 as key terms in 3.20–1 (οὐρανοῖς, ὑπάρχει, μετασχηματίσει, σύμμορφον); the transformation of the one(s) characterised by ταπείνωσις; the structural relationship between 2.5–11 and 3.20–1, forming a pair of climactic, heavily Christological passages near the start and at the end of the main argument (1.27–4.1).

It is notable that Bormann, who takes Philippians 3 as a separate letter, still feels that the links between 3.20–1 and 2.10–11 are so strong that he can build a composite argument from the two passages.[64]

---

[62] Ibid., e.g. p. 78.
[63] D. E. Garland, 'The Composition and Unity of Philippians: Some Neglected Literary Factors', *NovT* 27 (1985), pp. 157ff.
[64] Bormann, *Philippi*, pp. 218f.

Figure 12   Reverse of (silver) denarius, Italy, c. 31–29 BC. The figure is probably Octavian. Obverse is a bust of Victory (*B.M.C.*, Augustus, 615)[65]

Figure 13   Ditto. Victory on globe. Obverse is head of Octavian (*B.M.C.*, Augustus, 602)

Figure 14   Aes (i.e. copper) as of Tiberius, Rome AD 35–6. Rudder and globe symbolising world power (*B.M.C.*, Tiberius, 117)

[65] See discussion in Sutherland, *Emperor*. The three coins are Pl. I nos. 10, 11 and Pl. VI no. 82 (see p. 112).

b. Christ is given universal authority

Jesus receives the Name above every name. All knees bow to him. Every tongue acknowledges him as Lord. A Graeco-Roman hearer would probably hear this as a comparison with the Emperor.

Many coins and inscriptions illustrate the Emperor's claim to world authority (see Figs. 12, 13, 14).

[Αὐτοκράτ]ορ[α Κ]αίσαρα [θ]εοῦ υἱὸν θεὸν Σεβαστὸ[ν πάσης] γῆ[ς κ]αὶ θ[α]λάσσης [ἐ]π[όπ]τ[ην]

The Emperor, Caesar, son of a god, the god Augustus, of every land and sea the overseer.[66]

ὁ τοῦ παντὸς κόσμου κύριος Νέρων

Nero, the Lord of all the world.[67]

The Emperor regarded every knee on earth as bowing to him. Christ gains the submission of every knee on earth (the meaning of 'every knee shall bow' is considered in more detail in section 3.e, below). This supersedes the Emperor's authority in the Emperor's sphere and even presumably includes the Emperor's own knee bowing. Christ goes on to claim a wider sphere of authority: under the earth and in the skies.

The list of those whose knees bow in 2.10 raises two immediate objections to this reading. First, Käsemann sees the terms ἐπουρ-ανίων, ἐπιγείων and καταχθονίων as referring only to angelic powers reigning over the various realms of the cosmos.[68] However, O. Hofius and others[69] have persuasively argued that the homage is universal: every knee bows, not only those of the spirits. We may also note the order in which the words of the verse are heard. The listener first hears, πᾶν γόνυ κάμψῃ, which would probably be heard as referring to all people (especially if the hearer knew

---

[66] *Inschr. von Pergamon* no. 381, from Augustus' lifetime, tr. in Deissmann, *Light*, p. 347.

[67] Ditt. *Syll.*³ no. 814, 31. Quoted in Deissmann, *Light*, p. 354. This is the first inscription in Greece (at Acraephiae in Boeotia) having Caesar as κύριος, my tr.

[68] E. Käsemann, 'A Critical Analysis of Philippians 2:5–11', tr. A. F. Carse, H. Braun et al., in R. W. Funk, ed., *God and Christ: Existence and Province* (*Journal for Theology and the Church* 5) (Tübingen: J. C. B. Mohr, 1968), pp. 78f.

[69] Otfried Hofius, *Der Christushymnus Philipper 2, 6–11* (WUNT, 17; Tübingen: J. C. B. Mohr, 1976), pp. 20–55; O'Brien, pp. 244f.

Isa. 45) or, possibly, to all creatures in the universe. This is then developed by ἐπουρανίων, etc. It would be surprising if the development was intended to exclude humans, the group who would most naturally have been heard as the referent of πᾶν γόνυ κάμψῃ.

A second objection is that even if those on earth are living people, those in the heavens or the underworld are not: this suggests a comparison with a figure other than the Emperor. This objection has particular force because Paul has taken Isaiah 45.23 (see below), which described the homage of the nations, and has specifically expanded it beyond them.

The proper first response to this is probably to say that, in any case, the picture painted is still that of homage to an emperor. Even if the comparison in 2.10–11 is with a god, the god himself is being painted in terms of an emperor. First-century hearers would undoubtedly think in terms of the Roman Emperor. Second, I am not aware of a divine figure in the Philippians' Graeco-Roman background who was likely to be heard receiving a homage of this type (for the Jewish background in Isa. 45.23, see below). Isis would seem too sectional an interest. Zeus might be possible but I am not aware of such a homage-tradition. Thirdly, even if there was a tradition of Zeus receiving such homage, the comparison with him seems excluded by verse 9. Zeus was not raised to authority by a third party on account of deeds performed. The strongest option seems to be that verses 10–11 would be heard by the Philippians as depicting an Imperial figure – but one with a far wider scope of authority than the Roman Emperor.

Two important questions have been left hanging here. Do the knees bowing really indicate submission rather than worship? Does my reading relate credibly to Isaiah 45.23, which is cited in verses 10–11? These questions will be picked up in section 3.e, below. What we can say is that a hearer in a Roman context would hear 2.9–11 as in some sense involving a grant of authority to Jesus that eclipsed the authority of the Emperor. The authority clearly eclipsed that of the gods too but the imagery employed would in the first instance evoke the idea of an imperial figure on his throne receiving homage from all those who had now been put under his authority.

c.   Authority granted for a reason

Christ's authority is granted to him, granted by a competent authority, granted for a reason and granted for a reason which is of a kind particularly prominent in legitimating the rule of emperors.

(i)   Granted authority

It is easy to think of the exaltation of verse 9 simply in terms of reward or vindication. It is, however, primarily a gaining of authority. Moreover, one of the most notable features of 2.5–11 is the change of actor at verse 9. Christ Jesus ἑαυτὸν ἐκένωσεν but it is ὁ θεὸς who αὐτὸν ὑπερύψωσεν. Christ did not raise himself to power, or crown himself, as Napoleon did. God granted Christ authority. The idea that the emperors' authority was granted to them was also an important element of imperial ideology.

The emperors were not regarded as holding usurped authority. Even those later emperors who did actually seize power by force went to great efforts to argue that their power was properly granted – one thinks of Hadrian producing the story of Trajan's deathbed adoption of him. In any case the Julio-Claudian emperors, even Claudius, could all put strong arguments for their power having been granted to them.

(ii)   Authority granted by the competent body

In our period, the competent authority for granting power was two-fold: the Senate voted to the Emperor his powers;[70] this was then ratified by the people of Rome gathered on the field of Mars.[71] Acclamation by troops, prior to all this, had great *de facto* force but no role *de jure* until Vespasian's time.[72] I do not think anything is to be gained by attempting elaborate parallels between God and the Roman Senate but the key point is that authority was conferred on Christ by the second party who had proper authority to do so.

---

[70] Blanche Parsi, *Désignation et Investiture de l'Empereur Romain (Ier et IIe siècles après J.-C.)* (Paris: Librairie Sirey, 1963), pp. 70, 78, 130f.

[71] Ibid., pp. 78ff., 94, 97, 119.

[72] Ibid., pp. 210f. Cf. the *Praetorianus Receptus* coin of Claudius: Sutherland, *Emperor*, p. 113 and Pl. VII No. 102.

(iii)   Authority granted for a reason

One of the features of 2.5–11 which has proved hardest for exegetes to handle is the phrase διὸ καί in 2.9. This has probably followed mainly from the overemphasis on verse 9 as reward rather than as granting of authority. This has produced dogmatic difficulties, over merit and grace, and ethical difficulties, over the possibility of Christ acting out of long-term self-interest. Both these worries actually seem misplaced but, in any case, if 2.9 is mainly about the granting of authority then the διὸ καί has a different function: it shows that verses 6–8, or part of them, provide a *reason* for God granting Christ authority. Irrespective of our current interest in a possible comparison with the Emperor, it is clearly important, for the exegesis of verse 9, for us to investigate first-century thinking on what were the proper reasons for granting extensive authority to someone.

It considerably strengthens the case for there being a comparison with the Emperor that the authority in verse 9 is granted for a reason at all. This pattern (authority granted for a reason) is a particularly marked feature of Roman Imperial authority – in contrast, for example, to that of the Persian empire. We can exemplify this pattern from three angles. One angle is the material on saving and power, discussed above: power was granted in order to give the chosen man the means to carry out his saving task. A second is constitutional. A third concerns interaction with the candidate at the time of accession.

Constitutionally, Rome remained nominally a democracy in the modern sense, i.e., rule by those elected by the people. The people's assembly might have lost the power to do anything except cheer, but it remained their approval that technically put the Emperor on the throne.[73] Moreover, the emperors always wanted to argue that the *consensus universorum* stood behind their coming to power.

The coin shown in Fig. 15 carries the legend, *Imperatori Caesare Augusto communi consensu* (To the Emperor Caesar Augustus by universal agreement), with a *cippus* or altar and, on the other side, *Iovum Optimo Maximo Senatus Populusque Romanus votum susceptum pro salute Imperatoris Caesaris quod per eum respublica in ampliore atque tranquilliore statu est* (The Senate and People of Rome made a votive offering to Jupiter Optimus Maximus for the

[73] Parsi, *Désignation*, pp. 78ff., 94, 97, 119.

Figure 15   Reverse of (silver) denarius showing
cippus or altar, 16 BC, Rome (*B.M.C.*,
Augustus, 92)[74]

safety of Emperor Caesar because by him the state is enlarged and
more peaceful[75] – but somewhat abbreviated on the coin!). Shipley
cites this coin to illustrate Augustus' own assertion that 'the entire
body of citizens with one accord, both individually and by munici-
palities, performed continued sacrifices for my health at the
couches of all the gods.'[76] The coin illustrates the general point of
Augustus being emperor by common agreement. Augustus himself
notes that, at the time around Actium, he received 'the absolute
control of affairs' *per consensum universorum*.[77] As well as citing
general agreement for specific offers of power made to him,
Augustus suggests the idea of the *consensus* by, for example, noting
the unprecedented crowds that gathered for his election as *Pontifex
Maximus*.[78] Tacitus writes that it is the *consensus* which ensures the
libertas of the people.[79] As Blanche Parsi notes, 'The Emperor is
merely the interpreter of the general will'.[80]

Also from a constitutional angle, the position of emperor was
technically only a temporary one, designed to meet the needs of
Rome in a period of crisis (see above). This technical status had
even had a recent practical proof in the attempt to restore republican government at Caligula's death. This status and the general
democratic idea involve the concept of the Emperor's power being
granted for a reason.

[74] Sutherland, *Emperor*, Pl. IV no. 54.
[75] My tr.
[76] Augustus, *Res Gestae*, 9 and p. 361 note a, tr. F. W. Shipley.
[77] Ibid., 34, p. 299.
[78] Ibid., 10, p. 361.
[79] Tacitus, *Hist.* 1.16.
[80] Parsi, *Désignation*, p. 11, my tr.

This conclusion is reinforced by a common (although not universal) motif in imperial accessions (and one which carried through into the Church hierarchy), that of the refusal of power. Béranger has shown that this device was part of a dialogue designed to reinforce the legitimation of the Emperor's power. The Emperor does not slide unobtrusively into power, as he could if he felt that he acquired his power simply by right of adoption.[81] He says, no, and the Senate and people (and the gods) demand that he accept it. There is then no doubt that his position is legitimate.[82] We can see this at work in the case of Tiberius. Velleius Paterculus wrote that, after Augustus' death,

> There was, however, in one respect what might be called a struggle in the state, as, namely, the senate and the Roman people wrestled with Caesar to induce him to succeed to the position of his father. (2.124.2, p. 313)

In legitimating his position, the process draws sharp attention to the idea of power being granted for a reason. The Senate and people are so aware of the vital nature of the task to be done, and of the uniqueness of this man's qualifications for the task, that they must go against his will and compel him to take it on.[83]

There are two senses in which authority was granted for a reason. First, there was a necessitating reason. A task needed carrying out so authority had to be given. Second, there was a reason that legitimated a particular candidate as the one who should be given authority. For Philippians 2, we are interested in the second type of reason. In the Roman system, the second type flowed from the first.

(iv)   Authority granted for a reason which is prominent in legitimating the authority of an emperor

How would the Senate and people know that a particular candidate was the person who would carry out the necessary task? The answer is that he would have demonstrated various characteristics. These then also legitimate the person's rule once he is Emperor.

---

[81] Béranger, *Recherches*, p. 147, sees refusal as not characteristic of genetic children of emperors (but such children being given the throne were, of course, rather thin on the ground in our period).

[82] Ibid., pp. 147–68, esp. pp. 152–4.

[83] Cf. the quotation from Dio Cass. 36.27.6, above.

The characteristics to which contemporary writers draw attention fall under four rough headings: abilities needed for the saving task; connections with previous rulers and the gods; universal agreement that a person should rule; moral excellence. The fourth of these is most relevant to Philippians 2. I will briefly survey the first three, so as to place the fourth in context.

Military victories demonstrated the most vital ability required of an Emperor, the ability to protect Rome against her enemies. Such ability was repeatedly cited.[84] As our above quotation from Béranger indicated, the Romans went beyond the simple weighing of evidence of military skill shown by victories to making the religious inferences that, first, there was a superhuman element in that skill,[85] second, that the gods specially favoured the person, in particular in granting him a full and reasonably steady supply of *fortuna*[86] and, third, that the gods had sent the person concerned into the world to perform tasks such as the one in question.[87]

The importance of this military aspect of legitimation can, paradoxically, be seen in the case of Claudius who had no prior victories to recommend him: he described his initial acclamation by the Praetorian Guard as his first 'triumph'[88] – thus gaining a military victory without stepping beyond Rome. More generally, our point is made by the monopoly which the emperors and their successors seized of the ceremony in which troops saluted a victorious general after battle as *imperator*.[89] Non-military acts could also add to a leader's case. Velleius Paterculus cites Tiberius' good management of the grain-supply.[90]

The second legitimating factor was connection to previous rulers and to the gods. Claudius had nothing obvious to recommend him except connection to the ruling dynasty. He seems to have had charismatic gifting inferred from his establishment as Emperor, rather than *vice versa*.[91] Even in more normal cases, however,

---

[84] For Augustus, see the denarius (Pl. I no. 10) shown above. For Tiberius: Vell. Pat. 2.94.2ff. For Claudius: Sutherland, *Emperor*, Pl. VIII no. 114. Cf. Pompey: Cicero, *De Imp. Cn. P.* 27–35.

[85] Cicero, *De Imp. Cn. P.* 37f.

[86] Ibid., 47: *divinitus adiuncta fortuna* – although Cicero is really somewhat nervous about speaking of *fortuna*, it being the prerogative of the gods.

[87] Ibid., 42, 49.

[88] Robert Combès, *Imperator* (Paris: Presses Universitaires de France, 1966), pp. 186ff.

[89] Ibid., p. 4.

[90] Vell. Pat. 2.94.3.

[91] Parsi, *Désignation*, pp. 21f.

connection to the previous ruler was clearly important. Velleius Paterculus indicates Tiberius' connection to Augustus in his usual restrained terms. As well as adopting Tiberius and conferring many offices on him, Augustus died 'with the arms of his beloved Tiberius around him, commending to him the continuation of their joint work . . .'.[92] Blanche Parsi describes various ways in which adoption by (or real sonship of) the present ruler helped the son towards the throne. The son inherited wealth, which was necessary for exercising *liberalitas*, especially for supporting one's clientele and (above all) for paying the soldiers.[93] Sonship conferred rights of patronage and clientele. During Octavian's civil war this was tangibly vital. Later it was institutionalised, the Emperor becoming the universal patron.[94] The son inherited the prestige of the dynasty.[95] Prestige, among both enemies and allies, was regarded by Cicero as essential for a leader.[96] The son was nominated as successor. If there was more than one adoption, they could be distinguished. Tiberius and Agrippa Postumus were both adopted but only Tiberius' adoption was *rei publicae causa*.[97] The nomination had no legal force but it must have had a wide range of means of being effective. From the point of view of legitimating a successor, one can imagine it having effect through the predecessor being viewed as an *optimus*, and therefore his choice being reliable, or through the predecessor being viewed as the 'providential' man, and able in some way to hand on his 'providentiality'.

Connection with the gods was also asserted. Julius Caesar was regarded as descended from Venus and Anchises.[98] The gods were also involved by predestining certain people to rule and by giving signs to show that predestination.

> As he [sc. Octavian] approached Rome . . . men saw above his head the orb of the sun with a circle about it, coloured like the rainbow, seeming thereby to place a crown upon the head of the one destined soon to greatness.[99]

[92] Vell. Pat. 2.123.2.
[93] Parsi, *Désignation*, pp. 3, 145, and see *Res Gestae*.
[94] Parsi, *Désignation*, p. 23.
[95] Ibid., p. 24.
[96] Cicero, *De Imp. Cn. P.* 43f.
[97] Vell. Pat. 2.104.2; Parsi, *Désignation*, p. 12.
[98] Vell. Pat. 2.40.1; cf. inscription to Caesar, above.
[99] Vell. Pat. 2.59.6. Cf. Suetonius, *Tiberius*, 14: the incident of the igniting altars at Philippi.

Evidence for the third legitimating factor, universal agreement that the person should rule, has been noted above. With a measure of ingenuity, each of these three factors could be quarried out of Philippians 2.5–11. However, since verses 6–8 are providing the reason for the διὸ καί, and especially given the paraenetic context in verses 1–4, it is the moral form of legitimation of power which is likely to be heard by the Philippians – and probably not any of the others.

Emperors' claims to moral qualities are again illustrated well by coinage. As well as the coin in Fig. 16, Tiberius issued coins celebrating his justice and his piety.[100]

Figure 16   Reverse of (aes) dupondius AD
18–21, Rome. Records the giving of honorific
shields in recognition of *clementia* and *moderatio*.
(*B.M.C.*, Tiberius, 85)[101]

In his *Res Gestae*, Augustus announced to the world his generosity and his self-effacement. The very title of the book speaks of 'the amounts which he expended on the state and the Roman people'. He fed people in a grain crisis (5), gave to rebuild earthquake-shattered cities (Summary, 4), and provided largesse which reached a quarter of a million people (15). He declined the dictatorship twice (5), refused the coronary gold at his triumphs (21), and

[100] Sutherland, *Emperor*, Pl. VI nos. 80–1. Cf. Sutherland, *Coinage*, pp. 27 (Augustus), 150 (Nero).
[101] Sutherland, *Emperor*, Pl. V no. 77, see pp. 110f.

removed eighty statues of himself from Rome (24). In a masterpiece of double-think, he announces,

> The Capitolium and the Theatre of Pompey, both works involving great expense, I rebuilt without any inscription of my own name. (20)

He also celebrates his magnanimity in victory (3) and his piety (19, 24).

Seneca discusses the precise issue of reasons for raising to power in *De Beneficiis*, in a passage where he defends God for raising to power various unworthy people such as Caligula. His defence is that God may have wished to repay the worthy actions of an ancestor. These can be the heroic saving of Rome but often they are moral – in some cases even such as directly to preclude military victories:

> God says: 'Let these men be kings because their forefathers have not been, because they have regarded justice and unselfishness as their highest authority, because, instead of sacrificing the state to themselves, they have sacrificed themselves to the state (*quia non rem publicam sibi, sed se rei publicae dicaverunt*). Let these others reign, because some one of their grandsires before them was a good man who displayed a soul superior to Fortune, who in times of civil strife, preferred to be conquered than to conquer, because in this way he could serve the interest of the state (*quoniam ita expediebat rei publicae, vinci quam vincere maluit*).' (4.32.2, tr. J. W. Basore)

> 'How can these critics know that hero of old, who persistently fled from the glory that followed him, who, going into danger, had the air that others show when they return from danger, who never separated his own interest from that of the state (*numquam bonum suum a publico distinguentem*)?' (4.32.4)

Such moral qualities come down to Seneca from the Republic.[102] Thus the moral qualities for which Cicero commends Pompey in *De Imperio Cn. Pompei* are openness to those below him (41) and, above all, self-control in not using warfare for financial gain (37f).

---

[102] See Béranger, *Recherches*, p. 216, on Cicero's influence.

Similarly, the moral qualities for which Velleius Paterculus particularly commends Tiberius are care for the soldiers under him – he was preoccupied by the health of each of them (2.114.3) – and moderation in accepting honours (2.122).

Just as military victories were the natural practical recommendation of a leader, concern for others and lack of self-interest were the natural ethical recommendations – although, as we have seen, others could also come in. The leader was raised up in order to carry out his task which was for the sake of the people: it was clearly vital that he too should view matters that way.[103]

My aim, in this sub-section, has been to show that aspects of what became systematised in the second century AD in the idea of the *optimus* as the ruler, had pervasive roots in the publicly presented Imperial ideology of the first century.[104] Such ideology found many forms of expression, including coins, inscriptions such as the *Res Gestae* and, no doubt, also speeches made at games during Imperial festivals. The Emperor was presented as the self-effacing man, devoted to others. He was therefore the right man to rule.

In Philippians 2.6–8, Christ refuses to seek his own interest, lowers himself and suffers obediently. Therefore, in verse 9, God grants him supreme authority. When the Philippians heard this and felt, as they no doubt did, 'Yes, this logic is appropriate', it seems probable that they felt this because of their experience of Imperial ideology. Among a church with a Jewish background, we would tend to look for the basis of the logic in the Old Testament. For the Gentile church in the Roman colony of Philippi there is a much more familiar logic to look at – and a logic which fits 2.5–11 well. The fit between moral excellence as legitimating power and verses 6–8 as legitimating verse 9 looks very natural. This is particularly so since the most prominent form of moral excellence seems to be concern for others and lack of self-interest.

The situation is also deeply ironic. Christ's self-lowering makes his accession to power fit a prominent pattern of legitimation of Imperial authority. Yet Christ's self-lowering led to crucifixion, the

---

[103] See ibid., pp. 169f. and esp. p. 216: 'Il la justifie [sc. sa délégation de pouvoirs] en affichant un dévouement absolu au bien public' (He justifies it [sc. the delegation of powers to him] by displaying an absolute devotion to the public good), my tr.

[104] As Parsi argues, the Julio-Claudian commitment to dynasty, *per se*, rather than selection of a candidate purely on grounds of excellence, precludes their commitment to it as a complete theoretical system (*Désignation*, II,1).

fate furthest from the career of a candidate for the Imperial throne. A writer would not have composed verses 6–8 as a depiction of an ideal candidate for rule. I will argue, in chapter 6, that the specific shape of verses 6–8 actually comes from the needs of the Philippian situation. However, when Paul reaches the end of verse 8, he turns round and points out that what Christ has done legitimates his being given universal authority. *Pace* Bornhäuser, I do not think that a Philippian hearing verses 6–8 would think of the Emperor. It is the use of verses 6–8 in the logic of verse 9 that would sound like a legitimation of authority, a legitimation cast in the Imperial mould.

    d.   Universal submission and the central Imperial saving task for the world

In 2.10, every knee bows to Jesus. If, as for example Hofius has argued,[105] this submission and the acclamation in verse 11 involve the salvation of all concerned, then Jesus' role here is unavoidably reminiscent of the Emperor. The point which legitimates to the world the Emperor's power over it is his bringing of salvation through universal submission to him. The specific content of this salvation is peace through harmony. Although the topic of harmony is not raised in 2.10–11, the possibility that Christ is bringing salvation through universal submission means that we ought to sketch the outline of the Imperial version of this.

The theme is central to Rome's legitimation as an Imperial power so there are many sources which exemplify it. It has recently been considered by Eberhard Faust in his book, *Pax Christi et Pax Caesaris: Religionsgeschichtliche, traditionsgeschichtliche und sozialgeschichtliche Studien zum Epheserbrief*, in which he argues that the setting of that letter is the aftermath of the Flavian declaration of universal peace, i.e. of inter-ethnic harmony, the application of which was destructively anti-Jewish in Asia. Ephesians 2 presents Christ as the only one who can properly bring this harmony.[106]

We can divide the subject of harmony in Imperial ideology into two parts by considering first the practical content of the harmony and then the philosophical and religious ideas surrounding it.

---

[105] Hofius, *Christushymnus*, pp. 66f.

[106] E. Faust, *Pax Christi et Pax Caesaris: Religionsgeschichtliche, traditionsgeschichtliche u. sozialgeschichtliche Studien zum Epheserbrief* (Freiburg: Universitätsverlag; Göttingen: Vandenhoeck & Ruprecht, 1993), esp. p. 475.

Philo shows the way in which the Roman Empire, and in particular the Emperor, was seen as saving the world by bringing practical harmony. There had been wars everywhere,

> so that the whole human race exhausted by mutual slaughter was on the verge of utter destruction, had it not been for one man and leader Augustus whom men fitly call the averter of evil . . . This is he who not only loosed but broke the chains which had shackled and pressed so hard on the habitable world . . . who reclaimed every state to liberty, who led disorder into order . . . He was also the first and the greatest and the common benefactor in that he displaced the rule of many and committed the ship of the commonwealth to be steered by a single pilot . . . 'It is not well that many lords should rule.'[107]

Augustus is also celebrated in the Priene inscription which notes that,

> he has given a different aspect to the whole world, which blithely would have embraced its own destruction if Caesar had not been born for the common benefit of all. Therefore people would be right to consider this to have been the beginning of the breath of life for them . . .[108]

Similar is Seneca's fear that the vast throng of people 'would crush and cripple itself with its own power' without the ruler's wisdom.[109] This all finds varied iconographic expression, such as on the altar of Augustan Peace where, among the reliefs, *Pax* and *Concordia* are seen as having an epiphany in the person of Augustus.[110]

Also on the altar, Mother Earth is seen sitting amidst symbols of peace and plenty.[111] Inter-ethnic peace brought increased prosperity to the Empire in general, prosperity fostered by what J. R. Fears argues was the restoration under Augustus of the *pax deorum*, between gods and men, the breaking of which had been indicated by the civil war.[112] Ethnic harmony was also linked to religious harmony. The emperors wanted peace between religious

---

[107] Philo, *De Legatione ad Gaium*, 144–9, tr. F. H. Colson. Philo's quotation is from *Iliad*, ii, 204.
[108] Quoted more fully above; Price, *Rituals and Power*, p. 55.
[109] Seneca, *De Clem.* 1.3.5, tr. J. W. Basore.
[110] Fears, 'Ideology', p. 105.
[111] Ibid.
[112] Ibid.

groups – a policy which accommodated the exclusivist Jews only with some unease, and which ran into problems with the exclusivist Christians.

The value of unity, obvious in practical terms, was also undergirded by philosophical/religious views among which two are prominent: the theoretical value attached to harmony and the particular theoretical position which the Emperor was given.

The value attached to harmony could be illustrated widely. In Philo's quotation above, he seems to be moving from practical considerations towards theoretical ones as the lines progress. Plutarch approvingly cites the argument of Zeno that men should be considered as one community and have a common life and order.[113] Plutarch makes this into a driving force for Alexander,[114] who was a type to whom the Emperors commonly and self-consciously likened themselves.[115] From a different philosophical tradition, Diotogenes writes on harmony in a characteristically Pythagorean way:

> Now the king bears the same relation to the state [πόλιν] as God to the world; and the state is in the same ratio to the world as the king is to God. For the state, made as it is by a harmonizing together of many different elements, is an imitation of the order and harmony of the world, while the king who has an absolute rulership, and is himself Animate Law, has been metamorphosed into a deity among men (αὐτὸς ὢν νόμος ἔμψυχος, θεὸς ἐν ἀνθρώποις παρεσχαμά-τισται).[116]

As Goodenough argues, Diotogenes' point is that the ruler is a god among men because the ruler performs among men the same harmonising function that God does in the Universe.

Béranger sums up the philosophers' concerns as being that they saw unity and order as perfection: therefore division was a scandal and,

> Réciproquement, celui qui assure l'ordre du monde accomplit oeuvre salvatrice, dont dépend le sort des humains. La

---

113 Plutarch, *De Alex. fort.* 329A–B.
114 Ibid., e.g., 330D.
115 Faust, *Pax Christi*, pp. 306f.
116 Stob. IV, 61, tr. Goodenough, 'Philosophy of Kingship', p. 68.

division, c'est le mal, la mort; l'harmonie universelle, la condition préalable de la félicité des peuples.

Conversely, he who ensures the order of the world carries out a saving task on which the fate of humans depends. Division is evil. It is death. Universal harmony is the precondition for the happiness of peoples.[117]

The practical and theoretical desire for harmony both contributed to and was supported by the philosophical position given to the Emperor. He was seen as the mind (or soul or head) for which the Empire was the body. Seneca expresses this very powerfully in an argument that it is not folly for large numbers of people to be willing to die for the sake of one man, their ruler,

> . . . Nor is it self-depreciation or madness when many thousands meet the steel for the sake of one man, and with many deaths ransom the single life, it may be, of a feeble dotard. The whole body is the servant of the mind (*animo*) . . . In the same way this vast throng, encircling the life of one man, is ruled by his spirit, guided by his reason, and would crush and cripple itself with its own power if it were not upheld by wisdom . . .

> . . . he [sc. their emperor] is the bond by which the commonwealth is united, the breath of life which these many thousands draw, who in their own strength would be only a burden to themselves and the prey of others if the great mind (*mens*) of the empire should be withdrawn.[118]

This kind of idea has a long pedigree. Plato provides for the general concept a philosophical base which Goodenough summarises as follows:

> . . . every animal has a sort of soul and head, whose virtue is the saving principle of the animal. But the active principle of salvation in the soul is mind (νοῦς) . . .

> . . . on a ship the νοῦς of the pilot acts through the senses of the sailors to save the ship, while generals and physicians similarly control and save by projecting their νοῦς into the senses of their armies or patients. In like manner a true

---

[117] Béranger, *Recherches*, pp. 226f., my tr.
[118] Seneca, *De Clem.* 1.3.5–4.1.

statesman is such by virtue of his supreme νοῦς which
saves the city.[119]

Goodenough then sees such ideas working through into Hellenistic
political philosophy in passages such as the one from Diotogenes
quoted above.

Goodenough's seminal article does seem to have a weak point,
however, in the route by which he chooses to lead his ideas into the
first century AD. His appeal to III Maccabees 6.24 seems particularly strange. He argues that, in this verse, since there is a threat to
the King's 'spirit' but not to his life, the term 'spirit' should imply
the Hellenistic royal philosophical ideas.[120] Similarly, Goodenough
seems to overstretch the evidence in seeing the philosophy of
royalty of Ecphantus in Plutarch's *Ad Principem Ineruditum*.[121]
Although the King does have a special position for Plutarch – for
example he is the εἰκὼν θεοῦ τοῦ πάντα κοσμοῦντος (image of God
who orders all things) – some of the key ideas for Ecphantus, such
as the King being the λόγος, are radically transposed in Plutarch
because λόγος is something available via philosophy to all. Goodenough reveals how confusing the situation is when he writes,
'. . . apparently it is generalised in such a form that anyone whose
life is guided by reason might be represented as an Animate
Nomos-Logos or king':[122] he tries to extricate himself by saying
that while all who learn philosophy are royal, 'only a king can be so
in the full sense'.[123] However, Ecphantus and Plutarch seem to
differ in what they are driving at. Ecphantus says that the king has
λόγος because he is king. Ecphantus addresses subjects and calls
them to obey.[124] Plutarch addresses the king and points out that
because of his position it is essential that he should have λόγος.
Therefore the king ought to study philosophy.[125] My problem
with how far Goodenough pushes his case can be summed up
by comparing Fowler's translation of one clause with that of
Goodenough:

οὕτω τὸ ἐν πόλεσι φέγγος εὐδικίας καὶ λόγου τοῦ περὶ
αὐτὸν ὥσπερ εἰκόνα κατέστησεν. . .(Plutarch, *Mor.* 781F)

[119] Goodenough, 'Philosophy of Kingship', pp. 66f., from Plato, *Laws*, 957–62.
[120] Ibid., pp. 92f.
[121] Ibid., p. 98.
[122] Ibid., p. 95.
[123] Ibid., p. 97.
[124] Ecphantus, Stob. IV, 7.65, Goodenough, 'Philosophy of Kingship', p. 89.
[125] Plutarch, *Mor.* 782A.

'just so he has established in states the light of justice and of knowledge of himself as an image . . .' (Fowler, Loeb, p. 65)

'so he has established in the state the effulgence of high justice and of his attendant Logos like a picture . . .' (Goodenough, p. 96)

Notwithstanding all this, Goodenough is clearly correct in his central point that the description of the King as being the state's λόγος, or mind, or soul, or Animate Law, or head, clearly does carry through from Hellenistic political philosophy into the ideas commonly linked to the Roman Emperor. We have seen it in the Seneca quotation above. Goodenough also has a useful contemporary piece from Musonius Rufus on Kingship (and hence presumably on the Emperor):

> . . . the good king must be sinless . . . since he must be what the ancients call Animate Law (ἔμψυχος νόμος), creating a law-abiding spirit and unanimity, and thrusting out lawlessness and strife . . .[126]

This kind of thinking was known in at least some Hellenistic Jewish circles, as G. F. Chesnut has shown in citing Philo who, in presenting Moses as the image of an ideal king, describes him too as νόμος ἔμψυχος.[127] Any of these descriptions of the position of the king can, as for example the Musonius quotation shows, have as one corollary the bringing of harmony in the body of which he is the head.

The ideal king brings harmony. The Emperor brings harmony. For the provincial, such as Philo, this means inter-ethnic harmony brought about by submission to a single head. It is this harmony that legitimates the Emperor's rule over the provinces. In Philippians 2.10 we have submission to a single head. Does this show Jesus carrying out, on a universal scale, the Emperor's central saving task, that of bringing harmony through universal submission?

I am not sure. It depends on whether verse 10 carries an idea of salvation for the Cosmos. However, one factor in favour of the idea that there is salvation in verse 10 is the allusion to Isaiah 45.23.

---

[126] Stob. IV, vii, 67, tr. Goodenough, 'Philosophy of Kingship', p. 94.
[127] Philo, *Vita Mos.* i, 162; Glenn F. Chesnut, 'The Ruler and the Logos in Neopythagorean, Middle Platonic and Late Stoic Political Philosophy', *ANRW 17.2* (Berlin: Walter de Gruyter, 1978), p. 1327.

e.   The use of Isaiah 45 in 2.10–11

There is no doubt that verses 10–11 cite the LXX of Isaiah 45.23.
The verse reads

... ἐμοὶ κάμψει πᾶν γόνυ καὶ ἐξομολογήσεται πᾶσα
γλῶσσα τῷ θεῷ

There is a textual question over ἐξομολογήσεται in LXX. Kreitzer
follows B and ℵ* in preferring ὀμεῖται, in line with the Masoretic
Text. He suggests that the author of Philippians 2.10–11 may have
substituted ἐξομολογήσεται for ὀμεῖται because of the liturgical,
confessional nature of the 'hymn'.[128] However, Fee's arguments,
for taking ἐξομολογήσεται (as in A, Q and ℵᶜ) as original to the
text of LXX that Paul read seem convincing. Paul uses ἐξομολογήσεται when quoting the same text in a different context in Romans
14.11. The transposition of πᾶσα γλῶσσα to before ἐξομολογήσεται suggests that Alexandrinus is not an adaptation to Paul,
whereas ὀμεῖται could easily be an adaptation to the MT. Fee
thinks that the reading, ὀμεῖται, was created in Origen's Hexapla.[129]

Paul (or the author of the passage, if someone else) is definitely
citing Isaiah 45.23. The question is what he is saying by doing so in
this way. Given my evidence so far, I was naturally driven to ask
whether Paul was using Isaiah 45.23 because its terminology
coincided with that used in imperial acclamations. I looked at the
phrases γόνυ κάμψῃ and ἐξομολογήσεται ὅτι.

Given how natural an expression for submission κάμπτω γόνυ
appears to be, given its use for reverent submission in LXX (the
term covers actions performed in a variety of contexts: it can be
used in preparation for thanksgiving (1 Chron. 29.20) as well as for
petition) and given the frequency of both γόνυ and κάμπτω in
secular Greek, it is a great surprise that the phrase does not appear
to be used for submission or worship in secular Greek. The only
usage of the two words together is as an expression meaning 'to sit
down and rest'.[130]

Traps abound in this area. Going down on one's knees, as an

[128] Larry J. Kreitzer, '"When He at Last is First!": Philippians 2:9–11', in Ralph
P. Martin and Brian J. Dodd, eds., *Where Christology Began: Essays on Philippians 2*
(Louisville: Westminster John Knox, 1998), p. 120.
[129] Fee, p. 223 n. 28.
[130] See H. G. Liddell and R. Scott, *Greek-English Lexicon*, revd H. S. Jones
(Oxford: Clarendon Press, 1940, 1968) and H. Schlier, *TDNT III*, both on κάμπτω.

action, is used in pleas for mercy. Vercingetorix, πεσὼν ... ἐς γόνω, begs for mercy from Caesar (Dio Cass. 40.41.2). Herod's various sons have occasion to do the same, both from Herod (Jos. *Ant.* 17.94) and from Caesar (17.248). However, although in LXX the terrified captain ἔκαμψεν ἐπὶ τὰ γόνατα αὐτοῦ κατέναντι Ηλιου (4 Kings 1.13), the apparent interchangeability of κάμπτω and πίπτω in this LXX usage does not occur in secular Greek. The only non-LXX example seems to be *Sib. Or.* 3.616f., but this is a religious text and from second-century BC Egypt,[131] i.e., is of about the same provenance as the LXX itself. The second trap is that κάμπτομαι means 'I submit' in secular Greek[132] but this represents an entirely different conceptual area from the LXX's κάμπτω γόνυ. κάμπτομαι is the passive of a very simple metaphorical sense of κάμπτω's basic meaning, 'I bend'. Thus Plato writes ἐπειδὴ δέ σου ἀκούω ταῦτα λέγοντος, κάμπτομαι καὶ οἶμαί τί σε λέγειν: 'but when I hear you speak thus, I am swayed over, and suppose there is something in what you say'.[133]

New Testament use of κάμπτω with γόνυ is almost restricted to citation of the LXX (Rom. 11.4; 14.11). The exception is Ephesians 3.14. However, the high-flown language here seems likely to be strongly inspired by the LXX (cf. 1 Esdras 8.70). The first independent use seems to be 1 Clement 57.1, κάμψαντες τὰ γόνατα τῆς καρδίας ὑμων. Presumably the language has come into Clement's vocabulary from the NT or the LXX.

For ἐξομολογέω, as for κάμπτω, I have found no examples of its use in material on the accession of emperors. The same is true of ὁμολογέω (the prefix ἐξ- seems to emphasise the public aspect of the act, if anything[134]). The closest is the Greek text of *Res Gestae*, 6, where the Senate and people ὁμολογ(ο)ύντων, ἵνα ... χειροτον-ηθῶι ('agreed that I should be elected', tr. Shipley) as overseer of laws and morals. However, this was 11 BC and Augustus was already in power; this was an office which (in name) he declined, so ὁμολογέω cannot have constituted part of an accession here; and the grammatical construction is rather different from Philippians 2.11. The sense seems to be the common one of 'agree' rather than any idea approaching acclamation.

---

[131] J. J. Collins, 'Sibylline Oracles', *The Old Testament Pseudepigrapha, Vol. 1,* ed., J. H. Charlesworth (London: Darton, Longman & Todd, 1983), p. 355.
[132] Liddell and Scott, IV.
[133] Plato, *Prot.* 320b, tr. W. R. M. Lamb.
[134] O. Michel, ὁμολογέω, *TDNT V*, p. 204.

The LXX has various unusual religious usages in praise or penitence but in Philippians 2.11, with ὅτι, the meaning seems to be in the area which the LXX shares with secular Greek: 'admit', 'agree', 'acknowledge', 'confess'. Josephus, *Ant*. 3.332, is a good example of this use: καὶ τοὺς μισοῦντας ἡμᾶς ὁμολογεῖν, ὅτι . . . ('even our enemies admit that . . .', tr. Thackeray). As in this example, ὁμολογέω ὅτι in Josephus carries a sense of reluctance (*Ant*. 17.57; *C.Ap*. 2.224). However, it would probably be unwise to drive a wedge between the verb with and without ὅτι. Without ὅτι there are examples of willing, even volunteered acknowledgement, most notably the crowd's fatal call to Herod Agrippa I, '. . . τοὐντεῦθεν κρείττονά σε θνητῆς φύσεως ὁμολογοῦμεν' ('. . . henceforth we agree that you are more than mortal in your being', *Ant*. 19.345, tr. L. H. Feldman).

We can conclude that, while πᾶν γόνυ κάμψῃ and πᾶσα γλῶσσα ἐξομολογήσηται are very suitable for describing reactions to an Imperial figure, Paul has not chosen them because they coincide with material about the Emperor. Although suggestive of the Emperor, the language is purely that of the LXX.

The LXX of Isaiah 45 reads,

[20]συνάχθητε καὶ ἥκετε, βουλεύσασθε ἅμα, οἱ σῳζόμενοι ἀπὸ τῶν ἐθνῶν. οὐκ ἔγνωσαν οἱ αἴροντες τὸ ξύλον γλύμμα αὐτῶν καὶ προσευχόμενοι ὡς πρὸς θεούς, οἳ οὐ σῴζουσιν.

[21]. . . τότε ἀνηγγέλη ὑμῖν Ἐγὼ ὁ θεός, καὶ οὐκ ἔστιν ἄλλος πλὴν ἐμοῦ· δίκαιος καὶ σωτὴρ οὐκ ἔστιν πάρεξ ἐμοῦ.

[22]ἐπιστράφητε πρός με καὶ σωθήσεσθε, οἱ ἀπ᾽ ἐσχάτου τῆς γῆς· ἐγώ εἰμι ὁ θεός, καὶ οὐκ ἔστιν ἄλλος.

[23]. . . ἐμοὶ κάμψει πᾶν γόνυ καὶ ἐξομολογήσεται πᾶσα γλῶσσα τῷ θεῷ

[24]λέγων Δικαιοσύνη καὶ δόξα πρὸς αὐτὸν ἥξουσιν, καὶ αἰσχυνθήσονται πάντες οἱ ἀφορίζοντες ἑαυτούς·

[25]ἀπὸ κυρίου δικαιωθήσονται καὶ ἐν τῷ θεῷ ἐνδοξασθήσονται πᾶν τὸ σπέρμα τῶν υἱῶν Ισραηλ.

Israel are in exile under the Babylonian empire. Isaiah encourages and exhorts the exiles by portraying Israel's God, the only God, on a throne with all the nations streaming to him and bowing down to him. They submit to God and worship God. They acknowledge him as the only one who can rescue. All other gods are futile. Babylon's gods and Babylon's emperor are shown to be powerless.

How much of this does Paul use? How much would the Philippians hear? At least the unusual phrase γόνυ κάμψη would be likely to make the passage sound scriptural. Given that, many might realise that in Scripture the bowing would be to God. In Philippians 2.9–11 God stays in the picture. God grants Jesus the authority (verse 9) and God receives the glory (verse 11). The Philippians might well realise that a scriptural vision of all coming to bow before God is being fulfilled by means of all bowing to Christ. God reigns and receives honour through Christ's reigning and receiving honour.[135] With Paul we are on more secure ground than with his hearers. He knew the passage in Isaiah (cf. Rom. 14.11) and presumably believed that God's plan expressed in that text in Isaiah was being fulfilled through Christ.

But which of two pictures predominates? We could see the worship of Revelation 6, as Richard Bauckham suggests.[136] Alternatively, we could see the subject peoples of a conquering emperor coming to swear allegiance. Bauckham argues that, in the case of God, the acknowledgement of his ultimate authority is actually the foundation of worship.[137] Indeed, in Isaiah 45.23 submission and worship cannot be distinguished from one another. Bauckham argues that the universal submission to Christ makes Christ the object of worship.[138] Simon Price links worship and submission in the provincial attitude to the Roman emperors. The rituals of the imperial cult expressed the Greeks' acts of locating the power of the Emperor in their picture of the Universe.[139] The bowing to Jesus conveys universal submission and that presumably does carry an idea of worship. However, I do not think that the main significance of 2.9–11 is cultic. In particular, I do not think that parallels with

---

[135] Richard Bauckham, 'The Worship of Jesus', in Ralph P. Martin and Brian J. Dodd, eds., *Where Christology Began: Essays on Philippians 2* (Louisville: Westminster John Knox, 1998), pp. 133–4. Kreitzer has recently drawn attention to ways in which 2.11 makes the passage end on a note that carries something of subordination in it: 'When He at Last is First!', p. 121.

[136] Bauckham, 'Worship of Jesus', p. 131.

[137] Ibid., p. 129.

[138] Ibid., p. 130.

[139] Price, *Rituals and Power*, pp. 25, 29f., 248.

the Emperor in the passage would specifically refer to the imperial cult.[140] Submission to God, Christ or the Emperor has areas of significance beyond liturgy. For Christ to be on the Isaianic throne receiving the submission of not just the nations but all the Cosmos would imply worship. But it would imply authority of every other kind too. As the Philippians heard the text they might get caught up in worship of Christ. But, faced with the crisis reflected in 1.27–2.4, they would also see Christ's authority as having social and political consequences. In Christ, God's project of putting the right authority in place over the Cosmos had come to fruition. The social and political authorities, under whom the Philippian Christians faced the social pressures that threatened perseverance and unity, had been relativised by Christ. Christ, not the Emperor, was now the true figure of authority. Not only worship but the key imperatives for living each day were changed by this.

If the Philippians knew the Isaianic context, as they might if this kind of eschatology was part of Paul's general teaching, then they would know that the imperial figure there is also a saviour. This would then also support the possibility of Christ being heard as carrying out the imperial saving task of bringing harmony by submission to him.

f.   The naming in verse 9

The giving of the names *Augustus* and *Pater Patriae* was a vital part of the process of accession of an emperor. These names were exclusive to the Emperor in this period, clearly distinguishing him from any co-regent.[141] The earliest point at which they were shared was under Marcus Aurelius, with his introduction of the double principate. There was an earlier sharing of a substantial name under Vespasian, who accorded to Titus the *praenomen imperatoris* while he remained only a co-regent.[142] However, this is still too late for our letter. In Roman political terms, in the Julio-Claudian period, the 'name above every name' could only belong to the Emperor himself.

Clearly, there are alternative possibilities within the Jewish tradi-

---

[140] Seeley, 'Background', p. 10, cites evidence that bowing was not a standard feature of the imperial cult. However, Seeley's ideas of what Caligula wanted to happen in the cult seem unlikely to have been sufficiently prominent in Philippian thinking for their minds to have turned to the cult because of Caligula when they heard the description of the scene from Isaiah 45.

[141] Parsi, *Désignation*, p. 41.

[142] Ibid., pp. 55–9.

tion. In particular, there is the exalted naming in the Enochic material but, while these traditions could well affect the writer of 2.5–11, we have little reason to suppose that they were likely to be familiar to Philippian hearers. However, many Philippians must have had some familiarity with the OT and so could well hear in verse 9 some connection with the name of God. In the LXX tradition, of course, this means a connection with the title κύριος,[143] which appears in verse 11. The title κύριος itself, however, was likely to provide a further link back to the Emperor.

g. The title κύριος

From an Imperial point of view, κύριος is a very interesting title to crop up in 2.11. It seems to represent not an officially promulgated title – *dominus* seems to have been resisted at this period (Suet. *Caesar*, 53)[144] – but a name used by ordinary Greek-speaking people. It is mainly testified to by ostraca and papyri giving a date for something:

> ζ (ἔτους) Τιβερίου Κλαυδίου Καίσαρος τοῦ κυρίου (P. Oxy. I.37.5f.)

> Νέρωνος τοῦ κυρίου (P. Oxy. II.246)

> τοῦ κυρίου Νέρωνος Κλαυδίου Καίσαρος Σεβαστοῦ Γερμανικοῦ Αὐτοκράτορος. (P. Lond. 280, 6)[145]

Popular usage of this kind is more relevant evidence for the NT than is official or literary usage. Turning, however, to the former we do have the interesting inscription to ὁ τοῦ παντὸς κόσμου κύριος Νέρων.[146] In literature we have an example of κύριος as one of the titles with which an Emperor was acclaimed (Dio Cass. 72.20.2)[147] but this is from a much later time (of Commodus) when *dominus* had come into Imperial use.[148] It would therefore be incorrect to see this as evidence of the title's use in first-century acclamations. Furthermore, the conclusion that verse 11 cannot represent the acclamation of the Emperor by the people of Rome, which constituted part of Imperial accession, is reinforced by the

---

[143] O'Brien, pp. 237f.
[144] Cited by Foerster, κύριος, p. 1056.
[145] All three cited by Foerster, κύριος, pp. 1054f.
[146] Ditt. *Syll.*³ no. 814, 31. See above.
[147] Foerster, κύριος, p. 1056 n. 76.
[148] Béranger, *Recherches*, pp. 61ff.

use of Isaiah 45. The context in Isaiah precludes the idea of those who are 'confessing' having any role in the election of the figure on the throne.

In contrast with κάμπτω and ἐξομολογέω, κύριος is an example where central LXX terminology probably coincides with a common term connected with the Emperor. However, the title is not a *novum* in Philippians 2 but must have already been familiar to the Philippians as a title attributed to Christ. Any special significance in a particular use of it must therefore come from the context. The immediate context here is both heavily Septuagintal and heavily Imperial. This seems an occasion when the title could be heard with strong connotations in both areas. If hearers missed the connotations in one of the areas then, for most of the Philippians, it seems more likely to be the Septuagintal connotations which would go unnoticed.

h. A leader who defines his people's ethics by example

Goodenough cites the Hellenistic philosopher Philolaus for the point that, just as the Universe is an expression of the activity of God, 'In the same way the state here is a product of the character of the king'. The king creates and shapes his state and he is what holds it together: he is its creative law.[149] This kind of idea is another, central aspect of seeing the king as the λόγος, mind, head, etc., of the state. Archytas of Tarentum held that 'laws are of two kinds, the animate (ἔμψυχος) law, which is the king, and the inanimate, the written law'.[150]

The king, of course, shaped the state by making laws and taking other actions which his power enabled. However, many writers emphasise particularly a second means of shaping, namely, by example. Diotogenes shows both elements of this pattern:

> . . . the king should harmonize together the well lawed city like a lyre. Knowing that the harmony of the multitude whose leadership God has given him ought to be attuned to himself, the king would begin by fixing in his own life the most just limitations and order of law. And besides issuing public decrees the good king should present to the state proper attitudes in body and mind.

[149] Goodenough, 'Philosophy of Kingship', p. 69; see Stob. I, 20. 2.
[150] Goodenough, 'Philosophy of Kingship', p. 59.

> So will he succeed in putting into order those who look upon him, amazed at his majesty, at his self-control, and his fitness for distinction. For to look upon the good king ought to affect the souls of those who see him no less than a flute or harmony.[151]

There are clear instances of the idea of example from the early imperial period:

> But just as a rule, if it is made rigid and inflexible makes other things straight when they are fitted to it and laid alongside it, in like manner the sovereign must first gain command of himself, must regulate his own soul and establish his own character, then make his subjects fit his pattern. (Plutarch, *Ad Principem Ineruditum*, 780B, tr. H. N. Fowler)

> . . . fair play has now precedence over influence, and merit over ambition, for the best of emperors teaches his citizens to do right by doing it, and though he is greatest among us in authority, he is still greater in the example which he sets. (Velleius Paterculus, 2.126.4, on Tiberius)

> We are pleased to hope and trust, Caesar, that in large measure this will happen. That kindness of your heart will be recounted, will be diffused little by little throughout the whole body of the empire, and all things will be moulded into your likeness. It is from the head that comes the health of the body . . . (Seneca, *De Clem.* 2.2.1, on Nero)

It is inevitably much more difficult to trace the pervasiveness of ideas such as these than it is for the previous ideas in this chapter. The other ideas tended to have some expression in public presentation of imperial ideology – through coins, inscriptions, etc. For the idea of example, we are rather limited to élite literary sources. One appeal that we can make is to the general first-century concept of leaders as example. This concept is displayed particularly prominently in the Pauline churches. Another appeal is to the general tendency of first-century groups to imitate others. For example, there is the way in which the institutions and patterns of behaviour of *collegia* followed those of the city, which followed those of Rome.

---

[151] Stob. IV, 7.62, tr. Goodenough, 'Philosophy of Kingship', p. 71f.

I think it is safe to say that, while the degree of regard for the idea of the Emperor as example will have varied sharply across the social spectrum, the concept that he was supposed to be a defining example, as Seneca and others argue, was probably very widespread and probably familiar to many in the Philippian church.

We need then to ask whether the Philippians are likely to have heard Christ as example in 2.5–11. This is involved with more general questions of the exegesis of the passage and will be deferred to the next chapter..If Christ is heard as example, this, of course, need not mean that he is compared with the Emperor. However, the Emperor would seem to provide a familiar figure who, precisely in his unique acts, acted as example for his people. This would then seem a background against which the Philippians could comfortably hear Christ as example.

4. Conclusions

Various of the Philippian hearers are bound not to have picked up various of the points noted in my arguments. I think that most hearers were Greeks and certainly do not expect that they would have read Seneca. However, Imperial ideology was all around: on coins, in statues, in processions, games and feasts, in pictures and in inscriptions. We know the text of Augustus' official autobiography, his *Res Gestae*, in Greek as well as in Latin because the entire book was inscribed in Greek on the outside of the Imperial cult temple at Ankyra. Sections of the text have also been found in various other places.

Whatever they would have made of the details of verses 9–11, the hearers are likely to have heard the Imperial shape of the events, i.e., at their most basic level: raised to power on account of deeds, universal submission, universal acclamation as Lord. This shape fits an Imperial figure much more closely than it does any other figure. Furthermore, if they did hear such a socio-political comparison being made with Christ, this would seem much more relevant to the concerns immediately being addressed in chapter 2, than would any purely religious comparison. We must now look at these concerns.

6

CHRIST AND THE PHILIPPIANS

My reading of both the situation in the Philippian church and the letter as Paul's response to that situation centres on the themes of suffering and unity. These themes are intertwined in 1.27–2.4 in particular. Paul then throws into this mesh the weighty contribution of 2.5–11 (and the following argument to 2.18). Probably the key test for my account of suffering and unity in Philippians is, therefore, the way in which it handles the issue of the relationship between suffering and unity in 1.27–2.4 and the way in which it sees 2.5–11 as addressing the agenda of the preceding passage.

Various scholars have, however, argued either that the issues of suffering and unity in 1.27–2.4 are not connected, or that one of them is not an actual problem at Philippi. Geoffrion sees unity as not an issue in its own right but a standard element of a call to stand firm. He sees the passage as reflecting, in particular, calls for the citizens of a Greek *polis* to stand against external attack. Central to these is a call for the citizens to band together. The same is true of calls addressed to Greek armies.[1] However, Geoffrion's view does not fit the intensity of Paul's rhetoric. The passion with which he calls for unity in 2.1–4 suggests that unity itself must be an issue in the church at Philippi. The issue may, as I have argued, stem from a situation of suffering, but it must be an actual issue rather than a topic brought in simply because it is a standard part of a call to stand firm. The rhetoric is too focused for that to be the case.

Mengel argues that the issues of suffering and unity cannot be shown to be connected. His target is probably Lohmeyer's view that an idea of the perfection of the martyr was producing pride among those who had suffered heavily and was thus splitting the

---

[1] Geoffrion, *Rhetorical Purpose*, pp. 24, 36, 65, 105, 111f.

church.[2] Mengel's criticism of Lohmeyer seems correct. It is not likely to be early martyrological ideas that are producing disunity. It is more likely to be a result of the concrete pressures of suffering. However, Mengel's conclusion that suffering and unity are not connected seems incorrect. He himself comments on how closely entangled is the material on suffering and unity[3] and it is difficult to see how he can avoid connecting them.

In Collange's approach, the language about suffering in 1.27–30 is accounted for by a dispute about the place of suffering in Christianity rather than by actual suffering at Philippi.[4] This has been criticised above. The passage reads much more naturally as one in which actual suffering is taking place – suffering about which Paul needs to give interpretative comment (and to deal with problems). However, we must go some way with Collange since Christians at Philippi must have had differing views on the place of suffering in the Christian life.

The intertwining of suffering and unity in 1.27–2.4 can be seen in the pattern of the passage and its context: Paul's suffering (1.12–26); stand firm under opposition, united (verses 27–8); the Philippians' suffering (verse 29); Paul's suffering (verse 30); be united (2.1–4); Christ's suffering (verse 8); do not have disputes (verse 14); suffering of Paul and the Philippians (verses 17–18). Although the theme of suffering runs through every part of the letter (see chapter 3, above), and must therefore be vital to the understanding of it, when the theme comes in this central appeal, it is heavily surrounded by calls to unity. The practical outcome of standing firm under suffering is intended to be precisely unity.

So, one issue to be tackled is the way in which the main practical outworking of the call to stand firm under suffering is a call to unity. The other issue to be tackled is the way in which Christ's example of loss of status and obedient suffering (see below), and the depiction of Christ raised to the position of universal Lord, are brought in by Paul as appropriate means of adding weight to the call to unity – and maybe also to the call to stand firm. It is not immediately obvious how Christ's example relates to unity. Clearly

---

[2] Lohmeyer, p. 4; Berthold Mengel, *Studien zum Philipperbrief: Untersuchungen zum situativen Kontext unter besonderer Berücksichtigung der Frage nach der Ganzheitlichkeit oder Einheitlichkeit eines paulinischen Briefes* (WUNT 2:8; Tübingen: J. C. B. Mohr, 1982), pp. 244f., 249f., 291.

[3] Mengel, *Studien*, pp. 249f.

[4] Collange, pp. 11, 72f., 75f.

verses 3–4 are important, but in what way? Should, for example, obedient suffering be linked in some way to considering the interests of others? Why bring Christ's Lordship in at all? We need to consider whether the view of Philippians, people and letter, for which I have been arguing, provides convincing solutions to these questions.

1. The shape of the appeal in 2.1–4

The first issue to be considered with regard to 2.1–4 is probably the meaning of the word πολιτεύεσθε, in 1.27, which can influence the reading of the verses. Bruce Winter has recently introduced a more nuanced way of trying to maintain something of the πολιτ-concept in the word. He does adopt R. R. Brewer's translation, 'live as citizens', but sees the central concept not in being a πολίτης but in living in πολιτεία.[5] He sees πολιτεία as 'the whole of life in the public domain of a city, in contrast to private existence in a household'. This public domain was particularly to do with the local council, assembly and law-courts.[6] Winter's main concern is over civil litigation as a means of social manoeuvring by church members but he does draw the boundaries of πολιτεία widely enough to allow it to include criminal court action. He writes of the troubles that Paul experienced in Philippi 'in the legal area of *politeia* (Acts 16.19ff.)' and of Christ who submitted himself 'to condemnation and death in *politeia* before a Roman court'.[7]

I wonder, then, whether Winter's research can be used to support a reading of πολιτεύεσθε as an instruction to do with the church's existence in the public life of Philippian society – 'public life' interpreted broadly enough to cover all the Christians' dealings with outsiders, although maybe particularly those with people such as magistrates. In that case, verse 27a acts as a natural heading for the material in verses 27–8 on standing firm under external opposition.

Such a reading of the term would seem to have the advantage over most of the other suggested options. 'Live as a good πολίτης of Philippi' would probably not fit most of the hearers since they

---

[5] Winter, *Seek the Welfare*, p. 82.
[6] Ibid., pp. 2, 93, the latter citing C. P. Jones, *The Roman World of Dio Chrysostom* (Cambridge, Mass.: Harvard University Press, 1978), p. 99.
[7] Winter, *Seek the Welfare*, pp. 98, 99.

would not have been citizens. 'Live as citizens of heaven'[8] looks, from the point of view of a first hearing of the passage, like an illegitimate import from 3.20 (πολιτεύεσθε would, however, seem likely to have carried overtones of this on later hearings). 'Live in community', referring to the communal dimension of life in the local church,[9] again seems to import an unexpected referent for the πολιτ- element of the word. Surely the πολιτ- element would be normally heard as about either life in Philippi, or public life in general, rather than life in the church? E. C. Miller's redefined Jewish usage, with the Gospel as a new law replacing Torah, seems very unlikely to be heard by Gentile Philippians.[10] Straight synonymity of πολιτεύομαι with περιπατέω[11] must be a possibility but Paul's use does look rather pointed.

Moving on from πολιτεύεσθε, we need to consider the effect on 2.1–4 of the anticipation of the theme of unity in 1.27b and, possibly, in 1.28. The unity theme is first raised explicitly with the verbs of struggle here: στήκετε ἐν ἑνὶ πνεύματι, μιᾷ ψυχῇ συναθλοῦντες . . . As O'Brien argues, ἐν ἑνὶ πνεύματι should probably be taken as synonymous with μιᾷ ψυχῇ and, thus, be read as a reference to humans rather than to the Holy Spirit.[12]

Two consequences for the theme of unity seem to follow from its introduction in 1.27f. First, it is unity for action. The Christians are called not simply to be united but to work unitedly for the Gospel. Given the note of struggle (συναθλοῦντες) and the topic of fear (πτυρόμενοι) which is introduced here, the Philippians seem quite likely to hear a comparison with the situation around Paul, where the Christians τολμ[ῶσιν] ἀφόβως τὸν λόγον λαλεῖν (1.14). Hence, the action to which they are likely to hear themselves called would be some sort of public witness for the Gospel. If there was danger simply in maintaining unity with those suffering, then there would be far more in joining them in the kind of public witness that the dynamics of 1.12–18 make clear to have been happening around Paul. In fact, whether or not 1.27f. refers to evangelism, it must surely envisage a willingness to be seen, in the public sphere, to stand alongside suffering sisters and brothers. The second conse-

---

[8] O'Brien, p. 145.

[9] Beare, pp. 66f., takes this type of line.

[10] E. C. Miller, 'Πολιτεύεσθε in Philippians 1.27: Some Philological and Thematic Observations', *JSNT* 15 (1982), pp. 86–96.

[11] See the discussion in Geoffrion, *Rhetorical Purpose*, p. 43.

[12] O'Brien, p. 150.

quence is that the unity is precisely in the context of opposition. In unity there is the need to stand firm, to strive, not to be panicked by the opponents (πτύρομαι seems quite likely to carry the connotation of being panicked into disorder and disunity[13]). Since unity is presented in the context of external opposition, the probability is increased both that it was heard, and that it was intended, to fit problems of disunity which were actually caused by opposition.

Philippians 1.28–30 also raises the topic of suffering and salvation, which we have discussed above. The verses carry an assurance that the way of suffering is actually the way – the only way indicated – of safety. The hearers of the dangerous calls of 2.3–4 (and 6–8) would hear those calls with the reassurance of 1.28–30 already in their minds. Philippians 1.30 ought also to link them back to taking Paul's attitude to suffering, in 1.12–26, as a model for theirs.

On 2.1, Beare writes, 'Paul now appears to be casting around for any and every kind of thought, feeling, and Christian experience to which he may appeal, that may move them to respond to his plea for unity.'[14] As Beare implies, the rhetoric is very intense. However, the ideas invoked by Paul might not be random. The first three clauses, with their . . . Χριστῷ . . . ἀγάπης . . . κοινωνία πνεύματος, are reminiscent of the concluding formula in 2 Corinthians 13.13, giving a rather Trinitarian feel to the set.[15] This would be appropriate since Paul seems to be trying to encompass the range of God's goodness experienced by the Philippians. I agree with Beare that it is possible that, after the trio, 'mercy and compassion' might slip out of the parallelism and be an appeal to Philippians possessing such qualities.[16] However, they too could be interpreted in terms of benefits from God.[17] I disagree with Beare when he effectively prevents verse 1a being a straightforward benefit by translating παράκλησις as 'exhortation'.[18] O'Brien argues that 'consolation' or 'comfort' is by far the most frequent sense of the noun, παράκλησις, in Paul.[19] It also seems best to maintain the parallelism of at least the first three clauses as describing benefits

[13] See Geoffrion, *Rhetorical Purpose*, pp. 66ff., for a discussion of the term.
[14] Beare, p. 70.
[15] Fee, p. 179.
[16] Beare, p. 71.
[17] O'Brien, p. 176.
[18] Beare, p. 70.
[19] O'Brien, p. 170.

received by the Philippians. This, too, suggests we read παράκλησις as 'consolation'.

For benefits received to be a motive to grateful action is natural in any culture and was particularly so in Graeco-Roman culture. The receipt of a gift tied one into a relationship with strong mutual obligations.[20] The acknowledgement of gifts from God should produce obedience not only out of gratitude but also because of a moral obligation that acceptance of God's gifts involves. Philippians 2.1 thus provides a very powerful foundation for the rhetoric of verses 2–4.

More specifically, someone who had heard the motivating argument of 2.1 would, in the first instance, expect that Paul was going to appeal to them to provide παράκλησις, παραμύθιον and κοινωνία, and to demonstrate σπλάγχνα καὶ οἰκτιρμοί. We would thus expect the appeal following the verse to be directed at people in a position to help certain others and to be a call for that help. This provides support for my view that economic suffering is a key element of the problems over unity faced by the Philippians. In contrast, suggestions that the disunity at issue in 2.1–4 is a more general church problem, such as a doctrinal dispute or a leadership struggle, seem not to pick up on the specific form of the rhetoric of 2.1.

Philippians 2.2a, πληρώσατέ μου τὴν χαρὰν, provides a further motive which is probably very similar to that of gratitude and obligation in 2.1. Again, the Philippians would probably feel that they were involved in the obligations of a relationship established through receiving benefits. This time, the relationship is with Paul. It goes unstated, as such, but is capable of carrying some of the force of the explicit argument of the σεαυτόν μοι προσοφείλεις of Philemon 19. There must be doubt, however, over whether the hearers would have responded to verse 2a in terms of obligation or simply affection. Their relationship with Paul seems to have been such that they would have wanted to give him joy because of their love for him. The specifics of verse 2 raise the issue of whether we ought to be placing it somewhere within the theme of Paul's joy in the letter. Paul's two weightiest expressions of joy (1.17; 2.17) are

---

[20] S. C. Mott, 'The Power of Giving and Receiving: Reciprocity in Hellenistic Benevolence', in G. F. Hawthorne, ed., *Current Issues in Biblical and Patristic Interpretation (Studies in Honour of Merril C. Tenney)* (Grand Rapids: Eerdmans, 1975).

both in the context of his suffering. However, it is unclear how this might affect our exegesis.

The rest of 2.2 consists of the four-fold exhortation to unity. If the four clauses carry an idea apart from unity, it would seem to be in a direction similar to that established by the theme of unity being introduced in 1.27, namely, as unity in a common purpose.[21] They may, however, not carry this idea since τὸ αὐτὸ φρονεῖν, at least, is a standard friendship-term.[22] Paul would then simply be piling up expressions about unity.

Such unity would itself be opposed by imperatives of Graeco-Roman society if, as was surely usually the case, a church covered a broad social range. Alan Mitchell argues, in the case of Acts 2.44–7 and 4.32–7, that 'Luke's appeal to friendship challenges the reciprocity ethic. He does this by suggesting how Lucan Christians can become friends across status divisions, thereby suspending the normal conventions of friendship in their day.'[23] We are in a methodologically difficult area here, that of looking for NT parallels to contemporary conventions and then arguing that the NT passage differs from the very convention which it is claimed to parallel. Such work is not necessarily doomed to failure (which is a good thing, since one could argue that, in principle, such work is the essence of New Testament scholarship!). It does, however, easily invite criticism. Bormann argues that conventions on 'friendship' are irrelevant, being an élite concept,[24] but this argument wears thin at the upper end of the social range in the church. Such people, even if few were themselves of élite status, must have been close enough to the ideas of the élite to have known the general shape of a major social concept such as the idea of friendship.[25] For such people, Paul's language in 2.2 would seem likely to carry a message that he was not merely instructing them, say, to take on poorer Christians as clients, but to go beyond that to a relationship which they would previously have only had with their own peers.

[21] Collange, pp. 78f.

[22] L. Michael White, 'Morality Between Two Worlds: A Paradigm of Friendship in Philippians', in D. L. Balch, E. Ferguson and W. Meeks, eds., *Greeks, Romans and Christians (Essays in Honour of A. J. Malherbe)* (Minneapolis: Fortress Press, 1990), p. 210.

[23] Alan C. Mitchell, 'The Social Function of Friendship in Acts 2:44–47 and 4:32–37', *JBL* 111:2 (Summer 1992), p. 259.

[24] Bormann, *Philippi*, p. 170.

[25] Aristotle, *Nicomachean Ethics*, VIII. Some outline of ideas resembling these seems likely to have been very widespread in Graeco-Roman society.

Of course, this issue must have arisen when Paul first established a church. It must, however, have needed reiterating periodically because – irrespective of whether suffering was present in the church, but especially if it was – there would be social pressures acting against this kind of unity.

Translating ἐριθεία (2.3) is a difficult task because the evidence on it is very limited. F. Büchsel argues that its basic meaning is 'the manner of a day-labourer (ἔριθος)', from which it developed pejorative senses in the area of self-interested activity.[26] Bruce Winter, on the other hand, takes κατ᾽ ἐριθείαν (2.3) as meaning 'through factions'.[27] His translation would not sit very naturally with my reading of 2.1–4.

Winter captures both the location of most of the evidence and its ambiguity by saying that ἐριθεία 'carries a variety of meanings in *politeia*',[28] i.e., to do with public life. In *Politics*, V, 2, Aristotle writes:

μεταβάλλουσι δ᾽ αἱ πολιτεῖαι καὶ ἄνευ στάσεως διά τε τὰς ἐριθείας, ὥσπερ ἐν Ἡραίᾳ (ἐξ αἱρετῶν γὰρ διὰ τοῦτο ἐποίησαν κληρωτὰς ὅτι ᾑροῦντο τοὺς ἐριθευομένους), καὶ δι᾽ ὀλιγωρίαν, ὅταν . . .

And revolutions in constitutions take place even without factious strife, owing to *election intrigue*, as at Heraea (for they made their magistrates elected by lot instead of by vote for this reason, because the people used to elect *those who canvassed*); and also owing to carelessness, when . . .[29]

In various other references (usually to verbal forms), it is difficult to work out quite the attitude that is attacked using the term ἐριθεία. It is certainly a fault among leaders or citizens[30] but whether, in these texts, the fault is simply self-interest, or whether it covers political manoeuvring or action on behalf of a faction, is hard to tell. The unexpected nature of the directions in which the word's development could go is shown by Symmachus' use (*c.* AD 200) of the term in translating עֶגְבָה (lust) in Ezekiel. 23.11. He also

---

[26] F. Büchsel, ἐριθεία, *TDNT II*, ed. G. Kittel, tr. G. Bromiley (Grand Rapids: Eerdmans, 1964), pp. 660–1.

[27] Winter, *Seek the Welfare*, p. 98.

[28] Ibid., p. 95.

[29] Aristotle, *Pol.* V, 2.1303a, 13ff., tr. H. Rackham. I have italicised Rackham's translations of ἐριθεία and its related verb. Cf. *Pol.* V, 2.1302b, 4.

[30] Philo, *De Legatione ad Gaium*, 68; Polybius, X, 22.9; Ditt. *Syll.*³ no. 526 n. 8.

used the verbal forms (with and without προσ–) to translate the related verb in verses 5, 9, 12.[31] Büchsel concludes his study by drawing attention to οἱ ἐξ ἐριθείας in Romans 2.8. There, it cannot mean 'faction'. He thinks that it probably refers to those 'who think only of immediate gain'.[32] He then applies this meaning in all the other NT occurrences. In particular, it 'is better than strife or contention in Phil. 2.3 [given verses 3–4 as a whole]. For this reason, it is best to understand ἐριθεία as "base self-seeking", or simply as "baseness", the nature of those who cannot lift their gaze to higher things.'[33]

This idea then has the advantage of matching the οἱ τὰ ἐπίγεια φρονοῦντες in 3.19. Whether or not we should follow Büchsel's line, it seems safe to assert that the term ἐριθεία (and also the term κενοδοξία, about which there is very little evidence indeed[34]) cannot be used as a substantial argument against a view of the passage as being linked to economic suffering. In fact, as Büchsel noted, the meaning of the unclear terms, ἐριθεία and κενοδοξία, ought to be considered in the light of the clearer, contrasting clause, τῇ ταπεινοφροσύνῃ ἀλλήλους ἡγούμενοι ὑπερέχοντας ἑαυτῶν.[35] This would seem to emphasise the possibilities of ἐριθεία as 'being concerned with one's own (social) advantage', and κενοδοξία as 'pride in one's high (social) position'.

Possibly the sharpest question in our discussion of 2.1–4 is that of the sphere in which the self-lowering involved in ταπεινοφροσύνη operates. Is it, for example, intellectual, with the call being to defer to each other in matters of opinion? Otto Merk has suggested that the sphere is that of social status.[36] This fits the surrounding text well. The action called for in verses 2–4 is social, not intellectual. I have argued (in chapter 3, above) that the action needed in first-generation Christian communities to tackle problems of economic suffering would carry both a risk of being seen as acting below one's status and a risk of actual loss of status. Part

[31] Origen, *Hexapla, in loc.*
[32] Büchsel, ἐριθεία, p. 661.
[33] Ibid. Cf. H. Giesen, ἐριθεία, *Exegetical Dictionary of the New Testament, Vol. 2*, ed. H. Balz and G. Schneider (ET; Grand Rapids: Eerdmans, 1991), p. 52.
[34] See, for example, the paucity of material in A. Oepke's entry on the word, κενός, *TDNT III*, ed. G. Kittel, tr. G. W. Bromiley (Grand Rapids: Eerdmans, 1965), pp. 659–62.
[35] Büchsel, ἐριθεία, p. 661 n. 14.
[36] Otto Merk, *Handeln aus Glauben: Die Motivierung der Paulinischen Ethik* (Marburger Th. St. 5; Marburg: Elwert, 1968), pp. 177f. Also, Mengel, *Studien*, p. 244; Friedrich, *in loc.*; O'Brien, tentatively, pp. 181f.

of Christ's example which reinforces the call of verses 2–4 is also, I will argue, of loss of status. Merk's suggestion also fits Graeco-Roman literary use of the term. However, as we will see, the term's use in early Christian paraenesis necessitates caution. Merk's specific exegesis of verses 3–4 is also open to question.

Klaus Wengst has undertaken a fairly full study of 'humility' in the Graeco-Roman, Jewish and early Christian contexts.[37] He sees Graeco-Roman and most OT views of humility as operating on a social axis. Both originate from being a label for those of low social position and develop various connotations from this – positive ones in the OT but almost exclusively negative ones in the Graeco-Roman literary tradition.[38] The central reason which he draws out for this difference is that, whereas the Graeco-Roman texts give a view from above (socially), the OT texts give a view from below. This, for Wengst, is a theological point rather than an accident of literary history: the view reflects God's partiality.[39] In some OT texts, those of the Wisdom Tradition, humility moves somewhat off Wengst's main social axis. Those who are rich but not violent use 'humility' to designate their modesty and gentleness.[40] In this unusual case, it is neither a property of the poor (as in the prophets and, partially, the Graeco-Roman sources) nor a moral failing of the rich people acting, inappropriately, in a manner like the poor (as in most Graeco-Roman sources).

Some of Wengst's arguments, particularly about how the term 'humility' gained connotations beyond simple social description, seem rather speculative. In writing about why the poor in Amos are 'righteous' he argues that they would not act as the violent rich do even if they could.[41] I cannot see grounds for this explanation. His general placing of 'humility' on a social axis does, however, seem to work well for OT prophetic and Graeco-Roman sources.

In the NT, there are thirty-one occurrences of ταπεινόω or related terms. Five of these refer unequivocally to low social position (Luke 1.48, 52; Rom. 12.16; Jas. 1.9, 10). On the other hand, there are three occurrences in paraenetic lists of virtues (Eph. 4.2; Col. 3.12; 1 Pet. 3.8). Although these letters are often argued to

---

[37] Klaus Wengst, *Humility: Solidarity of the Humiliated – The Transformation of an Attitude and its Social Relevance in Graeco-Roman, OT-Jewish and Early Christian Tradition*, tr. J. Bowden (London: SCM, 1988 (German 1987)).

[38] Ibid., pp. 4ff., 16ff.

[39] Ibid., p. 16 (cf. p. 4).

[40] Ibid., p. 30f., citing esp. Prov. 15.33; 18.12; 22.4; 29.23.

[41] Ibid., p. 20.

be somewhat late (a consideration with Luke too, of course), their evidence is definitely important, both because they use the ταπεινοφρο– root, whereas the previous references use only ταπεινο–, and because they are related to unity. This is particularly true of Ephesians 4, which has various links to Philippians 2 and the preceding verses:

> Παρακαλῶ οὖν ὑμᾶς ἐγὼ ὁ δέσμιος ἐν κυρίῳ ἀξίως περιπατῆσαι τῆς κλήσεως ἧς ἐκλήθητε, μετὰ πάσης ταπενοφροσύνης καὶ πραΰτητος, μετὰ μακροθυμίας, ἀνεχόμενοι ἀλλήλων ἐν ἀγάπῃ. σπουδάζοντες τηρεῖν τὴν ἑνότητα τοῦ πνεύματος ἐν τῷ συνδέσμῳ τῆς εἰρήνης. (Eph. 4.1–3)

This humility seems to represent a significant development beyond the basic social meaning, 'think (and act) in a way appropriate to those of low social status'. This is so, even if, from Judaism, one gives that a positive rather than a negative moral value. The term seems to have acquired a more general role as a virtue which is presumably to do, in some broader way, with having a modest view of oneself.

In other early Christian writing this trajectory extends much further. By the time of 1 Clement ταπεινοφροσύνη has moved a long way from possibly being a socially radical term. Wengst contrasts Clement with Paul: 'Whereas according to Phil. 2 the humiliation of Christ was the basis for comprehensive solidarity, and therefore the humility of Christians could only be reciprocal, here it becomes willingly taking one's place in the hierarchy . . .'[42]

Because of its role in early Christian paraenesis, it does not seem safe to argue that the word ταπεινοφροσύνη, on its own, would have been understood unequivocally as relating to social status held by the hearers. However, it does seem safe to argue that in a Gentile church, in the very early Christian period, the term will have held strong connotations along these lines. Given that 2.1–4 raises issues which would be a challenge in the area of social status, and given the nature of Christ's example in 2.6–8, these connotations seem likely to be prominent in the way that the verse was heard.

Merk's specific theory about the Philippian situation stems from the Graeco-Roman way of thinking in which 'die

---

[42] Ibid., p. 55. See 1 Clem. 63.1.

menschliche Qualität des Einzelnen nach seiner sozialen Stufe bestimmt wird' (the human quality of a person is determined by their social standing). This way of thinking is one 'das die Gemeindeglieder sich untereinander aufgrund ihrer sozialen Stellung menschlich disqualifizieren läßt' (that allows the members of the community to disqualify each other as human beings on account of their social position).[43] This then affects love in the church.

Merk's idea is reasonable in Graeco-Roman terms but I do not think that it is sufficiently explanatory of verses 3–4. 'Regarding others as greater than yourselves', 'looking not to your interests but also to those of each other' – these seem to be about involvement with others and about helping them practically rather than simply about removing a social concept which prevents you loving them. The focus in verses 3–4 seems not sufficiently to be on over-throwing the 'Stufenordnung' (social hierarchy), as a concept, for Merk's idea to be persuasive. This criticism is somewhat parallel to our earlier one of Collange on 1.27–30. That passage seems to be about actual suffering rather than the concept of suffering. In 2.3–4, there seems to be a call actually to endanger your status rather than to change your concept of status – although again, as with Collange, change in concept will be involved in the action. Another problem for Merk's view is the example of 2.6–8. This, however, is not surprising since Merk does not see verses 6–8 as an example.

In view of 2.4, ὑπερέχοντας ought to carry the sense of 'more important' rather than that of 'more virtuous' or 'more likely to be correct in their views'. The issue in verse 4 is not that of being willing to give up one's views on various issues in order to accept the ideas of other people in the church – as though there were a doctrinal dispute in the congregation. Nor is the issue one of deciding who will take the leading positions in the congregation (*pace* Winter[44]). The issue in verse 4 is one of help for others in the congregation.

Verse 4a is notable for the absence of an expected μόνον. The manuscript evidence suggests that 4a and 4b really are unbalanced: 'not . . . but also . . .'. If this is the right translation, then O'Brien is probably correct in seeing the καί as carrying a measure of

---

[43] Merk, *Handeln*, pp. 177f., my tr.
[44] Winter, *Seek the Welfare*, p. 99.

concession after the apparently absolute verse 4a.[45] However, Bockmuehl has recently cited persuasive parallels (e.g. Ezra 2.12 LXX) for translating as 'not . . . but rather . . .'.[46] This would leave no problem to solve. In any case, verse 4a is bound to be cast in absolute terms because τὰ ἑαυτῶν . . . σκοποῦντες is pejorative: it is not something which Paul could directly permit the Philippians to do. The obvious point of comparison is verse 21, οἱ πάντες . . . τὰ ἑαυτῶν ζητοῦσιν. Given our discussion of ἐριθεία, above, the phrase in 2.21, speaking about the people around Paul, could even be synonymous with their ἐριθεία in 1.17. In that case, the ἐριθεία forbidden to the Philippians in 2.3 could be synonymous with τὰ ἑαυτῶν σκοποῦντες in 2.4.

Various scholars have attempted to turn verse 4 in the direction of intellectual argument or of virtue.[47] However, O'Brien shows that τὰ ἑαυτῶν σκοπεῖν is synonymous with τὰ ἑαυτῶν ζητεῖν and must be handled entire, as an idiom.[48] The idiom covers seeking one's own interests in any of a variety of senses.[49] The call in verse 4 to seek not your own interests but those of each other could therefore, on the face of it, refer to any of a wide range of types of interest. However, this verse is the 'pay-off' of a call for unity in a suffering church. If, as we did in chapter 3, above, we think about the lives of the people involved, it is immediately clear that there is a kind of 'looking to the interests of each other' which is bound to be the predominantly important one, namely, the giving of mutual help, especially economic help. The shape of verses 1–4, ending with a call for considering each other's interests, combined with the passion that Paul puts into the call for unity, make it seem probable that what Paul has in mind is mutual practical help, in a situation where such practical help was vitally needed.

Paul has some knowledge of the current situation in the Philippian church: the specificity of the later reference to Euodia and Syntyche makes that clear. He knows the Philippians are suffering. When he raises the issue of their suffering he entwines it with a call to unity culminating in a call to consider each other's interests.

---

[45] O'Brien, pp. 164, 185.

[46] Bockmuehl, pp. 113f., citing J. P. Louw and E. A. Nida, *Greek-English Lexicon of the New Testament Based on Semantic Domains* (New York: United Bible Societies, 1989²), §91.11.

[47] Barth, p. 57; R. P. Martin, *Philippians* (New Century Bible; Grand Rapids: Eerdmans, 1980), p. 90.

[48] O'Brien, pp. 184f.

[49] Ibid.

Then he reinforces that call by means of a very particular retelling of the story of Christ.

2. The function of 2.6–11

Whether Paul brings in verses 6–11 from Christian tradition or composes them himself, he does so in order to address the agenda of 2.1–4 (or more broadly of 1.27–2.4). We need to consider the issue of how 2.5–11 functions in addressing that agenda. Ernst Käsemann's 1950 article, 'Kritische Analyse von Phil.2,5–11', marked a clear division of approaches to this issue into two schools. The distinguishing criterion was whether or not Christ is presented in the passage as an example. Käsemann's rejection of this has been followed with particular vigour by Otto Merk[50] and Ralph Martin.[51] Strong responses have come, first, from L. W. Hurtado, who argues that Jesus is being presented as 'Lordly example' (and hence authoritative example)[52] and, second, from Morna Hooker, who argues that even if Käsemann's exegesis is followed, Christ will still, inevitably, function as example.[53]

By trying to look at the passage from the hearers' angle, I will seek to defend a position related to those of Hurtado and Hooker. In a sense, however, my reading is akin to that of Käsemann. Chapter 5, above, has shown that I follow Käsemann in seeing the passage as culminating in a change of authority.

a.   Verse 5

Käsemann's addition of a verb to complete verse 5b produces,

$$\text{τοῦτο φρονεῖτε ἐν ὑμῖν}$$
$$\text{ὃ καὶ φρονεῖν δεῖ ἐν Χριστῷ Ἰησοῦ.}^{54}$$

He paraphrases this by saying that 'the Philippians are admonished to conduct themselves toward one another as is fitting within the

---

[50] Merk, *Handeln*.

[51] R. P. Martin, *Carmen Christi: Philippians 2:5–11 in recent interpretation and in the setting of early Christian worship* (Grand Rapids: Eerdmans, 1983 edn).

[52] Hurtado, 'Lordly Example'.

[53] Morna D. Hooker, 'Phil 2:6–11', in *From Adam to Christ* (Cambridge, 1990 (Orig. 1975)), pp. 90f., 93.

[54] Following Julius Kögel, *Christus der Herr* (Gütersloh, 1908), pp. 10ff., not available to me. Käsemann, 'Critical Analysis', p. 84.

realm of Christ'.[55] He argues that the ἐν Χριστῷ belongs to formulae which are originally Hellenistic and mystical and indicate 'an understanding of being, according to which man conceives his existence on the basis of the world that determines him'.[56] The 'hymn' in verses 6–11 announces salvation, that is, the fact that the sovereign authority over the world has changed hands, from the hostile powers to Jesus.[57] As the Christian community adopts the 'hymn' it proclaims Christ as *cosmocrator*. By doing this, 'the new world is already manifest in the community itself, and it becomes evident that the obedient one is himself the author of obedient ones'.[58] I think we can summarise Käsemann by saying that, in his view, verse 5 calls the community to acknowledge the events of verses 6–11. This means acknowledging that Christ, rather than the powers, is now Lord of the Cosmos. This itself constitutes obedience but it also calls the Philippians to live in the obedience which Christ's exaltation to sovereignty has freed them for. Philippians 2.6–11 shows that the Philippians are free. It shows that Christ has freed them. It shows also that the freedom is freedom for obedience. Christ thus enables them and calls them to the obedience which, in the immediate context, means the unity discussed in 2.1–4. On one thing Käsemann is sure: 'Paul did not understand the hymn as though Christ were held up to the community as an ethical example'.[59]

An approach from the angle of the hearers of the letter places verse 5 in a different light, even if we accept Käsemann's paraphrase, 'Conduct yourselves toward one another as is fitting within the realm of Christ Jesus who . . .'. A Philippian hears this and then hears a story of Christ's self-emptying, his self-lowering, his obedience through to death and his subsequent exaltation. As soon as the story starts, the hearer is thinking, 'What is this "conducting ourselves" that Paul is calling for?' They are bound to hear Christ's acts in verses 6–8 as exemplary. They are trying to think as someone in Christ's realm. Christ is their king. Christ lowers himself. They must be willing to lower themselves. Christ is obedient right through to death. They will be obedient in this way if it is necessary.

---

[55] Ibid.
[56] Ibid., p. 86.
[57] Ibid.
[58] Ibid., p. 87.
[59] Ibid., p. 84.

As we considered in the previous chapter, this would be a particularly natural way of thinking for a Greek or Roman hearer in the first century. Both Hellenistic kings and Roman emperors were regarded as providing ethical examples for their subjects – those who were in their realm. This also gravely weakens the arguments, forcefully put forward by Ralph Martin in particular, about the inimitability of Christ's acts.[60] The Emperor's moral qualities were shown specifically in the way he governed the Empire. His acts were, *ipso facto*, inimitable – yet they could be regarded as ethical example. In addition to emperors and kings, we should add more down-to-earth examples of leaders who were to be imitated. There is a range of authority-figures to whom allegiance could be felt and who were then imitated. For the Philippian hearers there was, in particular, Paul himself.

We need to add to our argument the effect that having heard verses 1–4 will have had on the hearer of verses 5–8. They have just heard a call to unity, to ταπεινοφροσύνη, to concern for others rather than themselves. If we add 1.27ff., they have also heard a call to stand firm under suffering. Even if τοῦτο in verse 5 does not explicitly refer backwards at all, the hearer is expecting that the content of 'conduct yourselves' is going to be somewhat along the lines that Paul has just been calling for. They will therefore be particularly listening out for anything in that area. They then hear of Christ's οὐχ ἁρπαγμὸν ἡγήσατο (cf. μὴ τὰ ἑαυτῶν ζητοῦντες, ἐριθεία, κενοδοξία, etc.), his ἐκένωσεν and ἐταπείνωσεν (cf. ταπεινοφροσύνη, etc.) and his ὑπήκοος μέχρι θανάτου (cf. στήκετε, μὴ πτυρόμενοι, etc.). They must hear these as exemplary.

We should also consider the concrete social situation in which the hearer is hearing the passage. One prominent factor is the suffering which Paul attests in 1.27–30. This is bound to lead a hearer to hear Christ's ὑπήκοος μέχρι θανάτου as exemplary.

Käsemann assumes an implausible level of conceptual sophistication among the hearers. He can reasonably argue that the hearers would have felt themselves, before conversion, to be under the dominion of hostile cosmic powers. He can also reasonably argue that the universal submission to Christ would have been heard as at least including the submission of these powers and hence the breaking of their authority over the converts. The unwarranted sophistication lies in supposing that the hearers would not hear

---

[60] Martin, *Carmen*, p. xiv.

Christ as being example in 2.6–8. Käsemann requires the Philippians to make distinctions that they seem very unlikely to have made. They are to imitate Paul. Surely they would also think that they should imitate their greater leader? They have been called to ταπεινοφροσύνη and then Christ clearly demonstrates it. Surely they will assume that Paul is depicting this aspect of Christ's life in order for them to imitate it?

Käsemann's completion of verse 5b with φρονεῖν δεῖ[61] is also difficult. The phrase is a complex one for the hearers to add. The simpler addition, φρονεῖτε, also seems unlikely since, as C. F. D. Moule argued, it renders the verse tautologous.[62]

In the context, the most natural way to read verse 5 is to take ἐν Χριστῷ Ἰησοῦ as paradigmatic – 'in the case of Christ Jesus'. This could operate using various supplied verbs, such as ἦν or Lohmeyer's βλέπετε, etc.[63] ἐν ὑμῖν could then mean either 'among you' or 'in your case'. If we follow the option of 'among you', the two occurrences of ἐν are not parallel. However, this is true of Käsemann's reading too. There, they are paraphrased as 'toward one another' and 'within the realm of Christ Jesus'. Lack of parallelism of the word in other readings ought not, then, to be a major criticism. In fact, there is a good, independent example of ἐν meaning 'among' followed by a paradigmatic ἐν which is attached to Christ. The example is from Justin Martyr's *Dialogue with Trypho*.

> Καὶ οὐδενὶ τῶν ἐν Ἰουδαίοις ποτὲ συμβεβηκέναι τοῦτο ἀποδεῖξαι ἔχετε, ἡμεῖς δὲ ἔχομεν ἀποδεῖξαι τοῦτο γενόμενον ἐν τῷ ἡμετέρῳ Χριστῷ.
>
> . . . you cannot prove that such a thing ever happened to any one among the Jews. But we are able to prove that it happened in the case of our Christ.[64]

If we take both occurrences of ἐν in 2.5 as meaning 'in the case of', they are parallel. They also use ἐν in a sense which Paul has used as recently in 1.30, οἷον εἴδετε ἐν ἐμοὶ καὶ νῦν ἀκούετε ἐν ἐμοί. A further example would be 1 Corinthians 9.15, οὐκ ἔγραψα δὲ ταῦτα,

---

[61] Käsemann, 'Critical Analysis', p. 83f.

[62] C. F. D. Moule, 'Further Reflexions on Philippians 2:5–11', in R. P. Martin, ed., *Apostolic History and the Gospel* (Exeter: Paternoster, 1970), p. 266; O'Brien, pp. 257f.

[63] Lohmeyer, *Kyrios Jesus*, p. 13; cf. also Moule, 'Further Reflexions', p. 265.

[64] Justin, *Dialogue with Trypho*, 77.3, tr. G. Reith; cf. *Protevangelium Jacobi*, 13.1.

ἵνα οὕτως γένηται ἐν ἐμοί. The problem with this option is the possibility that ἐν ὑμῖν is then redundant after φρονεῖτε. 'You' are bound to think 'in your case'. The redundancy would, however, be alleviated if ἐν ὑμῖν, 'in your case', is a marker that another case is about to be cited.

Martin uses translation of the word, φρονέω, to attack the idea that verse 5 points to Christ as ethical example.

> The call is for his readers to 'adopt a way of life' (φρονεῖν is more than 'to think'; it signifies a combination of intellectual and affective activity which touches both head and heart, and leads to a positive course of action) in their mutual relations (ἐν ὑμῖν), which is indeed (καί) how they should live 'in Christ Jesus'.

> . . . What counts is that the becoming human of a divine being is by definition – as Hurtado explicitly says in his note 48 – 'unique', and if this is the case, Christians cannot imitate it except in an attenuated way. Then, what becomes of the summons in verse 5: 'Act thus . . . as Christ acted'?[65]

Martin has over-translated φρονέω and has then built an argument on the over-translation. The verb φρονέω does not have an essential reference to acts. This is immediately seen from 1.7, καθώς ἐστιν δίκαιον ἐμοὶ τοῦτο φρονεῖν ὑπὲρ πάντων ὑμῶν. The essential reference of φρονέω is to thought, not action. Therefore, if two beings share the same attitude – say, humility – there is no problem in saying that they φρονοῦσιν the same thing, even if one shows his humility by becoming incarnate and the other shows it by becoming unemployed.

Does verse 5 in fact introduce verses 6–11 or only verses 6–8? Διὸ καί and verse 9 follow on so dynamically from verse 8 that it seems reasonable to see it as having been foreseen when Paul wrote verse 5, rather than being, say, a theological reflection suddenly provoked by consideration of Christ's action. However, even though verse 5 does seem to introduce the whole of verses 6–11, it does not seem essential for the referent of ὅ to extend beyond verse 8, as Käsemann and others wish it to do. It seems quite reasonable to see verse 5 as about an attitude which Christ had and which is demonstrated in verses 6–8. The link to verses 9–11 is that they show the outcome of Christ adopting that

---

[65] Martin, *Carmen*, p. xiv, referring to Hurtado, 'Lordly Example'.

attitude and show Christ's current position – and hence act as an encouragement to the Philippians (in a manner to be discussed below).

b. Verses 6–8

As they heard these verses, the Philippians will have been listening out for attitudes to adopt or, indeed, actions to take, especially any which related to Paul's calls in 1.27–2.4. They seem likely to have heard two broad imitable actions. This division into two actions needs defending grammatically. I will do this by putting a 'stop-motion camera' on the text, in a manner reminiscent of Stanley Fish.[66] It must be noted, though, that the methods do have a difference in principle since he asks what a hypothetical 'informed reader' hears, whereas I am asking what the Philippians are likely to have heard.

The hearers first hear a statement about a position that Christ occupies (verse 6a). This statement is clearly preparatory since its verb, ὑπάρχων, is a participle. It sets up the situation in which the action of the main verb will take place. A suitable main verb, ἡγήσατο, arrives immediately (verse 6b). However, the tone of voice of the person reading out the letter would presumably have indicated that the 'not' in verse 6b was going to be matched by a 'but'. In any case, having heard the 'but', the hearers will have readjusted any idea that θεῷ ended the sentence and will have linked the next main verb, ἐκένωσεν, back to the situation of verse 6a. The participle of verse 6a thus sets the scene for action which is described by an οὐχ . . . ἀλλά pair. 'Being in situation X, Jesus did not do A but instead did B'.

6a   ἐν μορφῇ θεοῦ ὑπάρχων
6b, c   οὐχ ἁρπαγμὸν ἡγήσατο τὸ εἶναι ἴσα θεῷ,
7a   ἀλλὰ ἑαυτὸν ἐκένωσεν

The action, however, is so far rather undefined. 'Did not take advantage',[67] 'emptied himself': it is hard to think what action is

[66] Stanley Fish, *Is There a Text in This Class? The Authority of Interpretive Communities* (Cambridge, Mass.: Harvard University Press, 1980), p. 28.
[67] Following R. W. Hoover, 'The Harpagmos Enigma: A Philological Solution' *HTR* 64 (1971), pp. 95–119; N. T. Wright, *The Climax of the Covenant: Christ and the Law in Pauline Theology* (Edinburgh: T&T Clark, 1991), pp. 62–90.

being described using these phrases.[68] Paul then supplies another participal clause, μορφὴν δούλου λαβών (verse 7b). The lack of any conjunction before this clause means that the clause is bound to be heard as dependent on the main verb of verse 7a (or, possibly, the verbs of verses 6b and 7a). This is strengthened by the unclear nature of ἐκένωσεν – the verb sets a problem on which the hearer will then look for help. μορφὴν δούλου λαβών provides help. The content of ἐκένωσεν is specified[69] as being that Christ took on μορφὴν δούλου. The hearer will undoubtedly compare this with ἐν μορφῇ θεοῦ and conclude that the content of ἐκένωσεν is some sort of lowering of position – in fact, a lowering of position which is about the most extreme that the Universe could offer.[70]

A little surprisingly, there is then another clause with a participle, ἐν ὁμοιώματι ἀνθρώπων γενόμενος. Again, there is no introductory conjunction. Because of this, the hearer is likely again to attach the clause to the immediately preceding one, as an explanation of it.[71] Again, this is easy for the hearer to do because μορφὴν δούλου λαβών is itself a rather mysterious explanation of ἐκένωσεν, given that the hearers know Christ to have been a free man rather than a slave. They will therefore still be expecting some further clarification. ἐν ὁμοιώματι ἀνθρώπων γενόμενος (verse 7c) provides it. Christ's profound lowering of position consisted in his becoming like humans.

Many scholars have baulked at this parallel. They argue that Paul's view of being human would not allow him to describe it as a whole as δουλεία.[72] This is supported by noting the high view of the human condition taken in parts of Jewish tradition such as the Psalms (e.g. Ps. 8.4–8). Rejecting the parallel between μορφὴν δούλου λαβών and becoming human leaves open two options. One is to say that μορφὴν δούλου λαβών represents joining a subset of humanity – δοῦλοι in some sense – rather than joining humanity as a whole. δοῦλος can then either represent those of low social status

---

[68] Although, if they were left hanging indefinitely, the hearer would presumably supply some content based on the tradition of Jesus' life and death.

[69] Beare, p. 82.

[70] Fowl, *Story of Christ*, pp. 53–8.

[71] O'Brien, p. 224, argues that the clause explains ἐκένωσεν rather than 7b. I think that the hearers are more likely to attach it to what immediately precedes. In any case, there seems unlikely to be any difference in effect.

[72] Ibid., p. 219.

within humanity (Wengst argues for this)[73] or be taken as indicating slavery to God and be used to represent those humans (or
the only human) who are obedient to God or who, more specifically, adopt the role of the Servant of the Lord.[74] The problem with
the option of seeing δοῦλοι in verse 7b as representing only a subset
of humanity is that it does not fit the sequence of the passage. Verse
7c explains or more sharply specifies verse 7b: verse 7b cannot give
the more narrowly specified group. If the δοῦλοι were a subset of
humanity, verse 7c would be entirely redundant. (If someone wrote,
'Harold Abrahams grew up to become the Olympic 100 metres
champion. He became an athlete', the second sentence would be
pointless.)

The second option is to see μορφὴν δούλου λαβών not as
generally synonymous with being human but as synonymous only
for Christ. This, again, usually takes the form of seeing Christ as
becoming the Servant of the Lord. The task which Christ took on
in becoming Servant was that of becoming incarnate – with its
various subsequent consequences.

Commentators who take the 'Servant' approach do not,
however, tend to accept verse 7c as specifying verse 7b, i.e., they do
not see incarnation as being the essential content of becoming the
Servant as Paul describes it here. Instead, they see the humbling
and obedient death of verse 8 as the essential content.[75] Verses 7d
and 8a, the statements about being like people, again become
redundant.[76]

There is, I would suggest, a better way of seeing verses 7b and 7c
as synonymous for Christ rather than synonymous in general. The
way is to link it back to our discussion of what is likely to have
been heard in the passage as far as μορφὴν δούλου λαβών, namely,
that Christ was portrayed as lowering himself by a vast distance.
The synonymity of this great lowering of himself with the process
of becoming human is completely natural in Christ's case, whatever

---

[73] Wengst, *Humility*, p. 50f.; cf. Hawthorne, p. 87. Moule, 'Further Reflexions',
p. 268, takes Christ as becoming someone without even basic human rights.

[74] For the δούλος as the Jewish obedient sufferer see E. Schweizer, *Erniedrigung
und Erhöhung bei Jesus und seinen Nachfolgern* (ATANT 28; Zurich: Zwingli, 1955).
For the Servant, see Lucien Cerfaux, 'L'hymne au Christ-Serviteur de Dieu (Phil., II,
6–11 = Is., LII, 13–LIII, 12)', *Recueil Lucien Cerfaux II* (Gembloux: Duculot,
1954), pp. 425–37.

[75] J. Jeremias, 'Zu Phil.2,7: ΕΑΥΤΟΝ ΕΚΕΝΩΣΕΝ', *NovT* 6 (1963), pp. 182–8,
cited in O'Brien, p. 194.

[76] Cf. O'Brien, p. 270.

might be Paul's view of the dignity of humanity. The crux is that it is not δουλεία which is synonymous with humanity, even in Christ's case. It is the distance between δουλεία and being like God that is synonymous, in Christ's case, with his becoming human. Between being like God and being like a slave, there is the widest status gap imaginable by Paul's hearers. Paul is saying that for Christ to become human meant that deep a drop in status.[77]

After verse 7c, the hearers hear a καί (at last!) and then yet another clause with a participle, καὶ σχήματι εὑρεθεὶς ὡς ἄνθρωπος (verse 7d). Leaving aside the intonation of the person reading the letter out (taking it into account would, in this case, be to prejudge the issue), the hearers' first reaction to the καί might be to expect further explanation of the μορφὴν δούλου λαβών (although they must have felt that the sentence was being rather over-elaborated). However, as they heard the clause, they would realise that it was synonymous with verse 7c,[78] except in terms of the point in time from which the action is being viewed (in verse 7c, Christ is becoming like humans: in verse 7d, Christ is already like a human). The hearers would therefore dismiss the idea of the clause developing verse 7b further and would conclude that the participle in verse 7d, like that in 6a, was setting the scene for a main verb which was coming.[79]

The story of verses 6–8 is therefore divided into two stages, each with its own main verb (or, in the case of verses 6–7c, an οὐχ . . . ἀλλά pair of main verbs). This, and the division after verse 7c, has found support from many scholars.[80] Most alternative views require a denial of the synonymity of verses 7c and 7d. This does not seem sustainable. A route which avoids this is to see the passage as consisting of pairs of lines which parallel each other, as they do in Hebrew poetry.[81] The problem with this is that it cuts across the way in which the grammar of the passage seems likely to be heard, especially in terms of the various conjunctions, which

[77] Fowl, *Story of Christ*, p. 58.
[78] Hawthorne, pp. 87f.; O'Brien, p. 226.
[79] Hawthorne sees 7d as co-ordinating with 7c to emphasise Christ's identification with humanity. The main problem with this is that verse 8a, with no conjunction, makes a very strange beginning for a sentence. 7d would also seem a weak reinforcement of 7c.
[80] E.g., J. D. G. Dunn, *Christology in the Making* (SCM: London, 1989[2]), p. 115; O'Brien, p. 226.
[81] Martin, *Carmen*, pp. 36–8.

must surely have a structural role.[82] In fact, the two-stage presentation of Christ's downward path must be one of the most distinctive features of 2.6–11. Elsewhere in Paul, the action happens in one movement (Rom. 8.3; 2 Corinthians 8.9). A consequence for the hearers is that they seem likely to hear in the passage two actions of Christ which they should imitate, that recounted in 2.6–7c and that in verses 7d–8.

The grammar of verses 7d–8 seems essentially to repeat that of verses 6–7c. σχήματι εὑρεθεὶς ὡς ἄνθρωπος sets the scene. ἐταπείνωσεν ἑαυτὸν provides the main verb. As in verse 7a, the object is ἑαυτὸν. Again, as in 7a, the main verb, ἐταπείνωσεν, is rather undefined and provides a puzzle. Verse 8b then follows without an initial conjunction and with a participle. It therefore seems to provide definition for verse 8a.[83] Furthermore, the participle in 8b is the same, γενόμενος, as that in verse 7c, the last clause of the first movement. Unique to verse 8, however, is the specifying expansion of the last term . . . θανάτου, θανάτου δὲ σταυροῦ. The structure of verses 6–8 can thus be set out as follows:

6a	ὅς
	ἐν μορφῇ θεοῦ ὑπάρχων
b, c	οὐχ ἁρπαγμὸν ἡγήσατο τὸ εἶναι ἴσα θεῷ,
7a	ἀλλὰ ἑαυτὸν ἐκένωσεν
b	μορφὴν δούλου λαβών,
c	ἐν ὁμοιώματι ἀνθρώπων γενόμενος·
d	καὶ
	σχήματι εὑρεθεὶς ὡς ἄνθρωπος
8a	ἐταπείνωσεν ἑαυτὸν
b	γενόμενος ὑπήκοος μέχρι θανάτου,
c	θανάτου δὲ σταυροῦ.

My resulting grammatical structure is actually very close to Lohmeyer's arrangement into stanzas. The only difference is that he begins a second stanza with ἀλλά at verse 7a, producing three three-line stanzas (τὸ εἶναι ἴσα θεῷ is a separate line and θανάτου δὲ σταυροῦ is omitted).[84] This difference does, however,

---

[82] Cf. Hooker, 'Phil 2:6–11', pp. 93ff.; Wright, *Climax*, p. 56 n. 1.

[83] Beare, p. 84.

[84] See now Colin Brown's exposition and assessment: 'Ernst Lohmeyer's *Kyrios Jesus*', in Ralph P. Martin and Brian J. Dodd, eds., *Where Christology Began: Essays on Philippians 2* (Louisville: Westminster John Knox, 1998). Brown sets out and translates Lohmeyer's reading on pp. 8f.

weaken Lohmeyer's structure grammatically. τὸ ἐιναι ἴσα θεῷ is not a new step in the argument in the sense that other lines are (ἡγήσατο cannot stand without it). The division into stanzas also creates a danger of losing sight of the fact that all of verses 6–7c are acted out from a starting-point defined by verse 6a. Exegetically the key structure of verses 6–8 is two movements. Division into three stanzas, or other poetic structures, tends to obscure this.

When Gordon Fee's commentary on Philippians appeared, I discovered that my structure was identical to his.[85] He analysed the passage using a directly grammatical method, with one eye on how it would have flowed as Paul dictated it. I suspect that my arriving at the same result as that of Fee has something to do with the influence of his earlier writings on the development of my understanding of Greek grammar.

Having defended, from the hearers' angle, a particular grammatical analysis of verses 6–8, we now need to consider how they are likely to have heard Christ's actions and what they would think they ought to do in response.

Since they had just heard verse 4, the first thing they probably heard was that Christ οὐ τὰ ἑαυτῶν ἐσκόπησεν. This is particularly clear in the translation of verse 6b as 'did not take advantage of', well argued for by Hoover and then Wright,[86] who handle the phrase as a whole as an idiom. However, most other translations, which handle ἁρπαγμός as a word on its own, also carry a forceful implication that regarding something as ἁρπαγμός would involve one's own gain. Conversely, not regarding it as such involves at least the refusal to make some gain for oneself. Thus Christ exemplifies verse 4a and possibly also a lack of ἐριθεία (verse 3a) – if we take that in the sense of selfishness or selfish ambition.

However, this first act, of not taking advantage, requires definition. In itself, 'not taking advantage', could involve any of a range of actions (or lack of action). Verses 7a–c provide the action which shows the specific form of Christ's 'not taking advantage'. The form which it took was that Christ lowered himself in terms of position – a great lowering, from being like God to being like a slave. Even before we reach the ἐταπείνωσεν of verse 8a, Jesus has

[85] Fee, pp. 194–6.
[86] Hoover, 'Harpagmos'; Wright, *Climax*, pp. 62–90.

clearly exercised some sort of ταπεινοφροσύνη. What this has meant for Jesus would probably have been perceived as a lowering of status.[87] I have argued, above, that a particularly likely way for a call to ταπεινοφροσύνη to be heard in a Graeco-Roman context was in connection with status – as acting in a way inappropriate to (and below) your status.[88] Christ's example of loss of status would greatly reinforce such a call. To obey a call to act below your status would seem likely, in the Graeco-Roman context, to be seen as carrying a risk of actual loss of status (possibly cf. the progression of Paul's presentation of himself in 3.7–8: ἥγημαι ζημίαν . . . ἐζημιώθην). Verses 6–8 greatly strengthen the probability that this is the kind of call that is being made in verses 3–4.

We have so far heard two elements of verses 1–4, μὴ τὰ ἑαυτῶν σκοποῦντες and ταπεινοφροσύνη, expressed in Christ's action of verses 6–7c, a single action of loss of status. This raises an obvious question. If Christ in verses 6–8 is an example for the paraenesis of verses 1–4, where is the main topic of verses 1–4, that of unity? Where, at minimum, is the expression of that topic in terms of concern for others, σκοποῦντες τὰ ἑτέρων (verse 4b)?

To say that the topic of unity is not, in itself, present in 2.6–8 may be the key point in discussing how these verses function as reinforcement of verses 1–4. One of the main features which distinguishes verses 6–8 from other Pauline comments on Christ's life and death is precisely that it is not described from the point of view of benefit for others. It is described solely from the point of view of what Christ did.[89] Verse 5 makes the hearers listen out for actions of Christ which reinforce the call to unity of verses 1–4. What they then hear in verses 6–7c is about Christ lowering his status. (On verses 7d–8, see below.)

The way forward, I would suggest, is to note that while verses 6–8 do not immediately match a call to unity, they do reasonably match the culmination in verses 3–4 to which Paul brings his call to unity. Since verses 3–4 form the climax of the call, it seems reasonable to see them as addressing the issues which Paul sees as hampering unity in the Philippian church. It then seems reasonable to see verses 6–8 as addressing the most pressing ones of those issues. The results of this fit the reconstruction of the situation in the Philippian church for which I argued above, that is, that in their

---

[87] Fowl, *Story of Christ*, pp. 53–8, cf. Schweizer, *Erniedrigung*, pp. 53f.
[88] Wengst, *Humility*, pp. 10–12.
[89] O'Brien, pp. 232, 252f.

situation of suffering, some in the church (who are suffering little and who tend to be of higher status) are failing to help (financially) others in the church (who are suffering more and who tend to be of lower status). For reasons described above, various imperatives of Philippian society would operate against the wealthier Christians offering this help. Such association could both endanger their status and be seen as acting below their status (even simply in associating with those of lower status to the close extent indicated by τὸ αὐτὸ φρονῆτε, etc.). The example of Christ who did not take advantage of his status but willingly lowered it is a reinforcement which would closely fit a call to unity in this particular kind of situation.

This conclusion is reinforced by a further feature of the passage. Although there is no mention of benefit for others from Christ's action, there is a pointed emphasis on Christ becoming like others. This too would be a good model for the Philippians if those who were comfortable were being called to come alongside, and identify with, those who were suffering.

In verses 7d–8, a downwards movement is again heard. Even as a human, Christ lowers himself further. He lowers himself to the lowest conceivable human level, crucifixion. In verse 8a we have the verb, ταπεινόω, and even Käsemann drops his guard sufficiently to allow a link between this and ταπεινοφροσύνη: '. . . the turn of the ages . . . when in the incarnation a ταπεινοῦν ἑαυτόν occurred, so that ταπεινοφροσύνη has now become the law of the new age . . .'[90] The Philippians, therefore, are bound to see in this second movement some further encouragement to lowering of oneself. However, in their situation of suffering, they are likely to interpret Christ's action more specifically, namely, as willing acceptance of suffering – all the way through to the most degrading death possible.

For the Philippians to hear a call to obedient suffering is quite probable, in view of 1.27–30 and Paul's example in 1.12–26. 'Obedience right through to death' is likely to have the same content as 'stand firm under suffering'. Each requires keeping going on the way of God despite attacks which harm and may even kill you. The call is also relevant in the situation of interlinked suffering and disunity which I have been arguing was the case. If people are holding back from unity out of fear of harm, in the social sphere or

---

[90] Käsemann, 'Critical Analysis', p. 87.

some other, this would be fear of suffering. Christ's example of obedient suffering could act against this fear.

Two imitable actions are likely to be heard by the Philippians in 2.6–8: Christ's lowering of himself and Christ's obedient acceptance of suffering. For these to function as a reinforcement to the call to unity in 2.1–4 suggests that the situation in the Philippian church is along the lines for which I have been arguing.

c. Verses 9–11

In verses 9–11, Christ cannot be an example to be imitated. The essential reason for this is not that his acts are inimitable but that he does not act. God acts and there is no call, in the context, for the Philippians to imitate God. Instead of providing an example to imitate, verses 9–11 probably function in two other ways: first, in offering the Philippians a hope that good will happen to them if they are faithful, as it happened to Christ; second, a function based on the unique authority or high status of Christ's position.

We seem to have a riddle here – a riddle that I would suggest is inherent in the passage. On the one hand, the Philippians, having mentally followed Christ down through his descent to the cross, and having resolved to follow him in their actions too, suddenly hear the joyful διὸ καὶ ὁ θεὸς αὐτὸν ὑπερύψωσεν. Christ's action was rewarded or vindicated by sudden exaltation. The Philippians will undoubtedly have heard that their following of Christ in his downward way would be rewarded too. On the other hand, verses 9–11 emphatically present Christ's position as unique. The Philippians cannot really share it (although 3.21 shows that they will, in some sense, share its glory). One possible way to solve the riddle is presented by the comparison between Christ and the Emperor.

(i) Reward

One of the most powerful dynamics of personal allegiance to leaders has often been the idea that, if one's leader was victorious and came to power, then his followers would gain by it. This was no doubt frequently true in Graeco-Roman politics, finding one sort of culmination in the careers of figures such as L. Clodius Pulcher, whom Bormann discusses.[91] The sole basis of allegiance to

---

[91] Bormann, *Philippi*, pp. 190ff.

this man seems to have been the hope of benefit for his followers. Another sort of culmination was reached in the careers of military leaders, whose followers counted on substantial gains if their man came to power.

The specific example to hand is, of course, Philippi itself (see chapter 1, above). Antony and Octavian's soldiers were promised and received great rewards after victory over the Republicans. Again, after the defeat of Antony at Actium, Octavian's soldiers gained: this time partially at the expense of some of Antony's veterans in Italy who had been rewarded earlier. Philippi ended up with a potent mix of Octavian's and some of Antony's supporters who had simply gained, many of Antony's supporters who had lost land in Italy but been given land at Philippi, and Macedonian and Thracian Greeks who had lost land to the followers of these generals. For each of these groups, the concept of followers gaining when a leader came to power was likely to be something potent.

There is no explicit promise in verses 9–11 of reward for the Philippians. However, Christ was exalted specifically because he followed his downward path (verse 9). The Philippians are bound to think that, if they faithfully follow Christ on this path, the 'therefore' will carry some effect for them too. Christ's exaltation to being Cosmic Emperor could, in the first-century Graeco-Roman world generally, and Philippi in particular, easily be heard as carrying such a possibility. It would do this without any suggestion that the Philippians were going to become emperors themselves. Further, it was Christ's exaltation to this Lordship which would enable the reward of the Philippians. Thus, the Philippians could hear both that, since Christ was rewarded, they too could expect a reward and that it was Christ's exaltation that would enable that reward to be provided. As Morna Hooker points out, in 3.20–1 salvation for the Philippians is explicitly provided on the basis of Christ's exaltation.[92]

My use of the word 'reward' has a polemic edge, as does my earlier use of 'imitate'. In each of these cases, NT scholars seem, for dogmatic, historical or ethical reasons, to have avoided the word which represents the way in which first-century hearers seem most likely to have understood the passage. Scholars commenting on the

---

[92] M. D. Hooker, 'Interchange in Christ', in *From Adam to Christ* (Cambridge, 1990 (Orig. 1971)), pp. 20f. I think she is wrong, however, to imply that the Philippians would not hear any promise of salvation in 2.9–11 itself.

Bible for modern audiences clearly do need to consider the resonances of terms for modern readers. However, as NT scholars, we should surely be seeking essentially to find words which best represent the first-century understanding, irrespective of whether we approve of their way of thinking.

In the case of 'reward', Martin excludes it on contextual grounds. Paul's paraenetic aim is to rebuke self-seeking. Surely the last thing he will do is to make the pursuit of self-interest the eschatological basis of the Christian life?[93] Martin's position, however, seems to represent Stoic ethics and not first-century Christian ethics. For Epictetus, the only reward for living a good life is living a good life and enjoying the 'freedom' that that brings. Yearning for a reward in some other sphere is like yearning for nursemaids when we are grown men.[94] For the writer to the Hebrews, on the other hand, belief in God's reward is central to faith itself:

χωρὶς δὲ πίστεως ἀδύνατον εὐαρεστῆσαι· πιστεῦσαι γὰρ δεῖ τὸν προσερχόμενον τῷ θεῷ ὅτι ἔστιν καὶ τοῖς ἐκζητοῦσιν αὐτὸν μισθαποδότης γίνεται. (11.6)

Scholars may not like this view but it seems quite implausible to say that it was not the general first-century Christian view. We only have to consider some of the more obvious parables, such as that of the talents (Matt. 25.14–30), or Paul's account of his own motivation based on the hope of eschatological reward (1 Corinthians 9.27; Phil. 3.14).

The use of 'imitate' rather than 'conform to' is a minor issue compared to this. As Hooker notes, 'the 'imitation' of Christ depends on union with him, and is a question of being conformed to his image, not of copying an external pattern . . .'[95] I think, however, that she is right to maintain the use of 'imitate', elsewhere in her book, rather than the theologically nuanced 'conform'. The Philippian Christians seem likely to have sought to follow 2.6–8 in terms of simple imitation rather than with the theological addition that produces 'conform'.

The idea of reward after faithful following of a leader seems a better option for the Philippians hearing a promise of reward in verse 9 than does the idea of God exalting the humble in general.

---

[93] Martin, *Carmen*, pp. xxxvii, 231ff.
[94] Epictetus, *Diss*. 3.24.51f. See Oakes, 'Epictetus', pp. 45ff.
[95] Hooker, *From Adam*, p. 7.

Lohmeyer sees verse 9 as exemplifying this principle.[96] This does not seem to work. In verses 6–8, although Christ lowers himself to an unheard-of extent, he does not end up in an unheard-of lowly position. If God exalts people because they are poor and crucified, he would have exalted others prior to Jesus. Conversely, there is no reason why he should have exalted Jesus from that position which others had held. Furthermore, God had not, since Christ's exaltation, started exalting everyone who was crucified. The crucial point for the Philippians lay in their following Christ and thus facing low status, rather than in their simply facing low status. They would be exalted because they faithfully followed their leader, despite the suffering, rather than because they suffered *per se*. The idea of verse 9 exemplifying a general principle does not give a good account, either, of the absolute level to which Christ is raised in verses 9–11.

(ii)   Sovereignty

Even though there does seem likely to be some thought of reward for the Philippians implicit in verses 9–11, our main exegetical concern must clearly be with what is explicit, Christ's accession to Lordship. Chapter 5, above, has already been devoted to this but we now need to ask how the material on Christ's sovereignty would function, as the Philippians heard it.

The Philippian Christians were probably mainly Greek non-citizens living in one of the most strongly Roman colonies in the eastern Empire. Almost all the Christians will have been economically dependent on Romans. A substantial number of Christians were suffering at the hands of Greeks or Romans, probably including the authorities. The Graeco-Roman social order imposed imperatives which would operate against unity between people of different status, especially in a time of suffering and particularly if some of those suffering had been in trouble with the authorities and hence were notorious as troublemakers. Paul calls for unity, then is heard to paint a picture of Christ being granted universal authority. Such a picture of Christ has a number of potential effects on hearers.

First, and probably most significantly, a Christ with universal authority relativises society's imperatives. In any conflict between Christ's imperatives and those of society, there can be no question about which carry more weight. The exegetical basis of this is the

[96] Lohmeyer, *Kyrios Jesus*, p. 48.

argument that the point of comparison in verses 9–11 is primarily political, not religious. I have argued for this in chapter 5, above. Of course, in the first century, religion and political power were inextricably entangled. However, there is a distinction that needs to be made. Käsemann, for example, sees Christ's sovereignty as being over the cosmic powers, the fates which controlled the chances of daily existence and of life and death.[97] This is not a political reading in the sense that a comparison with the Emperor would be.

For verses 9–11 to function in the social/political sphere fits the paraenetic needs of 1.27–2.4 far better than do the alternative suggestions in which the primary area of comparison in verses 9–11 is religious. If verses 9–11 are about victory over the powers, this has nothing more than a completely general link to the paraenesis – a link that it would equally have to any Christian paraenesis.[98] If, as R. R. Brewer argued, verses 9–11 are about Christ opposing the Imperial cult,[99] then some additional unstated element is needed in the situation addressed in 1.27–2.4 – an element to do with trouble on account of the Imperial cult.[100] In contrast, if we take the political and social view of verses 9–11 it directly fits the issues of standing firm under opposition from Philippian society and of pursuing unity, an aim opposed by the social imperatives of Philippian society. In both these issues, the key practical point is likely to be that the Christian has grown up thinking that following society's imperatives is the right thing to do and the safe thing to do. Although they will be keen to follow Paul's calls, the pressure of these social imperatives will be very great. For Paul to present Christ as the one who outdoes the lord of the political and social sphere seems a very appropriate rhetorical strategy. (It would not be so appropriate in various other Christian paraenetic contexts in which the actions called for would not contravene society's imperatives.)

Hurtado's suggestion of the Lordship of Christ acting to make Christ's example authoritative[101] is very important. However, it is probably too narrow in one sense and too broad in another. It is

---

[97] Käsemann, 'Critical Analysis', pp. 79ff.

[98] Fowl, *Story of Christ*, pp. 81f., criticises Käsemann on these grounds.

[99] R. R. Brewer, 'The Meaning of Politeuesthe in Philippians 127', *JBL* 73 (1954), p. 82.

[100] Verses 9–11 would actually, in practice, oppose the Imperial cult. Cult, however, seems not to be the issue at stake in 2.1–4 (although it would be a little more plausible in 1.27–30).

[101] Hurtado, 'Lordly Example', p. 125.

too narrow because he sees it specifically as validating the example. It seems likely, instead, to provide imperatives and encouragement for the paraenesis of 1.27–2.18 (and elsewhere) which operate beyond the example as well as through it. Hurtado's idea seems too broad because 'Lordship' in general does not provide the close fit to the paraenesis that is provided by Christ replacing the Emperor's political and social lordship. A third criticism of Hurtado is that to see Christ simply depicted as Lord treats verses 9–11 as the presentation of a static situation. Instead, verses 9–11 present the event of Jesus' accession and acclamation. Käsemann's concept of change of authority does more justice to this.

If Christ has replaced the Emperor as the world's decisive power then we are no longer in the established Graeco-Roman social world. Instead of a world under the high-status man, whose Roman Empire has commanded the hardening of an already stratified Mediterranean society into stone, the world is under a new lord whose command is τὸ αὐτὸ φρονεῖτε and who enjoins ταπεινοφροσύνη. The lord even exemplifies these things. The whole basis of Graeco-Roman society is done away with.

Just as I agree with Käsemann in seeing verses 9–11 as a proclamation of a new authority, it also seems possible to see them as carrying a proclamation of freedom, as he does. Again, however, he sees freedom from the fates, from Necessity. I see freedom from being bound by the constraints imposed by society. Again, the difference between Käsemann and myself flows from his seeing the point of comparison as religious and my seeing it as social and political.

Freedom is linked with confidence – freedom from fear of the constraints imposed by society. With Christ enthroned, following him is ultimately never dangerous, even if it comes to the point of being social and economic suicide. This would fit with the material on suffering leading to salvation, considered in chapter 4, above. It would fit in particular with a reading of 2.12 as Paul saying, 'Follow the (apparently dangerous) path I am calling you to: it is the way to bring about your salvation'. Conversely, one's position in Roman society is not a safe basis for confidence since Roman society is now no longer the social order commanded by the one who rules. The way in which verses 10–11 are picked up in 3.20–1 adds weight to the idea that verses 9–11 would convey confidence in the safety of following Christ's direction. In 3.20–1 the function of Christ's sovereignty is for him to apply it in rescuing the Christians.

The Christian community is also de-marginalised. It is the community belonging to the one in authority. If it is seen by certain 'authorities' as a maverick group, and consequently frowned upon, then the 'authorities' who frown on it are at odds with the real authority. The idea that verses 9–11 would affect the Christian community's perception of itself gains credibility from the raising of this issue in verses 15f.

These are four areas in which a depiction of Christ as Lord, and particularly of Christ above the Emperor, could function: authority, freedom, confidence and the church's view of itself. I think that these are the best candidates for the elements from which a combination would affect each hearer as they were faced by verses 9–11 (before moving back into the exhortation of verses 12–18, which I think broadly restates the call of 1.27–2.4). Which elements predominated would presumably vary from hearer to hearer. A poor, suffering Philippian might be most aware of the promise implicit in Christ's authority making Christ a safe basis of confidence. A wealthier Philippian who had suffered little might be struck most by the way in which Christ's imperatives ought to displace certain social imperatives which had, for them, been far too dominant.

In addition to these, a Philippian who was aware of the reference to Isaiah 45 in verses 10–11 might draw further strength for their situation from the idea that Christ was the one through whose action God was fulfilling his plan to bring the Cosmos under its proper authority. The Christian's allegiance to Christ would thus receive extra legitimation.

3. The nature of Philippians 2.6–11

The church at Philippi is suffering. Paul calls for a unity which means willingness to lower oneself and give help to others. He reinforces this, first, by Christ's example of self-lowering and of obedient suffering, then, second, by depicting Christ as the decisive authority in the Universe.

What conclusions ought my arguments to lead to with regard to the origin, form, backgrounds and Christology of the passage?

Essentially, my arguments have been about how the passage was likely to have been heard by the Philippians. Christ was heard to undergo the deepest possible loss of status. He was heard to suffer obediently the worst possible death. He was heard to be raised to universal authority. The logic of this was heard as natural because self-sacrificing, morally good acts were a common legitimation of imperial power. The Philippians (with the prompting of 1.27–2.4) inferred from 2.6–11 that they should be willing to lose status and suffer faithfully. They inferred that Christ's authority made his imperatives and security far outweigh those of the society in which they lived. Less directly, they heard the pattern of Christ's story as offering hope to those who followed him in the way of obedient suffering. For those with ears to hear the allusion to Isaiah 45, God was heard as fulfilling through Christ his plan to exercise sovereignty over the Cosmos.

If this is how it was heard, how was it written? It is either an existing story of Christ which Paul saw as fitting the Philippians' needs or it is a story newly formulated to fit those needs. However, the second option needs stating more carefully. Any newly formulated story is bound to be a reformulation of an existing story. Ralph Martin's suggestion that Paul re-orientates the passage by inserting the reference to the Cross[102] would be a reformulation at the minimum end. At the maximum end would be something like James Dunn's view[103] in which what really happens is reformulation by the combination of two stories, that of Adam and that of Christ. In fact, if we talk about the original composition of 2.6–11, by Paul or someone else, we must always be talking about a reformulation of an existing story of Christ. Although, in some readings, the story which gives the passage its most obvious shape and content is a story of a figure other than Christ, even in these cases, for the author of the passage, the passage will still be a reformulation of what he or she believed to be a true story of Christ.

What this means is that, whenever the passage was composed, it bears witness to Christology earlier than itself. For example, the passage could only be written by someone who already believed that Christ now held a position of high authority. The reformulating of the story of Christ can, however, constitute some Christological development. For example, if the author was the first to retell the story of Christ's accession to authority in terms of Isaiah 45, this represents a substantial move both in terms of relationship to Judaism (as Seeley – rather too caustically –

---

[102] Martin, *Carmen*, p. xvii.
[103] Dunn, *Christology*, p. xxxiv n. 21.

observes[104]) and in terms of movement towards Trinitarian theology.

Since Paul's writing down of Philippians 2.6–11 must either be re-use or reformulation of a story, or stories, of Christ, questions of background and Christology cannot be done away with by an argument that the passage is especially appropriate to the Philippians. What may happen, however, is that certain kinds of argument from the text could become invalid. Consider the detailed arguments about the meaning of μορφή in verse 6.[105] These arguments depend on the assumption that the term conveys relatively precise information about the position of Christ or some other figure in a story on which 2.6–11 is based. However, if we take a maximal view of the implications of my argument and suppose that the passage was formulated specially to fit the Philippians' needs, then ἐν μορφῇ θεοῦ ὑπάρχων and μορφὴν δούλου λαβων could be fairly imprecise formulations, designed to convey to the Philippians a social change immeasurably beyond any that they might be called upon to undergo. The specific shaping would come from the needs of the Philippian situation rather than from precise Christological formulation. Christology is still there but, in order to understand the Christology conveyed by the passage, we might need to work in looser terms than some scholars have done. Ernst Käsemann might criticise me as excluding serious theological readings of the passage.[106] I would deny the charge. We do need serious theological readings – serious Christological readings – of the passage. But serious theology must give due weight to context and if, as I am arguing, the context may have shaped the terminology of a passage, this must be acknowledged.

Taking my arguments at their minimum, the passage could be a pre-Pauline hymn. It would be composed on the basis of early Christian testimony about Jesus. For verses 6–8, Jesus would have been seen as fitting the pattern of a story of some other scriptural or non-scriptural figure. For verses 9–11, Jesus would have been

---

[104] Seeley, 'Background', p. 3.

[105] See Gerald F. Hawthorne's useful summary of the state of discussion, 'In the Form of God and Equal with God (Philippians 2:6)', in Ralph P. Martin and Brian J. Dodd, eds., *Where Christology Began: Essays on Philippians 2* (Louisville: Westminster John Knox, 1998), pp. 97–101.

[106] See Robert Morgan, 'Incarnation, Myth, and Theology: Ernst Käsemann's Interpretation of Philippians 2:5–11', in Ralph P. Martin and Brian J. Dodd, eds., *Where Christology Began: Essays on Philippians 2* (Louisville: Westminster John Knox, 1998), p. 58.

seen as fitting into the story of Isaiah 45. Paul would have observed how closely this fitted the Philippians' needs and therefore introduced it as reinforcement of his call of 1.27–2.4.

My impression, however, is that the passage fits the needs of the Philippian situation so well that Paul has, at least, heavily reformulated it to meet those needs. I think that the likelihood is that Paul has taken his beliefs about Christ's self-lowering (2 Corinthians 8.9), his obedient death (Rom. 5.19) and his exaltation (1 Corinthians 15.24) and has carefully crafted a rhetorically powerful Christological reinforcement to his call, in 1.27–2.4, to stand firm and united. The passage does tell us vital things about Paul's Christology. In particular, it places Christ very precisely in Paul's mental map of the Universe. It places Christ relative to the earthly powers that Paul and his churches faced: Christ is above the Emperor. It places Christ relative to God in a way that is much more difficult to define. Christ sits on God's throne. But this brings glory to God so Christ's authority must in some way be the means by which Isaiah's vision of God's own sovereignty comes to fulfilment.

There are very few scholarly options that my study on 2.6–11 has absolutely excluded. It has, however, led me to think that the most likely view about the nature of the passage is that it was composed especially for the people at Philippi and, more specifically, for the letter written to their church.

CONCLUSION

How strongly has my model of the church affected my exegesis of the text? For an initial answer to that, we can look back at an alternative model of the church, that of Friedrich: 'In contrast to other places, the [Christian] community is probably composed not of the proletariat but mainly of members of the middle class . . . The veterans settled in Philippi are not slaves but free people, who mainly own their land . . . A church that is financially so well placed can give Paul material support.'[1] This model would not have led to an exegesis like mine. My exegesis certainly has some relationship to my model.

The actual numbers I arrived at in my model had little effect other than to make me dismiss lines of exegesis that were based on the assumption of a church predominantly of Roman citizens or, particularly, of veteran soldiers. In fact, the factor that has influenced my exegesis most has probably been the very act of modelling the church. Asking questions about who was likely to be in it, and in what proportions, has made me think about the dynamics of relationships among types of people within the church and between types of people in the church and those outside. Consideration of the dynamics of relationships was then combined with the exegetical conclusion that Philippian Christians were suffering at the hands of fellow-townspeople. The result of this combination was a series of exegeses of the word 'suffering' in terms of what it was likely to mean for each group in my model. This led to a global conclusion that the main long-term suffering was likely to be economic.

I then turned my attention to how this would relate to the issue of unity. My conclusion was that Paul was primarily calling for mutual economic help. This conclusion then affected my exegesis of

---

[1] Friedrich, pp. 92f., my tr. Quoted in German on p. 68.

2.6–11. Christ was seen as undergoing a loss of status greater than any that Philippians might risk by offering economic help. He was also seen as standing firm under suffering. He was also seen to have been given an authority which relativised the social imperatives of Philippi that might work against unity.

My exegesis of Paul's autobiographical passages is more loosely connected to my model. The main connection is probably that the conclusions that my model led me to, about suffering and unity, made me want to see the whole letter as centred on the issue. In particular, I wanted to see the Philippians' situation, not Paul's, as central to the letter. I studied the texts and became convinced that this was indeed the case. More tentatively, the texts seemed to offer support for the ideas that Paul modelled both loss of privilege and concern for others. These fitted my understanding of the situation of the church.

Looking at the broad field of Pauline studies, a general conclusion of my study is that Philippians ought to be moved more towards the main stream of Paul's letters. The Philippian church has long been seen as wealthy and unproblematic – both highly atypical for Pauline churches in receipt of letters. It has rather followed from this that Philippians has been seen as a somewhat disconnected, friendly 'chat', with a rather alien outburst in chapter 3. My study presents a suffering church with difficulties over unity – a church to which Paul needs to address a letter which is an extended piece of often passionate persuasion.

We may also be able to move Philippians 2.5–11 more towards the Pauline main stream. I have argued that the passage closely fits the requirements of the Philippians' situation. If this is the case, then it looks rather likely that the passage is a piece of rhetoric, constructed by Paul from his Christological beliefs specifically to fit the argument he wishes to make. This would be a far more typical Pauline move than would be the incorporation of a long, almost unedited, piece of prior Christian tradition.

Flanders and Swann once said, '. . . models of friendship are precious and rare: but the friendship of models is not!' My own experience has convinced me that models are very good at posing important questions. Wrestling with a model of the Christian community at Philippi has greatly deepened my appreciation of Christ and Paul as models for the life of the suffering Church.

BIBLIOGRAPHY: ANCIENT

For abbreviations of titles of classical works, see *The Oxford Classical Dictionary*, ed. S. Hornblower and A. Spawforth (Oxford: Oxford University Press, 1996³), xxiv–liv.

For other abbreviations, see *The SBL Handbook of Style*, ed. P. H. Alexander et al. (Peabody, Mass.: Hendrickson, 1999), 121–52.

Appian, *The Civil Wars, III–V*, tr. H. White (Loeb vol. IV; London: Heinemann, 1913).

Aristotle, *Historia Animalium, IV–VI*, tr. A. L. Peck (Loeb vol. II; London: Heinemann, 1970).

　Nicomachean Ethics, tr. H. Rackham (Loeb vol. XIX; London: Heinemann, 1926).

　Politics, tr. H. Rackham (Loeb; London: Heinemann, 1932).

Augustus, *Res Gestae Divi Augusti*, tr. F. W. Shipley (Loeb (with Velleius Paterculus); London: Heinemann, 1924).

B.M.C. = *Coins of the Roman Empire in the British Museum (Augustus to Vitellius)*, ed. H. Mattingly (London: British Museum, 1923).

Bettenson, Henry, ed., *Documents of the Christian Church* (Oxford: Oxford University Press, 1963²).

Cicero, *De Imperio Cn. Pompei (Pro Lege Manilia)*, tr. H. G. Hodge (Loeb; London: Heinemann, 1927).

　De Re Publica, De Legibus, tr. C. W. Keyes (Loeb; London: Heinemann, 1928).

　On Duties (De Officiis), tr. M. T. Griffin and E. M. Atkins (Cambridge: Cambridge University Press, 1991).

Dio Cassius, *Cassii Dionis Cocceiani, Historiarum Romanarum quae Supersunt*, ed. U. P. Boissevain (Berlin: Weidmann, 1931).

　Dio's Roman History, LI–LV, tr. E. Cary (Loeb vol. I; London: Heinemann, 1932).

Dio Chrysostom, *Discourses, I–XI*, tr. J. W. Cohoon (Loeb vol. I; London: Heinemann, 1932).

　Discourses, XII–XXX, tr. J. W. Cohoon (Loeb vol. II; London: Heinemann, 1939).

　Discourses, XXXVII–LX, tr. J. W. Cohoon (Loeb vol. IV; London: Heinemann, 1946).

Orations, Vol. II, tr. J. W. Cohoon (Loeb; London: Heinemann, 1950).
Orations, Vol. IV, tr. H. L. Crosby (Loeb; London: Heinemann, 1962).
Diogenes Laertius, *Lives of Eminent Philosophers, Vol. II*, tr. R. D. Hicks (Loeb; London: Heinemann, 1925).
Dionysius of Halicarnassus, *The Roman Antiquities, I–II*, tr. E. Cary (Loeb vol. I; London: Heinemann, 1937).
Dittenberger, C. F. W., *Sylloge Inscriptionium Graecarum, Vols. 1, 2, 3* (Leipzig: Hirzel, 1915^3, 1917^3, 1920^3).
Dittenberger, W., *Orientis Graeci Inscriptiones Selectae, Vols. 1 & 2* (Leipzig: Hirzel, 1903, 1905).
Edmonds, J. M., *The Greek Bucolic Poets* (Loeb; London: Heinemann, 1950).
Epictetus, *Discourses*, 2 vols., tr. W. A. Oldfather (Loeb; London: Heinemann, 1925).
Eusebius, *The Ecclesiastical History, I–V*, tr. K. Lake (Loeb vol. I; London: Heinemann, 1926).
Granius Licinianus, *Reliqueae*, ed. Nicola Criniti (Leipzig: Teubner, 1981).
Heath, T. L., *Aristarchus of Samos* (Oxford: Clarendon Press, 1913, repr. 1959).
Hunt, A. S. and Edgar, C. C., *Select Papyri, II* (Loeb; London: Heinemann, 1934).
Ignatius, *Apostolic Fathers, II.II*, tr. J. B. Lightfoot (London: Macmillan, 1889^2).
   Die Briefe des Ignatius von Antiochia und der Polykarpbrief, tr. W. Bauer and H. Paulsen (Handbuch zum NT 18: Die Apostolischen Väter II; Tübingen: J. C. B. Mohr, 1985).
Inscriptiones Graecae ad Res Romanas Pertinentes (Paris: E. Leroux, 1906).
Inscriptiones Graecae, II.2, ed. U. Koehler (Berlin: Reimerus, 1883).
Inscriptiones Graecae, IV, ed. M. Fraenkel (Berlin: Reimerus, 1902).
Inscriptiones Graecae, VII, ed. W. Dittenberger (Berlin: Reimerus, 1892).
Inscriptiones Graecae, XII.7–8, ed. J. Delamarre (Berlin: Reimerus, 1908).
Johnson, A. C., Coleman-Norton, P. R. and Bourne, F. C., *Ancient Roman Statutes: a Translation* (Austin: University of Texas Press, 1961).
Josephus, *Against Apion*, tr. H. St. J. Thackeray (Loeb; London: Heinemann, 1926).
   Jewish Antiquities, tr. H. St. J. Thackeray, R. Marcus and L. H. Feldman (Loeb; London: Heinemann, 1930, etc.).
   The Jewish War, tr. H. St. J. Thackeray (Loeb; London: Heinemann, 1927, 1928).
Justin Martyr, *Vol. II, Dialogue avec Tryphon*, tr. G. Archambault (Paris: Picard, 1909).
Justin Martyr, tr. G. Reith (Ante-Nicene Christian Library, II; Edinburgh: T&T Clark, 1867).
Lewis, N. and Reinhold, M., eds., *Roman Civilization II* (New York: Harper & Row, 1955).
Lightfoot, J. B. and Harmer, J. R., *The Apostolic Fathers*, revd M. W. Holmes (Leicester: Apollos, 1991^2).
Lucan, *The Civil War Books I–X (Pharsalia)*, tr. J. D. Duff (Loeb; London: Heinemann, 1962).

Origen, *Origenis Hexaplorum I*, ed. F. Field (Oxford: Clarendon Press, 1875).

Ovid, *Tristia & Ex Ponto*, tr. A. L. Wheeler, revd. G. P. Goold (Loeb; London: Heinemann, 1988 edn).

Petronius, *Works*, tr. M. Heseltine, revd E. H. Warmington (Loeb (with Seneca, *Apocolocyntosis*); London: Heinemann, 1969 edn).

Philo, *De Decalogo*, tr. F. H. Colson (Loeb vol. VII; London: Heinemann, 1937).

De Iosepho, tr. F. H. Colson (Loeb vol. VI; London: Heinemann, 1935).

Life of Moses, tr. F. H. Colson (Loeb vol. VI; London: Heinemann, 1935).

On the Embassy to Gaius (De virtutibus prima pars, quod est De Legatione ad Gaium) tr. F. H. Colson (Loeb vol. X; London: Heinemann, 1962).

Plato, *Laches, Protagoras, Meno, Euthydemus*, tr. W. R. M. Lamb (Loeb; London: Heinemann, 1925).

Laws, VII–XII, tr. R. G. Bury (Loeb vol. II; London: Heinemann, 1961).

Pliny, *Letters & Panegyricus*, 2 vols., tr. Betty Radice (Loeb; London: Heinemann, 1969).

Plutarch, *Ad Principem Ineruditum, Moralia Vol. X*, tr. H. N. Fowler (Loeb; London: Heinemann, 1969).

De Alexandri magni fortuna aut virtute and *De Fortuna Romanorum, Moralia Vol. IV*, tr. F. C. Babbitt (Loeb; London: Heinemann, 1936).

Sulla, Lives Vol. IV, ed. B. Perrin (Loeb; London: Heinemann, 1950).

Moralia, Vol. I, tr. F. C. Babbitt (Loeb; London: Heinemann, 1927).

Moralia, Vol. XII, tr. H. Cherniss and W. C. Helmbold (Loeb; London: Heinemann, 1957).

Polybius, *The Histories, IX–XV*, tr. W. R. Paton (Loeb vol. IV; London: Heinemann, 1925).

The Histories, XVI–XXV, tr. W. R. Paton (Loeb vol. V; London: Heinemann, 1926).

Roman Provincial Coinage, Vol. I (44BC–AD69), Pts I and II, ed. A. M. Burnett, M. Amandry and P. P. Ripollès (London: British Museum Press, 1992).

Seneca, *Apocolocyntosis Divi Claudii (The Pumpkinification of Claudius)*, tr. W. H. D. Rouse (Loeb (with Petronius); London: Heinemann, 1969 edn).

De Beneficiis, Moral Essays Vol. III, tr. J. W. Basore (Loeb; Cambridge, Mass.: Harvard University Press, 1935).

De Clementia, Moral Essays Vol. I, tr. J. W. Basore (Loeb; London: Heinemann, 1928).

Septuaginta, ed. A. Rahlfs (Stuttgart: Deutsche Bibelgesellschaft, 1935, 1979).

Stobaeus, John, *Anthology, Vol. IV*, ed. C. Wachsmuth and O. Hense (Berlin: Weidmann, 1909).

Strabo, *The Geography*, 8 vols., tr. H. L. Jones (Loeb; London: Heinemann, 1917, etc.).

Suetonius, *Lives of the Caesars*, 2 vols., tr. J. C. Rolfe (Loeb; London: Heinemann, 1913, 1914).

'Sibylline Oracles', tr. J. J. Collins, in *The Old Testament Pseudepigrapha, vol. I*, ed. J. H. Charlesworth (London: Darton, Longman & Todd, 1983).

Tacitus, *The Annals of Imperial Rome*, tr. Michael Grant (Harmondsworth: Penguin, 1971 edn).

   The Histories, 2 vols., tr. C. H. Moore (Loeb; London: Heinemann, 1925, 1931).

Tertullian, *Apologia*, tr. T. R. Glover (Loeb; London: Heinemann, 1931).

   De Idololatria: Critical Text, Translation and Commentary, tr. J. H. Waszink and J. C. M. Van Winden (Supp. to Vig. Chr. I; Leiden: E. J. Brill, 1987).

Theophrastus, *De Causis Plantarum, V–VI*, tr. B. Einarson and G. K. K. Link (Loeb vol. III; London: Harvard University Press, 1990).

Velleius Paterculus, *Historiae Romanae*, tr. F. W. Shipley (Loeb; London: Heinemann; Cambridge, Mass.: Harvard University Press, 1924).

BIBLIOGRAPHY: MODERN

Abrahamsen, V., *The Rock Reliefs and the Cult of Diana at Philippi* (Diss. Harvard University; Ann Arbor: University Microfilms, 1986).

Alcock, Susan E., *Graecia Capta: The Landscapes of Roman Greece* (Cambridge: Cambridge University Press, 1993).

Alexander, Loveday, 'Hellenistic Letter-Forms and the Structure of Philippians', *JSNT* 37 (1989), 87–101.

Barth, K., *The Epistle to the Philippians*, tr. J. W. Leitch (Richmond: John Knox, 1962 (ET of 1947 edn)).

Bauckham, Richard, 'The Worship of Jesus', in Ralph P. Martin and Brian J. Dodd, eds., *Where Christology Began: Essays on Philippians 2* (Louisville: Westminster John Knox, 1998).

Bauer, W., Arndt, W. F., Gingrich, F. W. and Danker, F., *A Greek–English Lexicon of the New Testament* (Chicago: University of Chicago Press, 1979).

Bean, G. E., 'Abydos', *Princeton Encyclopedia of Classical Sites*, ed. R. Stillwell (Princeton: Princeton University Press, 1976), 5.

Beare, F. W., *A Commentary on the Epistle to the Philippians* (New York: Harper, 1959).

Béranger, Jean, *Recherches sur l'aspect idéologique du Principat* (Basel: Reinhardt, 1953).

Bloomquist, L. Gregory, *The Function of Suffering in Philippians* (JSNTSup 78; Sheffield: JSOT Press, 1993).

Bockmuehl, Markus, *The Epistle to the Philippians* (London: A. & C. Black, 1997).

Bormann, Lukas, *Philippi: Stadt und Christengemeinde zur Zeit des Paulus* (NovTSup 78; Leiden: Brill, 1995).

Bornhäuser, D. Karl, *Jesus imperator mundi (Phil 3, 17–21 u. 2, 5–12)* (Gütersloh: Bertelsmann, 1938).

Bowersock, G. W., *Augustus and the Greek World* (Oxford: Clarendon Press, 1965).

Brewer, R. R., 'The Meaning of Politeuesthe in Philippians 127', *JBL* 73 (1954), 76–83.

Brown, Colin, 'Ernst Lohmeyer's *Kyrios Jesus*', in Ralph P. Martin and Brian J. Dodd, eds., *Where Christology Began: Essays on Philippians 2* (Louisville: Westminster John Knox, 1998).

Browning, Robert, 'Prologue: Land and People', in R. Browning, ed., *The Greeks* (London: Thames & Hudson, 1985; Portland House, 1989).

Brunt, P. A., *Italian Manpower: 225BC–AD14* (Oxford: Oxford University Press, 1971, 1987).

Büchsel, F., ἐριθεία, *TDNT II,* ed. G. Kittel, tr. G. Bromiley (Grand Rapids: Eerdmans, 1964), 660–1.

Bunbury, E. H., 'Marsyas (2)', *Dictionary of Greek and Roman Biography and Mythology,* ed. W. Smith (London: Taylor & Walton, 1846).

Burford, Alison, *Craftsmen in Greek and Roman Society* (Ithaca: Cornell University Press, 1972).

Caird, G. B., *Paul's Letters from Prison (Ephesians, Philippians, Colossians, Philemon)* (New Clarendon Bible; Oxford: Oxford University Press, 1976).

Campbell, J. B., *The Emperor and the Roman Army, 31BC–AD235* (Oxford: Clarendon Press, 1984).

Carney, T. F., *The Shape of the Past: Models and Antiquity* (Lawrence, Kans.: Coronado Press, 1975).

Cerfaux, Lucien, 'L'hymne au Christ-Serviteur de Dieu (Phil., II, 6–11 = Is., LII, 13–LIII, 12)', *Recueil Lucien Cerfaux II* (Gembloux: Duculot, 1954).

Chesnut, Glenn F., 'The Ruler and the Logos in Neopythagorean, Middle Platonic & Late Stoic Political Philosophy', *ANRW 17.2* (Berlin: Walter de Gruyter, 1978).

Collange, J.-F., *The Epistle of Saint Paul to the Philippians,* tr. A. W. Heathcote (London: Epworth, 1979).

Collart, Paul, 'Inscriptions de Philippes', *BCH* 56 (1932), 192–231.

'Philippes', *Dictionnaire d'Archéologie Chrétienne et de Liturgie XIV:1,* ed. F. Cabrol and H. Leclerq (Paris: Librairie Letouzy et Ané, 1939), cols. 712–41.

Philippes, Ville de Macédoine: depuis ses origines jusqu'à la fin de l'époque romaine (Travaux et Mémoires, Fascicule V; École Française d'Athènes: Paris, 1937).

'Sanctuaire des dieux égyptiens', *BCH* 53 (1929), 70–100.

Collart, Paul and Ducrey, Pierre, *Philippes I: Les Reliefs Rupestres* (BCH Supp. II; Paris, 1975).

Combès, Robert, *Imperator* (Paris: Presses Universitaires de France, 1966).

Conzelmann, H., *Acts of the Apostles* (Hermeneia; Philadelphia: Fortress Press, 1987).

Coupry, J. and Feyel, M., 'Inscriptions de Philippes III (I)', *BCH* 60 (1936), 37–58.

Culpepper, R. A., 'Co-Workers in Suffering. Philippians 2:19–30', *RevExp* 77 (1980), 349–58.

Dahl, Nils A., 'Euodia and Syntyche and Paul's Letter to the Philippians' in L. M. White and O. L. Yarbrough, eds., *The Social World of the First Christians: Essays in Honor of Wayne A. Meeks* (Philadelphia: Fortress Press, 1995).

de Ste Croix, G. E. M., 'Why were the early Christians Persecuted?' *Past & Present,* 26 (1963), 6–38.

Deissmann, Adolf, *Light from the Ancient East: The New Testament Illustrated by Recently Discovered Texts of the Graeco-Roman World,* tr. L. R. M. Strachan (London: Hodder & Stoughton, 1927 edn).

Dodd, Brian, 'The Story of Christ and the Imitation of Paul in Philippians 2–3', in Ralph P. Martin and Brian J. Dodd, eds., *Where Christology Began: Essays on Philippians 2* (Louisville: Westminster John Knox, 1998).

Duncan-Jones, R., *The Economy of the Roman Empire: Quantitative Studies* (Cambridge: Cambridge University Press, 1982²).

Dunn, J. D. G., *Christology in the Making* (SCM: London, 1989²).

Ehrhardt, A. A. T., 'Jesus Christ and Alexander the Great', *JTS* 46 (1945), 45–51 = *The Framework of the NT Stories* (Manchester: Manchester University Press, 1964), 37–43.

Elliger, Winfried, *Paulus in Griechenland: Philippi, Thessaloniki, Athen, Korinth* (Stuttgarter Bibel-Studien; Stuttgart: Verlag Katholisches Bibelwerk, 1978).

Elliott, John, *Social Scientific Criticism of the New Testament* (London: SPCK, 1995).

Engels, D. W., *Roman Corinth: an Alternative Model for the Classical City* (London: University of Chicago Press, 1990).

Faust, E., *Pax Christi et Pax Caesaris: Religionsgeschichtliche, traditionsgeschichtliche u. sozialgeschichtliche Studien zum Epheserbrief* (Freiburg: Universitätsverlag; Göttingen: Vandenhoeck & Ruprecht, 1993).

Fears, J. Rufus, 'Rome: The Ideology of Imperial Power', *Thought*, 55 (March 1980), 98–109.

Fee, Gordon D., *Paul's Letter to the Philippians* (NICNT; Grand Rapids: Eerdmans, 1995).

Feldman, Louis H., *Jew & Gentile in the Ancient World: Attitudes and Interactions from Alexander to Justinian* (Princeton: Princeton University Press, 1993).

Finley, M. I., 'Freedmen', 'Peculium', 'Slavery', *Oxford Classical Dictionary*, ed. N. G. L. Hammond and H. H. Scullard (Oxford: Clarendon Press, 1970²), 447f., 793, 994–7.

Fish, Stanley, *Is There a Text in This Class? The Authority of Interpretive Communities* (Cambridge, Mass.: Harvard University Press, 1980).

Foerster, W. and Quell, G., κύριος, *TDNT III*, ed. G. Kittel, tr. G. W. Bromiley (Grand Rapids: Eerdmans, 1965), 1039–98.

σωτήρ, *TDNT VII*, ed. G. Friedrich, tr. G. W. Bromiley (Grand Rapids: Eerdmans, 1971), 1003–21.

Fowl, Stephen E., *The Story of Christ in the Ethics of Paul: An Analysis of the Function of the Hymnic Material in the Pauline Corpus* (JSNTSup 36; Sheffield: JSOT Press, 1990).

Frend, W. H. C., *Martyrdom and Persecution in the Early Church* (Oxford: Blackwell, 1965).

Friedrich, Gerhard, 'Der Brief an die Philipper', *Die kleineren Briefe des Apostels Paulus*, H. W. Beyer et al. (NTD (9th edn) VIII; Göttingen: Vandenhoeck & Ruprecht, 1962).

Garland, D. E., 'The Composition and Unity of Philippians: Some Neglected Literary Factors', *NovT* 27 (1985), 141–73.

Garnsey, Peter, *Social Status and Legal Privilege in the Roman Empire* (Oxford: Clarendon Press, 1970).

220   Bibliography: modern

Garnsey, Peter and Saller, Richard, *The Roman Empire: Economy, Society and Culture* (London: Duckworth, 1987).
Garnsey, P. and Woolf, G., 'Patronage of the rural poor in the Roman world', in A. Wallace-Hadrill, ed., *Patronage in Ancient Society* (London: Routledge, 1990).
Geoffrion, Timothy C., *The Rhetorical Purpose and the Political and Military Character of Philippians: A Call to Stand Firm* (Lewiston: Mellen Biblical Press, 1993).
Georgi, Dieter, *Theocracy in Paul's Praxis and Theology*, tr. D. E. Green (Minneapolis: Fortress Press, 1991 (Ger. 1987)).
    'Der Vorpaulinische Hymnus Phil 2, 6–11', in E. Dinkler, ed., *Zeit und Geschichte: Dankesgabe an Rudolf Bultmann zum 80 Geburtstag* (Tübingen: J. C. B. Mohr, 1964).
Giesen, H., ἐριθεία, *Exegetical Dictionary of the New Testament, Vol. 2*, ed. H. Balz and G. Schneider (ET; Grand Rapids: Eerdmans, 1991), 52.
Gnilka, Joachim, *Der Philipperbrief* (Herders Theologischer Kommentar, X:3; Freiburg: Herder, 1968).
Goodenough, Erwin R., 'The Political Philosophy of Hellenistic Kingship', *Yale Classical Studies* 1 (1928), 55–102.
Goodman, Martin, *Mission and Conversion: Proselytizing in the Religious History of the Roman Empire* (Oxford: Clarendon Press, 1994).
Grant, M., *From Imperium to Auctoritas* (Cambridge: Cambridge University Press, 1969).
Hawthorne, Gerald F., 'In the Form of God and Equal with God (Philippians 2:6)', in Ralph P. Martin and Brian J. Dodd, eds., *Where Christology Began: Essays on Philippians 2* (Louisville: Westminster John Knox, 1998).
    Philippians (Waco: Word, 1983).
Hays, Richard B., *Echoes of Scripture in the Letters of Paul*, (New Haven, Yale University Press, 1989).
Heichelheim, F. M., 'Latifundia', *Oxford Classical Dictionary*, ed. N. G. L. Hammond and H. H. Scullard (Oxford: Clarendon Press, 1980[2]), 579.
Hendrix, Holland L., 'Philippi', *Anchor Bible Dictionary, V*, ed. D. N. Freedman (New York: Doubleday, 1992), 313–17.
Hofius, Otfried, *Der Christushymnus Philipper 2, 6–11* (WUNT, 17; Tübingen: J. C. B. Mohr, 1976).
Hooker, M. D., 'Interchange in Christ' and 'Phil 2:6–11', *From Adam to Christ* (Cambridge: Cambridge University Press, 1990).
Hoover, R. W., 'The Harpagmos Enigma: A Philological Solution' *HTR* 64 (1971), 95–119.
Hopkins, K., *Conquerors and Slaves* (Cambridge: Cambridge University Press, 1978).
Houlden, J. L., *Paul's Letters from Prison* (PNTC; Harmondsworth: Penguin, 1970).
Hurtado, L. W., 'Jesus as Lordly Example in Philippians 2:5–11', in P. Richardson and J. C. Hurd, eds., *From Jesus to Paul: Studies in Honour of Francis Wright Beare* (Waterloo, Ontario: Wilfred Laurier University Press, 1984).

One God, One Lord: early Christian devotion and ancient Jewish Monotheism (London: SCM, 1998²).

Huttunen, Pertti, *The Social Strata in the Imperial City of Rome: A Quantitative Study of the Social Representation in the Epitaphs published in the Corpus Inscriptionum Latinarum Volumen VI* (Oulu: University of Oulu, 1974).

Isaac, Benjamin, *The Limits of Empire: The Roman Army in the East* (Oxford: Clarendon Press, 1992 (revd)).

Jeremias, J., 'Zu Phil.2,7: ΕΑΥΤΟΝ ΕΚΕΝΩΣΕΝ', *NovT* 6 (1963), 182–8.

Jewett, Robert, 'Conflicting movements in the early church as reflected in Philippians', *NovT* 12 (1970), 362–90.

'The Epistolary Thanksgiving and the Integrity of Philippians', *NovT* 12 (1970), 40–53.

Johnson, A. C. et al., *Ancient Roman Statues: a translation* (Austin: University of Texas Press, 1961).

Jones, A. H. M., 'Colonus', *Oxford Classical Dictionary*, ed. N. G. L. Hammond and H. H. Scullard (Oxford: Clarendon Press, 1970²), 266.

Jones, C. P., *The Roman World of Dio Chrysostom* (Cambridge, Mass.: Harvard University Press, 1978).

Käsemann, E., 'A Critical Analysis of Philippians 2:5–11', tr. A. F. Carse, H. Braun et al., in R. W. Funk, ed., *God and Christ: Existence and Province* (*Journal for Theology and the Church* 5) (Tübingen: J. C. B. Mohr, 1968), 45–88.

Jesus means Freedom: A Polemical Survey of the New Testament, tr. F. Clarke (London: SCM, 1969) (Der Ruf der Freiheit, J. C. B. Mohr, 1968³).

Kennedy, H. A. A., 'Apostolic Preaching and Emperor Worship', *The Expositor* (April, 1909), 289–307.

Kim, C.-H., *Form and Structure of the Familiar Greek Letter of Recommendation* (SBL Diss. Series 4, 1972).

Kloppenborg, John S., 'Edwin Hatch, Churches and Collegia', in B. H. McLean, ed., *Origins and Method: Towards a New Understanding of Judaism and Christianity: Essays in Honour of John C. Hurd* (JSNTSS 86; Sheffield: JSOT Press, 1993).

Koester, H., 'The Purpose of the Polemic of a Pauline Fragment (Philippians III)', *NTS* 8 (1961–2), 317–32.

Kögel, Julius, *Christus der Herr* (Gütersloh, 1908).

Koukouli-Chrysantaki, Chaido, 'Colonia Iulia Augusta Philippensis', in C. Bakirtzis and H. Koester, eds., *Philippi at the Time of Paul and after His Death* (Harrisburg: Trinity Press International, 1998).

Τυχαια Ευρηματα-Εντοπισμοι, *Archaeologikon Deltion* 42 (1987) Β΄ 2, Χρονικα (1992), 444.

Kreitzer, Larry J., '"When He at Last is First!": Philippians 2:9–11', in Ralph P. Martin and Brian J. Dodd, eds., *Where Christology Began: Essays on Philippians 2* (Louisville: Westminster John Knox, 1998).

Kurz, William S., 'Kenotic Imitation of Paul and of Christ in Philippians 2 & 3', in F. F. Segovia, ed., *Discipleship in the New Testament* (Philadelphia: Fortress Press, 1985).

Kyrtatas, Dimitris J., *The Social Structure of the Early Christian Communities* (London: Verso, 1987).

Lane Fox, Robin, *Pagans and Christians* (Harmondsworth: Viking, 1986).

Laqueur, 'Marsyas (9)', in G. Wissowa and W. Kroll, eds., *Pauly XIV (2)* (Stuttgart: Metzler, 1930), 1998–9.

Lazarides, D., Φίλιπποι-Ρωμαϊκή ἀποικία (Ancient Greek Cities 20; Athens, 1973).

Lemerle, Paul, 'Inscriptions Latines et Grecques de Philippes, 2', *BCH* 59 (1935), 126–64.

  Philippes et la Macédoine Orientale à l'époque chrétienne et byzantine: Recherches d'histoire et d'archéologie (Bibliothèque des Écoles Françaises d'Athènes et de Rome 158; Paris: Boccard, 1945).

  'Le Testament d'un Thrace à Philippes', *BCH* 60 (1936), 336–43.

Leveau, Philippe, *Caesarea de Maurétanie: Une Ville Romaine et ses Campagnes* (Collection de l'école française de Rome 70; Rome: École Française, 1984).

Levick, Barbara, *Roman Colonies in Southern Asia Minor* (Oxford: Clarendon Press, 1967).

Lewis, N. and Reinhold, M., eds., *Roman Civilization II* (New York: Harper & Row, 1955).

Liddell, H. G. and Scott, R., *Greek-English Lexicon*, revd H. S. Jones (Oxford: Clarendon Press, 1940, 1968).

Lightfoot, J. B., *St. Paul's Epistle to the Philippians* (London: Macmillan, 1885 edn).

Lincoln, Andrew T., *Paradise Now and Not Yet: Studies in the role of the heavenly dimension in Paul's thought with special reference to his eschatology* (SNTSMS, 43; Cambridge: Cambridge University Press, 1981).

Loh, I.-J. and Nida, E. A., *A Translator's Handbook on Paul's Letter to the Philippians* (London: United Bible Societies, 1977).

Lohmeyer, Ernst, *Der Brief an die Philipper* (Göttingen: Vandenhoeck & Ruprecht, 1928).

  Christuskult und Kaiserkult (Tübingen: J. C. B. Mohr, 1919).

  Kyrios Jesus: Eine Untersuchung zu Phil 2, 5–11 (Sitzungsberichte der Heidelberger Akad. der Wiss. 18:4; Heidelberg: Winters, 1928).

Louw, J. P. and Nida, E. A., *Greek-English Lexicon of the New Testament Based on Semantic Domains* (New York: United Bible Societies, 1989[2]).

MacMullen, Ramsay, *Roman Social Relations: 50BC to AD284* (New Haven: Yale University Press, 1974).

Malina, Bruce J., *The New Testament World: Insights from Cultural Anthropology* (London: SCM, 1983 (page refs. unless noted); Louisville: Westminster/John Knox, 1993 edn).

Mann, J. C., *Legionary Recruitment and Veteran Settlement During the Principate,* ed. M. M. Roxan (Occasional Publication No. 7; London: Institute of Archaeology, 1983).

Marshall, P., *Enmity in Corinth: Social Conventions in Paul's relationship with the Corinthians* (Tübingen: J. C. B. Mohr, 1987).

Martin, R. P., *Carmen Christi: Philippians 2:5–11 in recent interpretation and in the setting of early Christian worship* (Grand Rapids: Eerdmans, 1983 edn).

Philippians (New Century Bible; Grand Rapids: Eerdmans, 1980).

Mearns, Chris, 'The Identity of Paul's Opponents at Philippi', *NTS* 33 (1987), 194–204.

Meeks, Wayne A., *The First Urban Christians: The Social World of the Apostle Paul* (New Haven: Yale University Press, 1983).

'The Man from Heaven in Paul's Letter to the Philippians', in B. A. Pearson, ed., *The Future of Early Christianity: Essays in Honor of Helmut Koester* (Minneapolis: Fortress Press, 1991).

Meggitt, Justin J., *Paul, Poverty and Survival*, (Edinburgh: T&T Clark, 1998).

Mengel, Berthold, *Studien zum Philipperbrief: Untersuchungen zum situativen Kontext unter besonderer Berücksichtigung der Frage nach der Ganzheitlichkeit oder Einheitlichkeit eines paulinischen Briefes* (WUNT 2:8; Tübingen: J. C. B. Mohr, 1982).

Merk, Otto, *Handeln aus Glauben: Die Motivierung der Paulinischen Ethik* (Marburger Th St 5; Marburg: Elwert, 1968).

Michael, J. H., *The Epistle to the Philippians* (MNTC; London: Hodder & Stoughton, 1928).

Michel, O., ὁμολογέω, *TDNT V*, ed. G. Friedrich, tr. G. W. Bromiley (Grand Rapids: Eerdmans, 1967), 199–200.

Millar, F., *The Emperor in the Roman World* (London: Duckworth, 1977).

'The Roman Coloniae of the Near East: a Study of Cultural Relations', in H. Solin and M. Kajava, eds., *Roman Eastern Policy and Other Studies in Roman History,* (Commentationes Humanarum Litterarum 91; Helsinki: Societas Scientiarum Fennica, 1990).

Miller, E. C., 'Πολιτεύεσθε in Philippians 1.27: Some Philological and Thematic Observations', *JSNT* 15 (1982), 86–96.

Mitchell, Alan C., 'The Social Function of Friendship in Acts 2:44–47 and 4:32–37', *JBL* 111:2 (Summer 1992), 255–72.

Mócsy, A., *Die Bevölkerung von Pannonien bis zu den Markomannenkriegen* (Budapest: Verlag der Ungarischen Akademie der Wissenschaften, 1959).

Morgan, Robert, 'Incarnation, Myth, and Theology: Ernst Käsemann's Interpretation of Philippians 2:5–11', in Ralph P. Martin and Brian J. Dodd, eds., *Where Christology Began: Essays on Philippians 2* (Louisville: Westminster John Knox, 1998).

Mott, S. C., 'The Power of Giving and Receiving: Reciprocity in Hellenistic Benevolence', in G. F. Hawthorne, ed., *Current Issues in Biblical and Patristic Interpretation (Studies in Honour of Merril C. Tenney)* (Grand Rapids: Eerdmans, 1975).

Moule, C. F. D., 'Further Reflexions on Philippians 2:5–11', in R. P. Martin, ed., *Apostolic History and the Gospel* (Exeter: Paternoster, 1970).

NIV Study Bible, The (London: Hodder & Stoughton, 1987 UK edn).

O'Brien, Peter T., *Commentary on Philippians* (NIGTC; Grand Rapids: Eerdmans, 1991).

Oakes, Peter, 'Epictetus (and the New Testament)', *Vox Evangelica* 23 (1993), 39–56.

'Jason and Penelope Hear Philippians 1:1–11', in Christopher Rowland and Crispin H. T. Fletcher-Louis, eds., *Understanding, Studying and Reading. New Testament Essays in Honour of John Ashton* (Sheffield: Sheffield Academic Press, 1998).

'Philippians: From People to Letter' (unpubl. DPhil thesis, Oxford, 1996).

'Quelle devrait être l'influence des échos intertextuels sur la traduction? Le cas de l'épître aux Philippiens (2:15–16)', in D. Marguerat and A. Curtis, eds., *Intertextualités* (Geneva: Labor et Fides, 2000).

Oakman, Douglas E., 'The Countryside in Luke-Acts', in J. H. Neyrey, ed., *The Social World of Luke-Acts* (Peabody: Hendrickson, 1991).

Oepke, A., κενός, *TDNT III*, ed. G. Kittel, tr. G. W. Bromiley (Grand Rapids: Eerdmans, 1965), 659–62.

Orr, D. G., 'Roman Domestic Religion: The Evidence of the Household Shrines', *ANRW II.16.2,* ed. W. Haase (Berlin: de Gruyter, 1978).

Papazoglou, Fanoula, 'Macedonia under the Romans: Political and administrative developments', in M. B. Sakellariou, ed., *Macedonia*, various trs. (Athens: Ekdotike Athenon, 1983 (1982)).

'Quelques aspects de l'histoire de la province de Macédoine', *ANRW II.7.1*, ed. H. Temporini (Berlin: de Gruyter, 1979).

Les Villes de Macédoine à l'époque Romaine (BCHSup XVI; Paris: École Française d'Athènes, 1988).

Parsi, Blanche, *Désignation et Investiture de l'Empereur Romain (Ier et IIe siècles après J.-C.)* (Paris: Librairie Sirey, 1963).

Perdrizet, P. 'Voyage dans La Macédoine Première', *BCH* 21 (1897), 514–43.

Peterlin, Davorin, *Paul's Letter to the Philippians in the Light of Disunity in the Church* (NovTSup LXXIX; Leiden: E. J. Brill, 1995).

Pilhofer, Peter, *Philippi I: Die erste christliche Gemeinde Europas* (Tübingen: J. C. B. Mohr, 1995).

Plummer, A., *A Commentary on St. Paul's Epistle to the Philippians* (London: Robert Scott, 1919).

Portefaix, Lilian, *Sisters Rejoice: Paul's letter to the Philippians and Luke-Acts as received by First Century Philippian Women* (Coniectanea Biblica, NT Series 20; Uppsala/Stockholm: Almqvist & Wiksell International, 1988).

Price, S. R. F., *Rituals and Power: The Roman imperial cult in Asia Minor* (Cambridge: Cambridge University Press, 1984).

Ramsay, W. M., *St. Paul the Traveller and the Roman Citizen* (London: Hodder & Stoughton, 1925[15]).

Reed, Jeffrey T., *A Discourse Analysis of Philippians* (JSNTSS 136; Sheffield: Sheffield Academic Press, 1997).

Richmond, I. A. and North, J., 'Pomerium', *Oxford Classical Dictionary*, ed. N. G. L. Hammond and H. H. Scullard (Oxford: Clarendon Press, 1970[2]), 856.

Roger, J., 'L'enceinte Basse de Philippes', *BCH* 62 (1938), 20–41.

Rohrbaugh, Richard L., 'The Pre-Industrial City in Luke-Acts: Urban

Social Relations', in J. H. Neyrey, ed., *The Social World of Luke-Acts* (Peabody: Hendrickson, 1991).

Salmon, E. T., *Roman Colonization under the Republic* (London: Thames & Hudson, 1969).

Samsaris, D., Ερευνις στην ιστορια, την τοπογραφια και τις λατρειες των ρωμαικων επαρχιων μακεδονιας και θρακις (Thessaloniki, 1984).

'Τοπογραφικα Προβληματα της Επικρατειας της Ρωμαικης Αποικιας των Φιλιππων: τα Πολισματα Αγγιτης και Αδριανουπολη', *Ancient Macedonia, IV* (Thessaloniki: Institute for Balkan Studies, 1986).

Sarikakis, Théodore Chr., 'Des Soldats Macédoniens dans l'Armée Romaine', *Ancient Macedonia, II* (Thessaloniki: Institute for Balkan Studies, 1977).

Schenk, W., 'Der Philipperbrief in der neureren Forschung (1945–1985)', *ANRW II.25.4*, ed. W. Haase (Berlin: Walter de Gruyter, 1987).

Die Philipperbriefe des Paulus (Stuttgart: Kohlhammer, 1984).

Schlier, H., γόνυ, *TDNT I*, ed. G. Kittel, tr. G. W. Bromiley (Grand Rapids, Eerdmans, 1964), 738–40.

κάμπτω, *TDNT III*, ed. G. Kittel, tr. G. W. Bromiley (Grand Rapids, Eerdmans, 1965), 594–5.

Schmitz, H., *Stadt und Imperium: Köln in romischer Zeit* (Cologne, 1948).

Schottroff, Luise, 'Die Schreckenherrschaft der Sünde und die Befreiung durch Christus nach dem Römerbrief des Paulus', *Evangelische Theologie* 39:6 (1979), 497–510.

Schweizer, E., *Erniedrigung und Erhöhung bei Jesus und seinen Nachfolgern* (ATANT 28; Zurich: Zwingli, 1955).

Scramuzza, Vincent M., 'Claudius Soter Euergetes', *Harv. Stud. in Class. Philology* 51 (1940), 261–6.

Seeley, David, 'The Background of the Philippians Hymn (2:6–11)', *Journal of Higher Criticism* 1, (Fall 1994), 49–72; internet edition at http://daniel.drew.edu/˜doughty/jhcbody.html#reviews.

Sève, M., 'Philippes', *BCH* 106 (1982), 651–65.

Recherches sur les Places Publiques dans le Monde Grec du Premier au Septième Siècle de Notre Ère: L'Exemple de Philippes (Microfiche; Lille: Lille-Thèses, 1989, 1990).

Sève, M. and Weber, P., 'Le côté Nord du forum de Philippes', *BCH* 110 (1986), 531–81.

'Un monument honorifique au forum de Philippes', *BCH* 112 (1988), 467–79.

Sherwin-White, Adrian N., *The Roman Citizenship* (Oxford: Clarendon Press, 1973²).

Silva, M., *Philippians* (Wycliffe Exegetical Commentaries; Chicago: Moody, 1988).

Sutherland, C. H. V., *Coinage in Roman Imperial Policy, 31BC–AD68* (London: Methuen, 1951 (1971 repr.)).

The Emperor and the Coinage: Julio-Claudian Studies (London: Spink & Son, 1976).

Tellbe, Mikael B., 'Christ and Caesar: The Letter to the Philippians in the Setting of the Roman Imperial Cult' (unpubl. ThM thesis, Vancouver, 1993).

'The Sociological Factors Behind Phil 3:1–11 and the Conflict at Philippi', *JSNT* 51 (1994), 97–121.

Walter, Nikolaus, 'Die Philipper und das Leiden. Aus den Anfängen einer heidenchristlichen Gemeinde', in R. Schnackenburg et al., eds., *Die Kirche des Anfangs: Für Heinz Schümann* (Freiburg: Herder, 1978).

Watson, Duane F., 'A Rhetorical Analysis of Philippians and its Implications for the Unity Question', *NovT* 30 (1988), 57–88.

Wengst, Klaus, *Humility: Solidarity of the Humiliated – The Transformation of an Attitude and its Social Relevance in Graeco-Roman, O.T.-Jewish and Early Christian Tradition*, tr. J. Bowden (London: SCM, 1988 (Ger. 1987)).

Pax Romana and the Peace of Jesus Christ, tr. J. Bowden (Philadelphia: Fortress Press, 1987 (Ger. 1986)).

White, L. Michael, 'Morality Between Two Worlds: A Paradigm of Friendship in Philippians', in D. L. Balch, E. Ferguson and W. Meeks, eds., *Greeks, Romans and Christians (Essays in Honour of A. J. Malherbe)* (Minneapolis: Fortress Press, 1990).

Wilken, Robert L., *The Christians as the Romans saw them* (New Haven: Yale University Press, 1984).

Winter, B. W., *Seek the Welfare of the City: Christians as Benefactors and Citizens* (First-century Christians in the Graeco-Roman World; Carlisle: Paternoster, 1994).

Winter, Sean F., 'Worthy of the Gospel of Christ: A Study in the Situation and Strategy of Paul's Epistle to the Philippians' (unpubl. DPhil thesis, Oxford, 1998).

Wright, N. T., *The Climax of the Covenant: Christ and the Law in Pauline Theology* (Edinburgh: T&T Clark, 1991).

'Putting Paul Together Again: Towards a Synthesis of Pauline Theology (1 & 2 Thessalonians, Philippians & Philemon)', in J. M. Bassler, ed., *Pauline Theology, Vol. I* (Minneapolis: Fortress Press, 1991).

What Saint Paul Really Said (Oxford: Lion, 1997).

GENERAL INDEX

accessibility, 56–9, 60
Acts of the Apostles, use of, 55, 64, 87
Adam, 131, 135, 208
Alcock, Susan, 5, 28, 42
Augustus, 139, 145, 148, 152–3, 157–8, 161, 167

Béranger, Jean, 142–4, 154, 155, 162–3
Bloomquist, Gregory, 78, 113, 121–3, 128
Bockmuehl, Markus, 125, 187
Bormann, Lukas, 52–3, 132, 147
Bornhäuser, Karl, 51, 63, 130–1

Caligula, 131, 134, 158
Cicero, 138, 141, 156, 158
citizenship, 66–7, 71–3, 93, 138, 177–8
city, 30
Collange, Jean-François, 84–7, 176
colonies, 3
competing interests, 34–5
countryside, population of, 44–6

disunity, 123–4

economic rearrangement, 100–1, 199–200
élite, 27, 34, 43–4, 46–7, 57–8, 59, 60, 61–2, 93
Emperor,
  bringing harmony, 160–5
  cult, 129–30, 134, 137, 169–70, 205
Epictetus, 115–16, 203

farmers, commuting peasant, 28–9, 33, 42, 48–9, 60, 91–2
Faust, Eberhard, 132, 141, 160

Fee, Gordon, 136–7, 198
Fowl, Stephen, 104, 108, 126–7
freedmen/women, 92
Friedrich, Gerhard, 68
friendship, 181

Geoffrion, Timothy, 80, 100, 175
Georgi, Dieter, 132–3
Goodenough, Erwin, 145–7, 162–5, 172
Greeks, 18, 63, 73–4
  land loss, 19–20, 26–8, 29–30

Hadrianoupolis, 31
Hawthorne, Gerald, 87–9
Hooker, Morna, 188, 202, 203
humility, 183–6
Hurtado, Larry, 127, 188, 205–6

inscriptions,
  Greek and Latin, 35–40
  pre-colonial, 20

Jews, 58–9, 87–9

Käsemann, Ernst, 149, 188–93, 200, 205, 206, 209
Kurz, William, 109–10, 126

Latin, 74
Leveau, Philippe, 5, 42, 43
Lohmeyer, Ernst, 129–30, 138, 175–6, 191, 197–8, 204
Lydia, 59, 61, 64

Malina, Bruce, model of pre-industrial city, 40–6
Martin, Ralph, 188, 190, 192, 203, 208

227

INDEX OF BIBLICAL REFERENCES